wild ride

Sam Everingham lives and works in Sydney. Trained in psychology and research methods, he has spent over a decade as a social researcher understanding how we live and behave. He is a sixth-generation Australian and an amateur historian with a passion for Australia's hidden history.

THE RISE AND FALL
OF COBB & CO

SAM EVERINGHAM

To my godfather, Berkeley King,

for showing me secrets

First published by Penguin Group (Australia), 2007

This edition published Stethoscope Publishing (Australia), 2016

Cover design by Megan Baker © Penguin Group (Australia)
Text design by Karen Trump © Penguin Group (Australia)
Cover photograph by Rhys Allen

National Library of Australia
Cataloguing-in-Publication data:

Everingham, Sam.
Wild Ride: the rise and fall of Cobb & Co.

Bibliography.

ISBN: 9781925281736 (pbk)
ISBN: 9781925281743 (ebook)

1. Rutherford, James, 1827–1911. 2. Whitney, William Franklin, 1826–1894. 3. Cobb and Co. – History. 4. Coaching – Australia – History. 5. Transportation – Australia – Passenger traffic – History. I. Title.

388.32280994

Contents

From 'The Lights of Cobb & Co'

Not all the ships that sail away since Roaring Days are done –
Not all the boats that steam from port, nor all the trains that run,
Shall take such hopes and loyal hearts – for men shall never know
Such days as when the Royal Mail was run by Cobb and Co.
The 'greyhounds' race across the sea, the 'special' cleaves the haze,
But these seem dull and slow to me compared with Roaring Days!
The eyes that watched are dim with age, and souls are weak and slow,
The hearts are dust or hardened now that broke for Cobb and Co.

– Henry Lawson, 1897

Introduction

While this book tells the true story of the American entrepreneur Freeman Cobb and how he founded an Australian coaching firm that became a household name, Cobb had only a small part to play in the company's often convoluted history. Freeman Cobb ran the firm for just over two years before selling out and returning to America. The focus of this book is therefore trained on the lives of the personalities who over the next forty years expanded the business throughout Australia's eastern states, turning a road transport company into a conglomerate with major stakes in every significant Australian industry of the time.

The facts of the Cobb & Co story are complex. To further complicate matters, Cobb & Co was used as a trading name by a number of unrelated coach operators in nineteenth-century Australia and New Zealand. However, the account is somewhat simplified by identifying the three chief Cobb & Co firms which developed in Victoria, New South Wales and Queensland, each being managed by a different set of partners. The story begins with the founding of the original company in the colony of Victoria in 1853, and goes on to trace the extraordinary destinies of the men and women who became most central to Cobb & Co's development in New South Wales and Queensland – in particular James Rutherford, Frank and Bella Whitney, and Walter Hall. Queensland's Cobb & Co became the largest transport enterprise of its time, while the New South Wales business controlled not just road transport but also vast pastoral properties, iron, copper and gold mines, and lavish homesteads. In New South Wales and Queensland the company won enormous government contracts, taking control of thousands of miles of mail and constructing railways through some of the country's most impossible terrain.

My introduction to this untold history came through my godfather, a great-grandson of Frank Whitney. In the late 1970s his family property, Coombing Park, was a grand but faded museum; a place where old people lived. As a schoolboy it was here that I first stumbled upon the relics of an incredible past. I scraped back generations of dust and cobwebs from the cracked leather upholstery of once-grand carriages and buggies, and spelt out the words 'Cobb & Co' stamped indelibly on travelling trunks and hundreds of company ledgers. Real people had driven these once-famous coaches and owned this iconic business. Surely there was a story here. As the years passed, and I delved further into the legend, it became increasingly obvious that the full story of Cobb & Co had never been told.

The real driving force behind Cobb & Co was James Rutherford. After she was widowed in 1911, Ada Rutherford had written down the details of her late husband's extraordinary life, using his most private letters as one source. Five years later her manuscript and all of those vital letters were destroyed in a fire that swept through Ada's home.

William Lees, who had known James Rutherford well and was the editor of *Queensland Country Life*, wrote a short history of Cobb & Co in 1917, chiefly from records and newspaper cuttings supplied by members of the Rutherford family. James Rutherford's youngest son, George, wrote some notes of his own in 1949.

Joan Rutherford, the wife of Rutherford's grandson, was an amateur historian who spent a lifetime collecting Cobb & Co ephemera, and wrote an account of the firm in the late 1950s which she eventually self-published. In the meantime, historian Ken Austin contacted Joan about the book he himself was writing on the subject. As Joan was battling to have her own book accepted for publication, she was rather unwilling to cooperate and Austin received little help. Nevertheless, he wrote a meticulous yet dry account of the firm's operations, published in 1967.

What none of these writers had seen was a pile of letters dating from the late 1890s. For a hundred years they had been locked away, a dusty bundle of papers tied up with string. In the mid-1990s my godfather admitted that he and his family had secreted these letters in the Mitchell Library of New South Wales, along with a truckload of yellowed and cracked documents. James Rutherford's family had done the same with their family papers.

When I first gained access to these old letters I could make out perhaps three words in every five. My interest in deciphering the letters was spurred on not only by the occasional post-scripted 'do destroy this', which invariably provides a tantalising reason to do the contrary, but also by the absence of any thorough, objective narrative dealing with the drama of the Cobb & Co story.

Months of deciphering the anguished handwriting uncovered

personal jealousies, family tragedies, fear, triumph and anger that for the first time put a human face on the rise and fall of Australia's Cobb & Co. Long-hidden family vendettas emerged, which generations of descendants had gone to great lengths to conceal. They explained why not one but two lines of Cobb & Co descendants had locked away records, forbidding public access for decades.

As my research progressed, some family descendants warned me off digging up their past. I was refused access to crucial material that had been donated to a major library. Other key manuscripts mysteriously went missing from the same library's holdings before I could view them. It was the support of my mentors at Penguin Books that encouraged me to dig deeper.

I waded through innumerable periodicals and obscure government archives of the day to discover the truth. I journeyed across three states to visit descendants of the Cobb & Co partners. Fortunately, I was dealing with country families who had never needed to adopt the urban necessity of garage sales. Over the decades, these families had kept not only the most banal paperwork but also a rich physical record, including trunks of antique clothing and musty furnishings. Their attics and storerooms housed both essential and intimate details of their ancestors: where they wrote their letters; what cookbooks their staff used; what blacksmith they dealt with; how many sheep were shorn each season.

Slowly, a real-life drama revealed itself, played against a backdrop of drought, economic depression and a growing sense of nationhood. In a history with so many twists and turns, spanning more than sixty years, there were inevitably small pieces missing in this nineteenth-century jigsaw. Where I was unable to draw clear conclusions on a specific issue, based on the evidence, I have at times suggested reasonable possibilities. Occasionally, dates were not included on letters and I have estimated their time-frame from the events described therein.

All letters and excerpts from such are drawn from the papers locked away for generations by the Whitney descendants. Newspaper stories, maps and ephemera are taken from publications of the day. In order to build a more complete picture of the times in which Cobb & Co operated, I have drawn on accounts written not only by Cobb & Co's proprietors but also by those who worked for them (Bartie Boake), those who travelled in their coaches (Constance Ellis and Anthony Trollope) and those who relied on Cobb & Co's mail coaches for contact with family, friends and the outside world. Any dialogue that has been included is taken directly from contemporary written accounts of specific conversations.

Sam Everingham

Did your ancestor work for Cobb & Co or another Australian or New Zealand firm? Visit the website below to check or add your relatives:

https://sameveringhamwrites.wordpress.com/2010/12/19/cobb-and-cos-great-secret/

PART ONE

YOUNG ENTREPRENEURS 1853–1864

CHAPTER ONE

FREEMAN COBB

... a colony that had not one decent road to its name ...

With his short stature and pronounced limp – the legacy of a bout of rheumatic fever – wielding a pick and shovel was never going to be Freeman Cobb's forte. When word reached California of gold being discovered in the faraway colony of Victoria in 1851, the 21-year-old American was keen to see this new land for himself. However, the gold-diggings were never his goal; rather, it was the young colony's apparently booming young economy that drew him.

Freeman Cobb had grown up in Massachusetts, and he'd joined the Adams Express freight company as an earnest young clerk. Ambitious, he'd studied banking and commerce while in their employ, and had been sent to the west coast by the firm when the California gold rush had taken hold. Although still a junior, Cobb was eventually permitted to sail to Victoria with an older colleague, George Mowton, with the aim of expanding the Adams Express business. Goods that trickled into the young colony were being sold at outrageous prices to newly wealthy miners, drunk with their riches. Melbourne was obviously the place to be exporting goods and setting up services.

Mankind's greed for gold has always been strong enough to uproot whole populations. In the decade before the discoveries on the Victorian goldfields, thousands of hopeful gold-seekers had sailed to California from the Australian colonies in search of their fortune, selling everything they owned in exchange for passage to an unknown country on the other side of the world. This was an age when even the humblest ex-convict had the chance of leapfrogging into a class of wealth that less than a generation before had been the sole domain of a class of British citizen cocooned by inherited lands, titles and privilege.

News of the far larger gold finds being discovered in Australia sent waves of excitement rippling throughout the world. American newspapers and telegraphic dispatches waxed lyrical about the unprecedented wealth that lay there for the taking in the far-flung new colony called Victoria, which in 1851 had only just separated from New South Wales. Papers such as the *New York Herald* ran success stories of American miners accumulating instant fortunes from just five weeks' digging in Victoria's goldfields. Further fantastical tales of overnight wealth excited even the most cynical. Over the last five months of 1851, more than 211 000 ounces of gold had reached the Melbourne banks. The institutions were taking in such vast amounts of gold, so quickly, there was no way of calculating revenue, let alone what interest rates should be paid. As one American working on the Victorian diggings wrote to a local newspaper, hundreds of men were picking 'up more [gold] dust here in one week than they would in six months in California'.

By the first months of 1852, American ships were arriving almost daily in Melbourne. Only a few months earlier, few of the ships' occupants would have even heard of the shanty town's existence. Boatloads of hopefuls were also pouring in from Great Britain and China, unaware that they had little chance of finding a crew to sail them home if they tired of this unknown land. Of the nearly sixty ships arriving in January 1852, five hundred crew members – nearly three in every five men – deserted in search of their fortunes on the diggings.

Most gold-seekers were young – they had to be in order to cope with the harsh living conditions on the goldfields. One Melbourne-bound ship recorded its oldest American passenger as being thirty-three years of age. Most were not footloose adventurers, however. Many were formerly steady, industrious mechanics and clerks, come to make a fortune with their young families in tow.

Freeman Cobb would have paid between $200 and $250 for his first-class cabin on the American passenger ship that took him to the new colony in the first months of 1853. The regular fare included all meals, though passengers often had to provide their own alcohol, soap and towels. Some negotiated a cheaper passage – just $50 from San Francisco – by working their passage on the outward voyage.

Depending on their size, passenger ships carried between sixty-five and 265 travellers. Second-class passengers ate pork and hard bread, while meals in first class were more refined. To keep the appetites of their passengers sated during the four-month voyage, the ships carried preserved meat and a menagerie of animals as a living larder. One ship of 180 passengers loaded two slaughtered oxen, 360 live fowls, twenty live sheep and forty-two noisy pigs as well as mountains of bread, buckwheat and rice. En route, the beasts were killed as required. A small army of over thirty cooks, waiters and stewards were on hand to feed the vessel's hungry young passengers.

When Freeman Cobb and George Mowton arrived in Port Phillip Bay in April 1853, Melbourne had been governing itself for only two years. As their ship tied alongside the many other vessels of all sizes and nationalities crowding the port, jostling for their turn to unload, young Cobb's eyes would have quickly alighted upon the mounds of uncovered goods that lay in huge piles along the beachfront at the mouth of the Yarra River, waiting for a means to reach the goldfields. Williamstown, the town that had sprung up around the Port Phillip wharves, was an eyesore. There were a few grog shops and boarding houses, but the streets were bare dirt and houses were few. Debris and garbage from the ships and the thousands of new settlers choked the bay.

Like all arrivals in these gold-rush years, Cobb would have been assaulted by the sounds and smells of a poorer but still eager pit of humanity on the other side of the Yarra River from the main town of Melbourne: a tent city of transient shopkeepers, barbers, boot-solers, prostitutes, butchers, sail-makers and book-sellers, where dirty lanes pierced a ragged trail through a maze of tents tempting the delirious traveller.

Melbourne was obviously struggling to cope with the influx. No additional accommodation had yet been built, and the trickle of supplies coming into the colony was grossly inadequate to support the skyrocketing population. There were no powers to enforce existing laws, no railways, no gas, no telegraph system, no waterworks, no sawmills – not even properly functioning wharves. Dirt tracks passed for main thoroughfares in the young town, and were cut up so badly from the wheels of heavy wagons that only their central ridges retained some trace of navigability. Teams of putrid-smelling oxen heaving wagons laden high forced carts full of equally foul-smelling garbage to give way, veering off to the road's edge. In the wet winter months their axles would sink low into calf-deep mud. Horsemen too were forced to guide their mounts at a snail's pace through the treacle-like slop.

However, for many new arrivals any doubts they may have harboured about crossing the world in search of a fortune were soon drowned out by Melbourne's interminable motion. It was impossible not to be infected by the excitement in people's voices. There was such a mix of accents – German, Scots, Irish, Yorkshire, Cockney – and the Chinese were of course easy to spot.

Men strolled the streets gloveless and coatless in coloured shirts, cabbage-tree hats and wide-awakes – a felt hat sporting a low crown and wide brim. Some had a necktie casually knotted around their throat. Trousers were stuffed inside high jackboots or were worn over laced-up watertights.

Respectable females were hard to find in such a town. It was the loose women who made themselves visible, jostling men on the footpaths, elbowing their way through the stores and rattling along the streets in carriages hired at a guinea the hour. These women flaunted cheap jewellery, florid dresses of silk, sarcenet and brocaded satins. Bonnets stuffed with flowers and cornstalks, gaudy parasols, corpulent earrings and chains, handcuff-sized bracelets – nothing was too showy. Unaccustomed to the protective benefits of the parasol against the harsh sun, they carried them too often on the shady side of their accoutrement, leaving the sun's harsh rays to further age their already rough faces.

A riotous mix of dwellings lined the streets. Solid brick and stone houses sat side-by-side with weatherboard shacks, canvas tents and corrugated-iron huts. Horses were tethered to rings set into the walls outside local business houses. They waited patiently, but their legs often sank so deeply into the mud that their bellies would rest on the mire's surface, their chins knocking against the kerbstones. Rather than whinnying in panic, the horses seemed to quietly accept their fate, as if this happened every day.

Melbourne's hotels were jammed shoulder to shoulder along Collins Street. One in particular, the Criterion, was a little piece of American showmanship transported to the new colony. The American-owned hotel was the most elaborate and progressive establishment in the city. First-time patrons were awed by its billiard saloon alone, its grand and lofty elegance reminiscent of a Greek temple. The hotel boasted a barber's shop, a bathhouse with hot and cold steam and shower baths, a 500-person theatre and a bowling saloon.

Even the bartenders were a drawing card. They would toss about plain nobblers, whisky, ales and Old Toms – an especially potent English gin – with reckless abandon. The best of them could line up a string of tumblers along their forearm, and in a few quick twitches fling them to the correct customer without spilling a drop.

The Criterion owed its popularity to American patronage but, like many of its big-spending patrons, the hotel's fortunes were not to last. The hotel suffered a rapid decline when close to three-quarters of Melbourne's Yankee population swarmed out of town following reports of huge gold deposits at the headwaters of the Amazon in Peru. The Peruvian Swindle, as it came to be known, made profits for no-one but the unscrupulous transport speculators whose vessels shipped in holds full of guano as manure for Victoria's deficient soils and returned across the Pacific filled to the brim with hopeful gold-seekers.

It was hard not to be taken in by the torrent of wild tales and promises that swirled around the Criterion. Before the hotel's demise, it was quite possibly here that Freeman Cobb met the young men who were to partner with him, and thereby change his destiny.

It soon became obvious that the idea of setting up a domestic freight service in Victoria faced huge obstacles. The roads and infrastructure were in a shocking state, not only in Melbourne but throughout the colony. Little work had gone into building decent roads, and with the huge increase in traffic occasioned by the gold rush they were often impassable to all but plodding bullock trains and single horsemen. When it came to the haulage of goods, it was a hopeless situation. Horse-drawn wagons laden down with supplies constantly became bogged in the deep mud.

Undaunted, by early May 1853 George Mowton and Freeman Cobb had set up an office on the corner of Collins and Queen streets, despite the fact that their goods wagons had not yet arrived from the United States. On 6 May, determined to take advantage of whatever business they could find, they placed an advertisement for the Adams Express Company's *Great American and European Express* in the local paper, the Melbourne *Argus*. Without a wagon to their name, it was not local passenger or freight transport they could offer but overseas freight services:

We are prepared to give through receipts for gold dust, spe-
cie, packages, etc, to any part of the United States, Canada or
Europe.

The problem, of course, was that demand lay in the opposite direction. Fortunately, by mid-June an American ship called the *Eagle* had
landed a new boatload of young drivers, freight wagons and supplies
for Adams Express. Among the wagon drivers to disembark were
James Swanton, John Peck and John Lamber, important names in the
history of what would become Cobb & Co.

However, faced with the realities of life in a raw colonial town,
George Mowton declared that the Adams Express Company would
not go ahead with its domestic freight service in Victoria. His decision was perhaps unsurprising, given the fact that the colony's roads
were well nigh impassable. After spending only a couple of months in
the colony, Mowton sailed home to the United States, taking the firm's
expense account with him.

Freeman Cobb was bitterly disappointed, for he saw opportunity
amid the chaos. While it was true that freight was not currently viable, there was clearly a demand for passenger transport, despite the
dreadful roads. Cobb dug in his heels, refusing to return with his senior partner. When George Mowton's ship left Port Phillip Bay, this
small, pallid 22-year-old with the heavy dark moustache and thick
mop of unruly hair was left with a shipload of unwanted wagons and
a handful of out-of-work drivers in a colony that had not one decent
road to its name.

CHAPTER TWO

A LINE OF WELL-APPOINTED COACHES

The crushing, the misery, the suffocation of these public
conveyances!
– Clara Aspinall, 1860

Transporting people and goods to the goldfields, whether on foot or by vehicle, was critically important, so it was no coincidence that the best-paid jobs by far in the new colony were shoemakers, boot-closers, wheelwrights, coach- and carriage-makers, wheelers, coach-smiths, coach painters, trimmers and saddlers, all of whom commanded upwards of £2 a week. Freeman Cobb had not one of these skills. All he had to offer was a few years' experience as a junior clerk in a goods-carrying firm, but he was not to be dissuaded. He'd identified the desperate need for contractors to cart the tonnes of imported goods that had been dumped at Sandridge (now Port Melbourne) the few miles upriver to Melbourne.

At an age when most twenty-first-century Australians are still living at home with their parents, Cobb prepared to start his own freight business. However, he needed partners. Somehow, he had to convince the handful of new arrivals who'd sailed to Melbourne on the *Eagle* not to run off to the goldfields but to invest their labour and capital in his business proposition.

Twenty-three-year-old John Peck had already driven for the famous US coach company Wells Fargo, and he was a talented horse-breaker. At five foot eleven, he was broad-shouldered and as strong as a horse. His ancestors had come to America in 1637 as pioneer Boston settlers, though Peck had grown up in New Hampshire. James Swanton, an Irish-born American, was also a first-rate horse-breaker and driver with similar experience to Peck. John Lamber had a background as a book-keeper for freight-carrying firms in America. He was a small man from a frontier town west of the Missouri River in Kansas. It is quite likely that Lamber had watched hundreds of covered wagons heading west across Kansas during the recent Californian gold rush.

Cobb convinced the three men – all of them aged in their early to mid-twenties – to join him in starting up a business ferrying goods between the port and Melbourne. Cobb assured his new chums he would find the money to finance the venture and attract business. His first task was to negotiate the purchase of the now-redundant Adams Express wagons that had arrived on the *Eagle*.

Only a little more than two months after Cobb had set foot in the colony, his new team had a hauling business using horse-drawn wagons. Peck and Swanton drove, while Lamber ran the supply side of the business. However, nothing went to plan, and the wet of winter caused the dirt track from the port to Melbourne to deteriorate so badly it was impassable in a heavy vehicle. Their new haulage business soon ground to a standstill. Nothing larger than hand-carts could get through the sludge, and the expensive teams of horses Cobb had purchased were useless. Perhaps Mowton had been right after all.

Running a haulage business without suitable roads was impossible.

To compound their problems, the colonial government was about to open the country's first steam railway between the port and Melbourne, the very same freight route Cobb had identified. If they were to continue in business, Cobb and his partners would need to find another opportunity. The answer was obvious: passenger coaches.

The potential market was huge, not least because of the continual stream of human traffic moving between the goldfields and Melbourne. Several firms were already offering a service to the goldfields, but their heavy English coaches were slow, unreliable and intermittent, and apt to become bogged in the muddy roads leading out of Melbourne. English coaches were fine for well-built, gentle country roads but totally unsuitable for unmade and steep terrain.

The need for a more efficient style of transport for passengers was clear. Such a vehicle needed to be fast, reliable and sturdy, capable of journeys on primitive tracks or virgin country, and flexible enough to move to another district as traffic demanded. It needed a compartment for carrying gold, one for mail and storage for luggage.

The American coaches Cobb was accustomed to were made of hickory and ash, much lighter wood than their English equivalents. Nevertheless, their bodies were strong, and instead of the heavy iron plates and stiff steel springs of the English model, the American coaches' rounded bodies were suspended on leather springs called thorough braces, cradle fashion, made from the hides of bison. The pliancy of the leather made all the difference to passenger comfort. Cobb was convinced it would significantly reduce the jarring experienced when travelling on Australia's rough dirt roads, creek beds and steep hill climbs.

An Englishman had recently begun running American-style coaches from Geelong to the Ballarat goldfields. Despite the enormous £10 fare each way, his vehicles were crammed full of passengers in each direction. The American coaches were fancy to the point of being festive, and were perfect for the routes to the rich goldfields.

Cobb knew what he had to do, but he would have to move swiftly if he was to launch a competitive American-style coach service. It would take too long to order the passenger vehicles he needed, and so Cobb and his partners improvised. Their Adams Express goods wagons were overhauled and cleaned. Cushioned seats were added, and they bought lighter horses and harnesses to make the switch to carrying passengers.

Public carriage transport in Australia dated from 1805, when William Robert began Australia's first land public transport service, a 'stage wagon' from Sydney to the Hawkesbury River. The journey took sixteen hours and cost seven shillings and sixpence, half a week's pay for some. It was a substantial investment of time and money. William Highland revived much the same route to the two Hawkesbury River towns of Richmond and Windsor in 1814. At first the service failed to thrive, for while the population was small there were sufficient horses to carry settlers faster, more cheaply and comfortably. A true stagecoach based on the English system, with quality carriages and regular staging of horses, was not introduced until 1819, between Sydney and Parramatta as well as between Hobart and Launceston – at the time the only two decent roads in Australia.

In 1824 competitors moved in with services from Sydney to

Parramatta, Windsor, Liverpool, Penrith and Bathurst. A firm called Ireland & Richards ran services from Sydney to Goulburn and Bathurst before going spectacularly bankrupt in 1834. Their collapse prompted the government to enforce regulations, setting fare rates and awarding mail contracts only to reliable firms. Such mail contracts became the basis of profitable coaching companies throughout the coaching era.

English coaches ran along the better roads near Sydney and between Hobart and Launceston, where there was sufficient mail and passenger traffic to operate daily services. These coaches typically cost £200 each and as much again for their sets of harness. Cleveland Bay horses were predominantly used, an English breed developed specifically for harness work. The horses combined speed with endurance, though they had nothing like the strength of the bullock teams that could haul heavily laden wagons in any conditions.

Coaching on these routes was fiercely competitive. One observer in the 1840s gave an account of the hotly contested run between Parramatta and Penrith. The public appreciated the competition, for it cut the fare down to five shillings instead of ten, but it also led to enmity between coach drivers. On one occasion, the rival firms Perry and Kendall each had a coach heading to Parramatta, each packed with passengers. Kendall's coachman decided to overtake the rival coach when he came to a bridge at the foot of a hill. Beyond the bridge was a great drop and it was here that he made the rush. Both coach teams came down the hill and onto the bridge at a full gallop, side by side. Kendall's driver pressed his horses against the opposition, and the side rail of the bridge gave way. The Perry horses remained on solid ground, but the back wheels of the rival coach spun over the chasm below. It was only the horses' momentum that yanked the coach to safety, narrowly saving the entire load of passengers from a nasty end.

New South Wales' and Tasmania's convict-built paved roads were remarkably good by the 1840s, featuring extensive earthworks and fine stone bridges. Coach travel was reasonably fast on these roads, typically covering nearly 60 miles (almost 100 kilometres) a day, even over mountainous terrain. This daily mileage became typical of the distance that separated towns in much of rural Australia, as coaching inns developed into townships. In the mid-1840s a weekly coach began running between Sydney and Melbourne, primarily to carry mail but also dropping off and picking up a few passengers at places along the way. Coastal steamers remained considerably faster, cheaper and more comfortable if you needed to travel the entire distance between the two capitals.

By 1853, Victoria's colonial government was finally doing something about the appalling state of the colony's roads. In desperation, they called in one of the best road builders from their sister colony, New South Wales. As a result, a number of good, all-weather roads to the goldfields around Ballarat and Bendigo were built, as well as a number of roads around Melbourne. For a very brief period, the new colony boasted some of Australia's best roads.

On 30 January 1854, the first advertisement for Cobb & Co's passenger coach to the goldfields appeared in the Melbourne *Argus*:

American Telegraph Line of Coaches
Daily communication between Melbourne, Forest Creek and

Bendigo.

Cobb & Co beg to announce to the public that they have determined to run a line of well-appointed coaches between the above places, starting from the Criterion Hotel every morning (Sunday excepted) at 6 o'clock, and from Forest Creek daily at the same hour.

The vehicles intended to run are the new American coaches, recently imported, and acknowledged to be the easiest conveyances in the colony.

That same day, Cobb & Co's first two-horse coach left Melbourne to make the 75-mile (120-kilometre) run to Forest Creek (now Castlemaine). Travelling at up to 15 miles an hour, the coach arrived in half the time of the heavier English competition. The new company soon slashed the Melbourne to Bendigo journey to an unheard-of ten hours. In a colony where men were falling over themselves to reach the goldfields quickly, the Cobb & Co service was an immediate success. Unlike their competitors, who often delayed departures until they had enough bookings to fill the seats, Cobb and his partners committed themselves to running to a regular timetable. Within a few months, their business was doing so well that they were able to acquire their competitor's service between Geelong and Ballarat, along with his American coaches.

Cobb & Co's fleet of coaches was soon augmented by Concord coaches, imported from America by one George Train, or so records from Melbourne's La Trobe Library would suggest. In a neat twist, it is likely that Train had made the journey out to Australia from the United States on the same ship as Cobb. These Concord-style coaches towered above the competition, both in height and suitability for the colony's rough roads. The top of each vehicle's hood was as high as a modern bus, the height accentuated by rooftop seating for passengers. A seat behind the driver provided additional room for a couple of extra passengers, along with luggage that was held in place by an iron railing. More luggage could be carried at the rear in a wedge-shaped boot.

The weekly swag of gold was initially carried in specially constructed wooden boxes, with the government seal affixed in a few places. However, they were too heavy to easily manoeuvre when coaches inevitably became bogged in the mud, and a lighter iron box was introduced, with a lid that could be clamped and secured with screws.

The box seats on top of the coach next to the driver were the most comfortable and popular positions, avoiding the often rank odours and discomforting closeness of fellow passengers inside the coach. It wasn't unknown for firms to ban women from sitting on the box seat, as these passengers were expected to assist with manning the brake on steep pitches and to hold the horses while drivers dealt with the mails. In smaller coaches, hours spent trapped inside a vehicle with your neighbour's questionable *toilette* was the grim alternative.

Coach body panels were painted red and detailed with floral motifs and gold scrolls. Fresh straw was often laid on the coach's floor to keep passengers' feet warm; it also came in handy for hiding small valuables in case of bushrangers. The brightly painted yellow wheels were positioned on wide axles well outside the coach's body to guard against the coach tipping on its side as it rounded a sharp corner at speed. Passengers onboard the new coaches must often have felt as if they were on a swing, rocked by the backwards and forwards rolling motion produced by the leather springs. One passenger described the sensation as like being on 'a baby camel in a hell of a hurry'. But the result meant a more constant speed, and the experience was a little less painful than having to deal with the sudden jerks and bounces of English steel-sprung coaches. Leather thorough braces meant coaches could handle rough conditions well, and if the braces broke they could be repaired at the roadside.

Each vehicle had a brake lever on the left and the right – a long-angled arm reaching from the wheelbase to the top of the coach where the driver sat. Despite their height and bounciness, the American coaches were considered to be very steady on the roads. Some of them did capsize, although many a disaster was averted by the driver commanding his passengers to throw their weight to one side to keep the vehicle balanced. Fatalities were rare, in Victoria at least, but minor accidents were frequent, both passengers and drivers sometimes breaking limbs.

Freeman Cobb knew his market. It was looking for a fast journey, whether to the goldfields to stake a claim or to the bank to cash in a find. For the gold-hungry, getting to a new digging fast might make all the difference between striking it rich and trawling through silted-up creeks and rubble pockmarked by weeks of human greed and feverish desecration. Travelling by coach was also the safest choice, particularly if you were carrying gold or other valuables.

Not just any old nag could pull a coach at the speed Freeman Cobb required. Cobb and his American friends well knew that horses could pull a laden coach at a canter if they were strong enough, though no harnessed team could possibly maintain such a pace for more than about 10 miles (16 kilometres) in hilly terrain. And there were certainly plenty of hills between Melbourne and the goldfields. Gambling on his customers' preparedness to pay for a fast journey, Cobb imported dozens of American thoroughbred horses, costing an average of £50 each, and he spent even more on purchasing the best American harness.

The horses were all thoroughbred trotters, though some drivers swore that a little draught-horse blood made for the best coachers; pure draught horses did not have enough stamina. Some felt that a mix of trotter mare and thoroughbred stallion made for an ideal coach horse. Over the years, there was even some crossing of Clydesdales, blood horses and Arabs in the quest to come up with the ideal Australian coach horse.

Some observers judged Cobb & Co's coaches to be better run than any they had travelled on in England or America. Unlike other operators, who tended to change their teams less often, Cobb set up 'change stations' every 10 miles or so along his new routes, employing a groom at each to have a fresh team harnessed and ready. These regular changeovers meant that each team could be pushed to run at a fast trot uphill and down. John Lamber set about renting stables and making arrangements with hotel-keepers for meals to be provided en route. As well as a harnessed team, feed and water also needed to be on hand. Grass wasn't enough to re-energise the powerful teams of coachers. The horses needed chaff, but as most Victorian farm labourers had deserted for the diggings, cut hay was hard to find. Like their competitors, Cobb and his young partners were forced to import hay from Tasmania at inflated prices of up to £35 a ton. The logistics involved in organising horses, feed, supplies and passenger bookings were complex, and Freeman's book-keeping skills must have proven useful. The key was to start with just a few routes and to charge high fares.

Cobb and his partners also made a point of only employing drivers who stayed sober on the job. Liquor was being abused in epidemic proportions in the Australian colonies, and there were too many stories of competitor coaches becoming stranded because the driver could not be woken from an alcohol-induced coma. Their policy paid off, and the company's reputation for reliable service soon became famous.

It wasn't only the quality of the coaches, drivers and equipment that made the new firm stand out. Its registered name – American Telegraph Line of Coaches – also captured attention. The word 'American' suggested progressiveness and 'telegraph' had almost magical associations for a population just coming to terms with the speed of telegraphic communication. However, the name was rather long to emblazon on each coach, and the phrase Cobb & Co fitted far better. It was also easier to remember, and those who argued it had a 'rolling, lurching rhythm like that of a thorough-brace coach in motion' were right, because by 1898 the name had became synonymous with coaches.

At £7 each way, Cobb & Co's 'glamour' route from Melbourne to Bendigo was hugely expensive. The fare was equivalent to four weeks' regular wages for many, and you could travel five times as far in first class by steamer to Sydney for significantly less than £6. Nonetheless, bookings kept pouring into the firm's Collins Street offices. Government representatives and wealthy diggers were prepared to pay a very good price for a safe journey at a time when police were scattered and armed bushrangers were hunting for coaches carrying thousands of pounds in gold.

The firm's service to Bendigo lasted only six months before the roads heading west became impassable once again with the winter rain. The most problematic section was the Black Forest, which became a muddy quagmire. Passenger traffic was far lower in the winter, as coaches had to be smaller and lighter (carrying eleven passengers compared to sixteen in the drier months) to avoid becoming bogged in the mud. It would be another two years before a plank road was laid in this section to prevent coaches from bogging. In just six months, however, the Cobb & Co service had created a premier reputation, and when the winter wet ended and the dirt tracks dried out, the firm was back on the road.

On 12 October 1854, the Melbourne *Argus* made the following welcome announcement:

> *Travellers to and from Castlemaine will be glad to find by the advertisement which appears in another column, that Messrs. Cobb and Co., who last season won golden opinions from all sorts of people for the punctuality and speed which characterized their mode of conducting their business as proprietors of passenger coaches between Melbourne and the diggings, have reappeared on the field of action.*

By the end of 1854, their first year in business, Freeman Cobb and his partners were running seventy thoroughbred horses on just four Victorian routes – to Castlemaine, Bendigo, Ballarat and Maryborough. Cobb's experience in California had shown him there would be no shortage of business in these gold districts, and he had been proven right.

To pay off the investment in expensive coaches and horses, Cobb & Co needed to win the government contract to carry the mail, thus ensuring income regardless of passenger numbers from one month to the next. In 1855 Freeman Cobb tendered to carry all the post-office mail on two routes: Melbourne to Bendigo, and Melbourne to Mount Blackwood. Cobb quoted the government the enormous sum of £10 000 to deliver the mail to Bendigo twice a week for one year, and not surprisingly both contracts went to competitor firms.

Without one mail contract, it was only the determination of diggers crazed with gold fever or rich from a big find that kept Cobb & Co's winter passenger numbers steady. There would soon be nearly 47 000 miners at the Ballarat fields alone, and by 1858 another 100 000 miners had arrived in the Victorian goldfields to stake their claim. In the ten years to 1860, the colony's population skyrocketed from 76 000 to over half a million.

With fares at a premium, Cobb & Co's passengers tended to be limited to newly rich diggers, policemen, young English royalty, famous writers, station managers, head stockmen, the postmaster or local schoolteacher. Those who couldn't afford to take the service walked. With instant wealth on the goldfields there for the taking, it wasn't just the 22-year-old Lord Robert Cecil (later Marquis of Salisbury and three times prime minister of Britain) who could afford to travel by coach from one goldfield to the next. Educated men travelled shoulder to shoulder with ruffians. The young Lord Cecil's diary entry of the day recalls a Californian gold prospector in the coach beside him:

> He was a coarse, hideous, dirty-looking man, without an attempt at ornament or even neatness in his dress; yet he wore in his ears a pair of earrings about the size and shape of a wedding ring. He wore a pair of pistols in his belt, and the words 'put a bullet through his brain' were continually in his mouth.

Coach travel held little romance for the passengers themselves. This was reserved for the townspeople waiting for mail, goods and loved ones. Nabbing a journey on the outside of a Cobb coach was often far more comfortable than riding inside, providing a full sensory experience: the crunch of wheels on gravel; the bite of the wind on your face; the *tock-tock* of the axle boxes; the smell of dew-soaked grass, wattle and gum, horse sweat and leather; the cry of magpies as they took wing from branches overhanging the track. If you were lucky enough to travel in fine weather and by daylight, coach journeys offered a wonderful view of the countryside. You would wear a greatcoat if the weather was cold, watching a cloud of steam rise from the team's flanks and the driver's breath condense into white vapour. From the box seat it was an experience like no other, being entertained by the driver's yarns, watching the landscape unfold, feeling the animal strength as the straining horses jerked on their traces and the unexpected lurch as the wheels dropped into a deep ditch. Bouncing around on hard wooden benches inside the coach was much less desirable, and travellers often kept the leather curtains inside rolled down to prevent the dust pouring in.

Cobb was a master at marketing before the concept even had a name. He assigned horses so each driver's team was a particular colour: Emanuel Levi's horses were black, W. P. Jackson's were grey, Harry Netherfield's were roans and Carter's were bays. Harnessed together, they had the visual impact that wily marketers can only dream of today. Teams did not remain so well matched through longer trips, where they were paired instead for strength and pace.

With horse teams changing every 10 miles, it was impossible for most drivers to know the name of every horse. Drivers harnessed their horses in pairs, each pair being called a span. In coaching, the right-hand side was not starboard but the off side, while the left was the near side. A six-horse team were named from front to rear – lead, swing and wheel teams – so each horse could be easily identified.

Where possible, changeovers were located at an inn, or an inn was built once the change station was operating, so that not only the horses but also the passengers could be refreshed. Bush inns were usually a long low building built of brick or weatherboard. There would be a verandah stretching along the length of the building and above it an ornamental signboard. Under the verandah awning a series of doors faced the road – one leading to the bar, one to the billiards room (or bagatelle if they could not afford a billiards table), then one or two private rooms and, at the end, bedrooms for paying guests. If space was tight, guests had to make do with a space partitioned from the innkeeper's own bedroom with hessian sacking. Often a married couple would run such an inn, the husband acting as groom, his wife serving meals to the travellers in the front room of their cottage. Some of the more solid of these nineteenth-century inns still pepper the Australian landscape.

Some inns offered passengers delicious homemade bread, butter, prickly-pear jam, eggs and dry hash (a meat rissole with gravy) for breakfast. At others, you would be lucky to get a slice of damper with treacle, or corned beef and tea could be considered standard breakfast fare. Afternoon tea might be tea and brownies, a cake made of yeast dough with currants, sugar, butter and any spice one could find.

Coach passengers usually paid twice the going rate for meals – two shillings instead of one – due to the inconvenience of having to be fed at whatever time the coach happened to arrive, which could be five in the morning or ten at night. It was unthinkable that the mails should be delayed, so drivers and their passengers were given their meals before other guests. Innkeepers saw this as justifying the premium price paid by passengers for meals, though some of them had a habit of using any ruse to delay a coach's departure if it meant they could squeeze some extra trade out of hungry or thirsty passengers.

For many years, drivers sounded a bugle to announce that the mail had arrived. At night, lamps flickered dimly in sockets high on the sides of the coach's body. Lamps were spring loaded so that as the wax burnt down, the flame remained neatly positioned in the centre of a reflector. Not all drivers bothered with lamps. Some drivers raced their vehicles through the blackness with nothing to guide them but a sliver of moon and a bush track that seemed at times to disappear completely into a maze of shadows.

Bushfires were a driver's worst nightmare. Fire could travel as fast as a galloping horse, and drivers needed experience to judge whether they were in danger of being trapped and burnt alive with their passengers. Horses could become unmanageable near fires, and a burning tree trunk crashing across the track could completely block an escape. Drivers would share tales of galloping their coach and terrified passengers down forest tracks with blazing trees roaring and crashing just 50 metres away. The air would be thick with smoke, flying ash and sparks. Both driver and box-seat passenger would be tied to their seats, the coach swaying on two wheels, inches from the massive gums. Meanwhile the other passengers, sweating from fear and the searing heat, were flung around inside the coach like so much chaff.

In the 1850s and '60s, when safe, fast vehicles were highly valued for the transport of gold, good drivers earned much more than trades-men. Freeman Cobb was initially paying his drivers £8 per week, and in years to come this rocketed to £14, such was the importance to the government of reliable coaches and mail; the wage later settled back to far lower levels. As an additional perk, drivers' meals and accommodation were paid for by the firm. Many drivers would earn a little money on the side by breaking in horses for local squatters. It was not unusual to see a load of passengers leaving a bush changing yard with a team composed of two unbroken horses, a bolter and a kicker.

An excellent memory was a handy attribute for drivers to possess, as they could earn a little extra if asked to call on a storekeeper in the next town and 'tell him to give you a couple of pounds of tea and some potatoes for me'. Another settler might ask a driver to 'pick up a pair of boots size three, for the missus' or myriad other items.

In these critical early days, coach driving became an opportunity to progress to serious wealth. John Fagan, a coach driver who was bailed up in the famous Eugowra hold-up by Frank Gardiner's gang, would become a rich publican and then a wealthy landholder in the Bathurst district of New South Wales. Hiram Barnes, one of Cobb & Co's most trusted drivers, would lead the firm's expansion into Queensland, having accumulated the capital to invest in a quarter share of the Queensland coach business.

Cobb & Co's drivers developed a reputation for trustworthiness, mixed with a rough-and-ready allure. Many of them tended to flirt – in a chivalrous fashion – with unaccompanied female passengers. Increasingly, it was the larger-than-life coach drivers who personified travellers' experience with the firm. Most of these early coach drivers had learnt their trade with American firms such as Wells Fargo, and were held in as much respect and awe as today's top racing-car drivers. They charmed their passengers, told a great story and were highly skilled with horses. Some were so accurate with the twelve-foot thong on their whip that they could cut a cigarette out of a fellow's mouth without the whip touching his nose.

One of the most famous of the firm's early drivers was Ned Devine, a Tasmanian nicknamed Cabbage Tree Ned after his characteristic wide and broad hat, made from the leaves of the cabbage tree. Ned was one of the first native-born drivers to match the Americans' skill, amazing his colleagues with his uncanny ability to handle huge teams of twelve horses on Cobb & Co's largest coach as if he were merely driving a pair. His skill and courteous manner made him extremely popular, and several entrepreneurs offered him the capital to run in opposition to his employers. The Cobb partners were forced to pay Ned Devine a huge £17 per week to guarantee his loyalty, and for fourteen years he drove the Geelong to Ballarat route. Devine claimed to have driven the Cobb mail coach past the Eureka stockade on the day of the famous battle in 1854.

In mid-1856, after just two and a half years in operation, Cobb & Co had by no means secured a monopoly over the Victorian routes. The company had failed to win a single mail contract, and was competing against at least three other firms running coaches to Castlemaine and Bendigo. They ran coaches on only a fraction of the routes operating in the colony at the time, leaving the routes from Melbourne to Beechworth, for example, to others. Nevertheless, their reputation for fast, reliable transport was unbeaten.

Melbourne was therefore shocked when, seemingly out of the blue, Freeman Cobb and his young partners sold up in May 1856. There is no record of why the decision to sell was made, although the huge price being offered (reputedly £16 000) must have been difficult to turn down. All four partners were still young, ambitious and restless for further adventures, for this was an age of discovery, a time when fortune favoured the brave. To move on to richer pastures was the mantra of the gold-digger, entrepreneur, squatter and publican alike.

CHAPTER THREE

A Business No-One Could Afford

Cobb, *n, sometimes used as equivalent to a coach.*
'I am going by Cobb'.

– Austral English, *1898*

A farewell dinner in Cobb's honour was held at Melbourne's Criterion Hotel on Friday evening, 23 May 1856, for over one hundred guests. Rather than waxing lyrical about Freeman Cobb, those who spoke on the night seemed more concerned that war between America and Australia would never ensue. The following day, three coach loads of friends accompanied Cobb to the port and toasted his future health and prosperity in champagne.

Cobb left a city that was outgrowing its close rival, Sydney. It had grand public buildings, gas lights, fine opera houses, nightly live theatre, a first-class public library and a new university boasting the country's first medical school. On his return to America, Cobb married and became a state senator in Massachusetts. Ever the risk-taker, he invested in some dubious American banks and mines, and lost much of his new fortune in the process. In 1871 he sailed for South Africa with a fellow American, C. C. Cole, who had also operated coaches in Victoria during the gold-rush years. Both were ready to capitalise on the great diamond discoveries in Kimberley. True to form, the pair raised £10 000 capital from Port Elizabeth businessmen and started running coaches between Port Elizabeth and the Kimberley mines.

Within three years, the company was in liquidation, as the promised fast schedules could not be maintained. Cobb continued operating the line on his own for another two years until, never in particularly good health, he died in South Africa in 1878 at just forty-six years of age.

Cobb's physical remains decayed in the cemetery at Port Elizabeth, but his name was to live on – not in his homeland, but in five Australian colonies and in New Zealand. The main road between Echuca in Victoria and Wilcannia in New South Wales was named the Cobb Highway after a man who had spent just three years of his life in Australia, never venturing more than a hundred miles out of Melbourne. Car parks and transport enterprises in Victoria and Queensland took on his name, as did a restaurant chain in New Zealand.

John Lamber returned to America, settling in Des Moines, Iowa. James Swanton worked with several other local Victorian coaching firms for a period, before moving to New Zealand, where he drove for an unrelated coaching firm that also used the Cobb & Co name. He eventually followed Freeman Cobb home to America.

Of the four founders, only John Peck settled permanently in Australia. He formed a stock and station agency in Melbourne, J. M. Peck & Co, and watched from the sidelines as other men grappled with the coaching business he'd once co-owned. He lived to see the last Victorian coach make its run, before dying in Melbourne in 1903.

The May 1856 purchase of the Cobb & Co business was secured by Thomas Davies, another American who already ran a coach line to Ballarat, but the firm subsequently became something of a hot potato. Davies held the coaches and routes for just one year before selling them on to Alex Walker. Unable to meet the repayments, in 1857 Walker rapidly sold the firm to George Watson, an Irishman, and Cyrus Hewitt, another lanky American, who was instantly recognisable about town in his black stove-pipe hat.

Bank notes were so scarce in the colony that, when large sums were involved, it was standard practice to pay just 25 per cent up-front in cash, with the remainder of the purchase price being paid six or nine months later. It is possible that not one of the new buyers had any intention of paying off the balance, looking instead for a quick profit.

Watson and Hewitt were adventurous businessmen, and by 1860 they'd expanded Cobb & Co's coaching routes towards Sydney. In fact, they *had* to expand in order to survive, as new railways out of Melbourne were threatening coaching routes to the goldfields. A private railway had already opened from Melbourne to Geelong in 1857, and new lines to Ballarat and Bendigo were almost complete, promising to make coaches redundant. Rich on the proceeds of gold, Victoria's colonial government was investing in a grand program of railway construction. It was to become one of the most extensive colonial railway networks ever developed.

The need for railways was considered more urgent than for roads, since trains provided far better solutions to transport problems. In terms of price and speed, coaches were no competition. The result was a gradual neglect of Victoria's roads, which lasted until well after the Great War. Roads became the responsibility of local government and, being perpetually under-funded, local councils saw no point in building or maintaining them for anything other than local traffic.

In contrast, the two goldfield railway lines were built according to the high standards of the English lines. The Bendigo route would take trains across the Great Dividing Range for the first time, and each line boasted double tracks, relatively easy grades, generous curves, fine bluestone stations and magnificent bridges – a bluestone viaduct at Malmsbury, an iron viaduct on stone piers at Taradale and the 1000-foot viaduct across the Moorabool River near Geelong.

Threatened by the railways, and disappointed by the returns on their expansion of routes north, Watson and Hewitt were forced to sell off their much-reduced Ballarat and Bendigo routes to repay their debts. The new purchasers of the goldfields routes were James Swanton, one of Cobb's original partners, and a fellow called Blake. The pair struggled to make a go of it, and soon the routes were back in the hands of Watson and Hewitt.

By the beginning of 1860, Watson and Hewitt must have turned the company around, for they had paid for the largest coach ever built in the country. The coach had been constructed in the Ballarat workshops of a coach-builder called Morgan over nine weeks, at the huge cost of £375, and it would serve the busy Geelong to Ballarat route. It made sense to run a larger coach on one of the colony's busiest routes, conveying more passengers in fewer journeys per day.

The coach had been originally commissioned by a group of over-enthusiastic miners as a fledgling business enterprise, and was christened the *Leviathan*, perhaps after the mine of the same name in Ballarat. The huge coach measured close to 5.5 metres long and

more than 3.5 metres from the ground to the rooftop seat. It weighed
a tonne and a half empty, and probably five tonnes when full. Inside
the coach were five rows of seats, each taking five passengers. The two
front rows were reserved for ladies, complete with a mirror so they
could check their appearance. On top of the coach were seven rows of
seats, seating another thirty-five and creating a total capacity of sixty
passengers – not counting those who hung off the sides.

The coach's many side panels were decorated with America's bald
eagle (perhaps in an attempt to win the favour of the many American
miners in the district), the stars and stripes and the E Pluribus motto.
The front panels were emblazoned with fancy paintings: a girl with a
vase and another of a woman wearing a ferocious expression about to
spear a lion in the mouth. The word 'Leviathan' was writ large across
the full length of the coach body.

Describing the coach's launch in Ballarat on New Year's Day 1860,
a bystander wrote in the *Star* newssheet:

> *At the moment of starting, Mr Morgan's men were hard at it,
> fixing a screw here and tightening another yonder or adjusting
> brakes, linings, hangings or some other of the many belongings
> of the great thing ... the ribbons taken by that veteran whip
> Sheppard, who tooled the great craft away from her moorings
> amid the acclamation of an excited crowd ...*

The writer went on to rave about the coach's 'deliciously easy motion,
comparable to nothing more than a comfortable first-class carriage
on an English broad gauge line of railway'.

The talented driver Ned Devine usually drove the great coach, wielding reins of more than 100 feet in order to reach the lead horses. The coach was variously pulled by eight to sixteen horses, depending on the skill of the driver and the strength of the horses – all light greys, splendidly groomed, their harnesses polished to a shine. Often the *Leviathan*'s horses were dressed up with pale blue rosettes in their ear buckles and saddle cloths of blue with silver mountings. For town locals, the departure of the coach – the guard blowing a horn – was the event of the day.

Fortunately for the poor horse teams who pulled the massive coach – some drivers nicknamed it the horse killer – the *Leviathan* was shelved after several years of service, for it was in fact totally impractical. It required strong horses, and as the heavier beasts tended to move more slowly than their lighter counterparts, the firm's fast schedules could not be maintained. The lead horses were so far ahead of the driver they could not be reached with a whip. Instead, Ned Devine was forced to fill a pocket full of small stones, throwing them at any lead horses requiring encouragement or correction.

Clara Aspinall, an Englishwoman living in Melbourne in 1860, penned her opinion of public coach travel into the interior to a friend:

Nobody ever travels up the country by coach if he or she can possibly travel in any private conveyance: but in the event of not having a private carriage, or of friends up the country not being able to drive down a hundred miles to meet him or her, there is no alternative . . . But oh! The crushing, the misery, the suffocation of these public conveyances! I am sure that a journey in a penny-a-mile Government train from London to Edinburgh would be the very refinement of luxury as compared with a journey of thirty miles in Cobb's coach. These vehicles are licensed to carry far too many passengers – from forty or fifty, including those outside. Inside they hold twelve to fifteen. I do not know how many inches are allotted to each passenger; I fancied that only about fifteen fell to my share . . . I know that I was condensed into a smaller compass than I could have imagined possible. I occupied a seat with two others. There were three passengers in front of us leaning against a leathern strap, at the same time pressing upon us and keeping from us the pure air which was admitted through the windows. Just as I was ready to faint, a lady who sat next to me actually did so, which event somewhat roused me up, turning my thoughts from my own misery – and so I rallied.

In a time before telephones, fax machines and email, being able to reply to a letter in time to catch the return mail coach that day was vital to country businesses. Government offices relied on the post more than anyone, so it was little wonder that they applied stiff penalties to coaching operators for late mail delivery. As a result timetables were scheduled to meet the needs of letter writers rather than passengers. In 1860s Australia, a letter posted in time for the Monday mail from Melbourne would reach a country town 200 kilometres away next day without fail. The recipient would pen a reply in time for the return mail and the original correspondent would be reading a reply by Wednesday at the latest. Today, the guaranteed standard delivery time of mail is at least twice as long.

Coach passengers accepted that their welfare came a distant

second to that of the mails their driver carried. Speed always came before customer comfort. When one Victorian coach broke down, the passengers – who were stranded on the roadside – insisted that the mail be sent onwards on horseback while they waited for assistance. Horses were pushed hard to ensure that the mail ran on time, and sometimes they collapsed from exhaustion. It wasn't unknown for a publican to greet a newly arrived coach, its horses frothing and snorting at their bits, then watch in dismay as one of the creatures fell down dead in front of him, almost capsizing the coach as it's heart gave out.

However, the reality was that every town the growing Victorian railway lines reached was one less route for coaches to service. Coach routes were forced to stretch beyond the railways, reaching into every remote part of the colony and feeding travellers to the railheads. To stay afloat, coach operators needed to have the flexibility to open new routes and close redundant ones from month to month. The most difficult Victorian coaching routes were those in the Otway district, the north-east and east of the colony. In the Gippsland forests there were swamps for the horses to negotiate, and the soil from Moe to Morwell was of a type that with a little rain became a sticky glue-pot. In time coach routes reached up into the cold and remote mountain camps of Walhalla, Woods Point, Dargo and Grant.

With its hundreds of horses, coaches and harness, and runs to Ballarat, Bendigo via Castlemaine, Beechworth and Mount Alexander, Watson and Hewitt's business was booming, and they had bought back many of the routes they'd earlier sold. Despite their success, in 1861 they put the business on the market once again. Their asking price was £23 000, a huge amount considering that a well-paid craftsman such as a coach-maker earned less than £150 a year. Perhaps they were relying on a successful gold-digger, blinded by his new riches, to buy them out.

As it transpired, it would be another American whose extraordinary drive would extend the Cobb & Co name into every part of New South Wales and Queensland. The man behind this monster was James Rutherford.

CHAPTER FOUR

JAMES RUTHERFORD

. . . I had no more idea of going to Australia than to Timbuktu.
– James Rutherford

James Rutherford liked to boast that he could do anything, but after spending several months on the Victorian goldfields, he'd had more than enough of greedy men, disease and death. He knew that there was money to be made in providing services to the mass of humanity around him.

Rutherford had followed a circuitous and often turbulent route to end up on the other side of the world. The second-oldest of thirteen children of a New York farmer, James had grown up near Amherst in the far north-west of New York State, not far from Niagara Falls. Although the runt of the Rutherford boys, he had developed a reserve of power as he'd grown, which made up for his lack of stature. His father hadn't wasted a fancy education on the boy. When James was aged seventeen he'd been sent to work on family land hundreds of miles away in Iowa, in the hope that he would take on its management. However, two years in Iowa was long enough. Young James was not the type to settle down.

On the opposite side of the huge continent, tiny Dunn's Corner in New Brunswick, Canada, was desperate for a new teacher. Rutherford was game for a challenge, and his lack of qualifications seemed no barrier to the town council, so in around 1846 he found himself teaching a class of more than twenty-five pupils in a bare wooden schoolroom in the frozen hills that bordered the Atlantic.

On his first day as a teacher, James Rutherford walked into the schoolroom to find total chaos. A dozen of his pupils were husky young farm boys only a year or two younger than himself, but Rutherford was strong with a strap and in that first week the boys soon learned to tone down their behaviour when their new teacher was in the room. They became even more circumspect when Rutherford heard reports that the boys were harassing elderly folks. Following the most troublesome lads home after school, he discovered an old man sitting crumpled in a chair on his porch, blood dripping through his beard. Six pairs of feet were sprinting out of sight.

The next day young Rutherford struggled to contain his fury as he looked at the boys the old codger had identified. The youngsters rose from their seats at his command, along with eight others, fourteen in all, who grinned quietly at each other. In an instant, ten boys lay bleeding and humiliated on the floor.

'You will respect others in this town or I will kill each one of you,' Rutherford thundered.

His students' eyes widened as one, for they had met their match. The town's doctor was called, and Rutherford would have been run out of town if there'd been any chance of finding a replacement for him. The boys' parents swallowed their anger and Rutherford finished the two terms of his contract, his charges silent as the sheaves of wheat in the surrounding fields.

James then moved to Buffalo, New York, where, in the first sign of his entrepreneurial talents, he raised enough money to take a lease on a hotel and made a good profit from the business. When Rutherford's brother Alexander, younger by some three years, wrote from California with fabulous stories of the goldfields, the time was ripe for James to move on. His kid brother Onias, just seventeen, was also up for adventure, so in February 1853 the pair travelled to New York City, only to find that the ship they hoped to sail on was fully booked. The next boat for California would be a month's wait.

Over the next few days, the boys wandered the freezing streets of the big city, impatient to get moving. The winds coming off the sea would have been icy, so finding a warmer climate must surely have been foremost in the lads' minds. Down on the wharves they noticed a cargo ship, the *Akbar*, a huge flag with the words 'Bound for the Australian Goldfields' in large white letters flying from its mast. The ship was crammed with a cargo of flour bound for Port Phillip, and was due to sail within a few days. There were just seven passenger cabins, and one of the berths was free.

Huge crowds were sailing to this new promised land of riches at the rate of five hundred a day, although Melbourne had only been settled sixteen years before. Even on the Californian goldfields men were packing up and hurrying off to find fares to Port Phillip – so did James Rutherford take the Australian ship on a whim? In his old age, he would admit that he had no more idea of going to Australia than to Timbuktu. Whatever the reason, James and his teenage brother took the berth to Port Phillip.

James Rutherford arrived in Melbourne in June 1853, two months after Freeman Cobb. There is no further mention of Onias Rutherford after his arrival in Melbourne. Unlike Cobb, Rutherford headed straight to the latest diggings, near Bendigo, probably on foot and apparently in the company of a Canadian he had met on the ship.

Once at the diggings, Rutherford paid a sizable monthly fee to claim an area of ground no larger than an average bedroom. At a newly opened goldfield such as this, new arrivals would find hundreds of desperate men lying on their backs, their legs and arms outstretched like yawning starfish. Many of them clutched a pistol in one hand and a knife in the other, for they were reserving as much ground as they could until a government surveyor arrived to peg out their claim legally. This policy of allotting every digger his own small patch meant that the alluvial gold, and that accessible with pick and shovel, was divided into thousands of hands. These goldfield allotments were particularly democratic, as no man had a monopoly.

James Rutherford and his friend sank their allotted shaft to a depth of around 4 metres, but without success. Rutherford soon tired of the work, perhaps realising that striking it rich would be long odds. He may well have contracted dysentery, as flies and maggots swarmed around human waste in the muddy ditches on the diggings. The newspapers regularly published long lists of diggers who had died intestate on the goldfields, with no known relatives. How many were crushed by earth falls, murdered by strangers or – drunk and asleep by the side of the road – run over by a bullock dray in the night? Perhaps James wondered how many charlatans came forward, posing as a relative of the deceased, to claim the poor fellow's gold and possessions. The temptation must have been strong.

There were suicides and fatal accidents on the diggings, but above all there was greed. Some fellows worked furtively on their claims, covering them with branches at night for fear a passer-by would take up ground alongside before they could determine which area was richest. On most fields the easily won surface gold was soon exhausted, with further finds only obtainable through the much harder work of digging a deep shaft. For many, taking the small chance of making a fortune on a new field was more attractive than staying put to work claims already turning up fairly good results.

When James Rutherford made his way back to Melbourne from the gold-diggings, he came across an advertisement for woodcutters required for a brick kiln. He applied and won the contract. After taking an axe to a tree, however, Rutherford soon realised that by enlisting the aid of some professional Yankee axemen he could get the job done far quicker. He also negotiated with a local trader for an order of explosives intended to blow up rock in the colony's catacomb of new mine shafts. No-one was using explosives to split logs, and Rutherford's American axemen must have stared at him as if he were mad. Nonetheless, to his employer's amazement, Rutherford had the job completed, his axemen paid and a nice profit for himself days ahead of schedule. It was another sign of the business acumen that was to make him rich.

According to biographical notes later recorded by his son, Rutherford's health 'broke down' just as the job was completed. Sickness was common and he could have been suffering anything from pneumonia to a bad back. In light of events to come, however, this episode may well have been the first sign of a problem that was to haunt James Rutherford and all who became close to him for the rest of his life.

A doctor advised him to leave the chaos of Melbourne for a time, so Rutherford sailed north to Brisbane.

If it was rest the doctor was prescribing, Rutherford found it impossible to comply for long. From Brisbane he left for Ipswich, bought a few horses, a cart, a gun, cigars and a pick and pan for prospecting (just in case), and engaged an offsider. His plan was to ride more than 2000 kilometres south to Melbourne, buying and selling horses en route. The trip was a success, with 120 horses purchased, and Rutherford began to become acquainted with the geography of inland Australia – its rivers, flood plains and climate. More importantly, the trip gave Rutherford something he often craved. Solitude.

Back in Melbourne, flush with profits from his trip, James decided to leave the colony in order to study at Edinburgh University. His forebears were Scottish, and he held the country in high esteem. He organised another horse-dealing trip, perhaps reasoning that it would cover the cost of his studies, and to accelerate matters he shipped the horses north to Sydney rather than mustering them overland. The trip was a disaster. A severe storm hit the Sydney-bound steamer, badly damaging it, and the horses, tethered on deck, were either strangled in the ropes that held them or washed over the side. The few that lived had broken legs and were useless. With nothing to show for the £1000 he'd spent on purchasing the stock, Rutherford returned to Melbourne, having blown all hope of a university education.

Undeterred, in early 1855 Rutherford went back to mustering herds overland, setting off alone on horseback to Port Fairy on the south-west coast of Victoria. This time he could afford just a dozen horses, which he purchased from a man named Kennedy. Apparently feeling out of sorts, he started his horses back for Melbourne and covered 40 kilometres before stopping at a public house for the night. In an account later conveyed by his son George, and confirmed by the subsequent legal case, Rutherford 'went off like a hurricane' at the bar that night. The two brothers who ran the hotel could not stop his vehement outburst and, losing patience, one of them demanded of the sergeant of police who was present at the bar – 'Off to the stable with him!'

Rutherford was rushed from the room, struggling. Seizing an old bullock's skull, he charged at his captors but was eventually overpowered. It is likely that all of the protagonists had drunk substantial amounts of alcohol, and as Rutherford cowered on his stomach, his hands protecting his face, the proprietors pummelled him. One of the fellows stood on Rutherford's back and danced a slow jig.

'They had a great time,' Rutherford recalled. He was later to testify in court:

They handcuffed me and stripped me of my clothes and tied me down on my back to one of the stable stalls, with my head in the manger so that I couldn't get up. It was a bitterly cold night, and I was entirely devoid of clothes with the exception of a singlet.

They left me there without a drink of water until 12 o'clock next day. I daresay that I would have died had there not been a 'pound sale' there that day, and had not Kennedy come down to attend it. He was the man who loosened me.

Kennedy found it hard to hide his horror when he discovered his client in such a bad way, calling to the publican and demanding that the fellow be released.

Rutherford hurriedly resumed his journey to Melbourne. That night he improvised a corral for the horses he had bought and used his saddle as a pillow. He fell asleep next to his campfire but during the night he woke to discover that every beast had broken out, his own mount included. The moon being bright, he picked up his saddle and set off after them. He walked until his legs were ready to collapse. He was nearly 300 kilometres from the nearest town, Geelong, and had no option but to continue walking. For eight days he struggled on, surviving on wattle-gum and water alone. Not until he was 50 kilometres from Geelong did he come across another white man to feed him. Only then did he realise his attackers at the public house had taken his wallet. Near Geelong he begged a meal from a hotel, but the publican refused, 'People like you are as thick as thieves along this road.'

Once in Geelong, Rutherford bluffed his way aboard a steamer bound for Melbourne. Back in the city, without a penny to his name, it was soon obvious that the journey had taken its toll, and Rutherford sickened once again. He was desperate to recoup his losses, but it would be six months before he was able to find the money for a horse and to retrace his steps towards Port Fairy in search of his lost animals. Amazingly, he found them only a few miles from where he had lost them. Perhaps his luck was turning.

Rutherford filed a lawsuit for ill-treatment and false imprisonment against the publican and his brother. He won the case, reported in the Melbourne *Age* of 11 August 1855, and was awarded a huge payout of £500 damages. However, the innkeeper and his brother declared themselves bankrupt, so Rutherford received just £200 plus expenses.

James Rutherford quickly bounced back from his run of bad luck, and in 1856 he spent six months managing routes for a local coaching firm, receiving the princely sum of £25 per week.

By 1857 Rutherford was working for Watson and Hewitt managing Cobb & Co's long coaching route out to Beechworth, near the New South Wales border. It is likely that Rutherford met Alex Robertson, John Wagner, William Bradley and Frank Whitney in Beechworth when these four men began running a coach in competition with Cobb & Co. Rutherford performed well, locating good American drivers to work for the firm and cutting operating costs. He also journeyed north to source horses for the new routes Watson and Hewitt were looking to open into New South Wales.

As a line manager, one of Rutherford's tasks was to ensure that the staff hired by the company were pulling their weight and working efficiently at every stage along the route. Every coaching firm needed reliable grooms, for with no-one to check on them for weeks at a time, a major risk was grooms becoming lazy and careless. A good groom knew to give horses just off a coach no more than a few mouthfuls of water before they had cooled down, as otherwise they risked getting gripe, a spasmodic bowel pain. If gripe and its colicky pain did ensue, each groom had his own remedy. Some swore by ground ginger, Epsom salts and spirits of nitre in a pint of hot water, poured over the suffering horse.

An important change station en route to Melbourne was in the village of Taradale, in the stable behind a hotel run by a Mrs Nicholson, who would one day become Rutherford's mother-in-law. The Taradale groom, a lad called Errow, was responsible for readying horses four times a day for the Melbourne coaches. This meant watering, feeding, brushing and cleaning each horse in time for the changeover. More often than not, young Errow was exhausted.

On one of his tours of inspection of the Taradale stables, Rutherford had a run-in with Errow, accusing him of not being man enough to do the job. When the boy came into the hotel bar to take his leave, Rutherford lunged at the lad, crazed with anger. Seizing him by the throat with one hand and punching out with the other, he caught the boy square on the jaw. The lad staggered and Rutherford lashed out with his boot, digging deep into the boy's ribs.

Errow collapsed to the wooden floor in agony, but Rutherford wasn't finished. He grabbed him from behind and frogmarched him along the passage and into the stables, kicking the boy's rear repeatedly as if it were a football. After his ordeal, the groom had to be carried to a local doctor, who examined and dressed his bruised body and wounds.

Errow pressed charges, backed up by four men who'd witnessed the attack in the hotel bar and who agreed to testify. When the case came before the Taradale Police Court in July 1861, Rutherford pleaded not guilty but the groom's statement was supported by the local doctor. Rutherford made a long and eloquent statement to the court, none of which disputed the truth or the violence of his actions, and he admitted how very sorry he was for his behaviour. The two magistrates nodded gravely and handed down a paltry fine of £10 damages and £5 costs.

Once again, James Rutherford had revealed his skill at getting himself out of a scrape, but there was also growing evidence of an uncontrollable temper. He seemed an unlikely candidate to bring together a successful business partnership.

CHAPTER FIVE

THE CONSORTIUM

. . . a willingness to risk everything . . .

Frank Whitney was a shy, self-effacing Canadian who loved working with animals. He was the kind of man who enjoyed a sing-along in the local bar, bringing a good voice and a jovial disposition to such occasions. An only son, Whitney had grown up on Montreal Island, at the confluence of the Saint Lawrence and Ottawa Rivers, and had run away to sea. A decade on, in September of 1852, he found himself in Hobsons Bay, Melbourne. Like his crewmates, Frank could not ignore the stirring tales of the riches that even a pauper could make in the Australian colonies, and for a time he tried his luck on the rough and tumble goldfields.

James Rutherford and Frank Whitney had become friends by the latter part of 1861, when it was common knowledge that Watson and Hewitt were looking to sell Cobb & Co. The asking price of £23 000 was enormous, but James Rutherford had been managing the firm's Beechworth line, so he well knew the capabilities of the business. If he and Frank Whitney could find roughly 25 per cent of the price – £5000 – they could secure the sale. The risk was whether they could make the money to pay the balance, as more than a few Cobb

& Co operators in the past few years had failed to do just that. But neither of them had anything like £5000: Rutherford could scrape together £1000 from the cash he'd saved managing the lines and selling horses, while Frank Whitney had just £500. Within a short time they had located five potential business partners with experience in coaching and the money to invest: Alex and Colin Robertson, Walter Hall, John Wagner and Charles Pollock.

Rutherford was to come to know Alex Robertson well. The eldest son of Scottish parents who had migrated to Canada, Alex had in turn sailed for Melbourne at the age of twenty-two, Like Rutherford and Whitney, he'd spent some time on the goldfields before making excellent profits as a carrier of goods to Bendigo and Beechworth. He had gone on to manage passenger routes, then gone into partnership running his own coaches with another young Canadian, John Wagner.

Walter Hall, an English fellow from the Cobb & Co booking office, would be useful, given his knowledge of the administrative side of the business. Hall had worked in Melbourne and in Beechworth, where Rutherford presumably met him while managing the coaching route for Watson and Hewitt. In fact, Walter Hall had shown the remarkable ability to escape from a tight spot seven years earlier at the Ballarat gold-diggings.

At the time, the government-administered Miner's Licence entitled the hopeful digger to work a claim by paying a fee of thirty shillings every month, regardless of the amount of gold recovered. The terms of the licence had been irksome to all diggers, but especially at Ballarat, where finding luck in the area's shallow mines was so uncertain. Adding fuel to the fire of discontent were the inadequate processes for settling countless claim disputes, the inconvenience and indignity of frequent 'licence hunts', the arbitrary and brutal physicality of these police searches and sly grog raids, and the atmosphere of privilege, patronage and corruption that permeated the goldfields' administration.

In September 1854, with his government under budgetary pressure, and concerned at the low level of licence compliance, Governor Sir Charles Hotham had secretly ordered an increase in the frequency of the hated licence hunts to twice weekly. A violent reaction seemed unavoidable at the volatile Bendigo field, but it failed to materialise. Instead, two events occurred in October over at Ballarat, once the most peaceful and industrious field, which inflamed the situation even further. The first was the wrongful arrest during a licence hunt, and the following conviction for assaulting a trooper, of the crippled, non-English-speaking Armenian servant of a Catholic priest. The second was the unpopular acquittal of James Bentley, the publican of the Eureka Hotel, charged with the murder of a miner. After an angry mob burned Bentley's Hotel to the ground, Commissioner Rede, resolving to reassert government authority and teach the miners a lesson, requested troop reinforcements.

Somehow, Walter Hall found himself sheltering behind a defensive stockade with a group of rebelling Irish and American miners. Government troops opened fire on the rebels, and Peter Lalor, the rebel leader, was shot in the arm. Hall pulled off his own necktie to bandage Lalor's wound and stem the bleeding, but as the massacre continued, and dozens of miners around him began screaming with the agony of bullet wounds, he decided the protest was not worth his life. He jumped the stockade and ran for several miles, chased by the

police, finally dodging them in a gully. Twenty-two diggers and inno-
cent onlookers were killed that day in the melee that became famous
in Australian folklore as the Eureka Stockade.

A wave of public indignation had coursed through Melbourne
and Ballarat against what was deemed a brutal overreaction to a situation caused by the actions of government officials. When thirteen
of the imprisoned stockaders were tried for treason in Melbourne
early in 1855, all were acquitted, to great public celebration. A formal
inquiry into the goldfields administration was damning in its criticism of the way the affair had been handled. Rapidly, most of the
miners' demands were met. The Miner's Licence was replaced by an
export duty on gold and a Miner's Right, which cost a small annual
fee. A system of mining wardens replaced the gold commissioners,
and police numbers were cut severely. The colony's citizens realised
they had a voice, and the government was prepared to listen. The pace
of reform was so fast that within a year, the rebel leader Peter Lalor
was representing Ballarat in the colony's legislative council.

Walter Hall was not to know it, but the carnage at the Eureka
Stockade became the catalyst for capitalism on Australia's goldfields.
Three decades on, the new goldfield laws and a great deal of luck were
to make him one of the country's richest men.

Within a week, James Rutherford had built on his own £1000 to raise
the cash deposit of £5000. He convinced Alex Robertson and James
Wagner to invest £1000 apiece (Alex had to borrow a little from Frank
Whitney to cover his share), and Colin Robertson (Alex's brother),
Frank Whitney, Charles Pollock and Walter Hall each put up £500.

Watson and Hewitt shook on the sale, with the remaining £18 000 to be paid in time. Some historians suggest that the pair were expecting the new enterprise to fail, and in fact many have wondered how Rutherford's consortium managed to pay off its huge debt in what was rumoured to be a mere six months when others had failed. The answers likely lay in good management, winning and keeping mail contracts, good timing and a willingness to risk everything in an aggressive policy of expansion.

Already proven to be a master at finding efficiencies, Rutherford quickly examined the company's operations and calculated that savings of 25 to 50 per cent in operating costs could be made. He lost no time reorganising the lines.

If Rutherford and his partners were to make their huge investment viable for years to come, they desperately needed to win government mail contracts. In the face of unpredictable passenger numbers, this would guarantee regular income from a resource that cost hundreds of pounds a day to run. The new partners were to become masters at winning such contracts, and the government proved to be the firm's major client. The conditions were sometimes tough. The Postmaster's Department would specify the rate of travel and include penalties for late arrival, with fines of ten shillings for every ten minutes a coach was over schedule often specified.

At the end of 1861, soon after their acquisition of Cobb & Co, the consortium's newly acquired transport business received a timely slab of publicity when promoters organising the first Australian tour by an English cricket team engaged the firm to transport the team around the colony. It is unclear whether it was the driving skill of Ned Devine or the reliability of the Cobb & Co name that helped win the firm the contract. The new proprietors agreed to dust off the problematic *Leviathan* coach to deliver the team onto the Melbourne Cricket Ground, where an enormous spectator stand had been specially constructed.

On Christmas Eve 1861, there was great excitement at the Sandridge wharves (Port Melbourne) when the ship carrying the English team docked. Three thousand cricket fans were waiting to cheer them ashore. Led by H. H. Stephenson, the captain of Surrey, it was not a truly national team as it was made up of professionals drawn from just a handful of counties, yet the locals were more than pleased. The English team played its first match on New Year's Day 1862 against the Melbourne and Districts XXII. Commanding twelve white horses, Cobb & Co's famed Ned Devine drove the English team right onto the ground to great cheers from the crowd.

Unfortunately, the scheduled three-day match was over within a day. Even though the Australians were allowed twice the number of cricketers as the English, they were all out in no time. The promoters – a catering firm – had a back-up in the wings to make up for this embarrassingly short match, staging a balloon ascent from the centre of the ground to amuse the crowd. The balloon was emblazoned with Queen Victoria on one side and the All-England XI on the other. Like the Englishmen's cricket score, it soared up and out of sight.

Ned Devine conveyed the English team to Geelong, Ballarat, Castlemaine and Beechworth, although the coach used in the countryside was probably a somewhat smaller version of the sixty-seater *Leviathan*. In every match, the English team were up against a 22-man side. Each Australian bowler could field six slips, four long stops and rank the rest of his fielders in rows on the leg and on sides. In Ballarat, six or more fielders would converge on each descending ball.

Some of the collisions were very nasty.

In Beechworth, the English team made 264, then finished off the locals for 76 runs. Once again, something had to be done to fill in the time, so George Griffiths, a fine English all-rounder, was picked to play a Beechworth eleven on his own at single-wicket cricket. He bowled the entire team out for one run. He only had to make two runs himself to win; hardly an exciting game.

At Castlemaine, the English were finally beaten, collapsing in their second innings with just 68 runs. Over five thousand bearded miners cheered their men on. At 18 wickets down for 93, victory was with Castlemaine. However, it later emerged that the cunning locals had plied the English team with so much lobster and champagne before the match, it had been a miracle any of them could stand upright on the field.

Ned Devine did very nicely out of the firm's contract. Before the English headed north to New South Wales, the match committee presented him with a purse of 300 sovereigns in recognition of his capable driving.

Rutherford and his partners received a further helping hand by way of lucky timing when news of a rich gold seam in New Zealand began to spread through Victoria early in 1862.

Those who had studied the Californian rush knew that gold-seekers were a fickle lot, and soon a steady stream of miners began to flow from the Victorian fields to New Zealand, further fanned by reports of rich gold on the beach at the mouth of New Zealand's Clutha River and at more than a dozen other centres. The miners would sell a potentially rich claim for just enough money to purchase the coach fare to Melbourne and the passage across the Tasman Sea. Cobb & Co couldn't move the miners fast enough, despite putting on seven coaches a day from Castlemaine down to the Melbourne rail terminus.

The New Zealand alluvial goldfields were soon worked out, and the firm made more money transporting miners back to the Victorian interior. Profits from the carriage of gold-diggers back and forth from Melbourne lined the pockets of the consortium over the next six years, helping to finance Cobb & Co's further expansion.

Perhaps the most important reason for the firm's success was Rutherford's enthusiasm to take on competitors in new markets. Cobb & Co were now making good profits in Victoria, and no other operators had yet taken the Cobb & Co name to New South Wales. When a new goldfield was opened on the Lachlan River near Forbes in New South Wales, they grabbed the opportunity to claim exclusive use. Profitable routes required volume – there was no money in just carrying shearers, station hands and the odd teacher – and fortune-hunters were flocking to the Lachlan goldfields, as well as those at Ophir near Orange and the Turon river.

In Victoria, Cobb & Co had partnership agreements with both the Bendigo Stage Company and the Western Stage Company. The latter firm was also keen to expand into New South Wales, so Rutherford and his partners joined with their partner company to take on the northern colony. Charles Pollock was replaced in the consortium by William Bradley from the Western Stage Company, giving the firm access to the additional coaches and teams they would need for expansion.

The question was where to base Cobb & Co's New South Wales

headquarters. While Sydney was the capital and major port of the colony, the Great Dividing Range west of Sydney presented a huge barrier to those wanting to easily access the goldfields on the other side. Bathurst was the closest town of any size to the Forbes goldfield; it was also a long way from Sydney, so it would take some time for a new railway to reach it. It made sense to fan out their routes from such a central point, instead of Sydney, and to cover settled districts that did not rely on coastal steamers. It also made sense to position trusted partners in Goulburn, Sydney, Orange and Forbes.

But there was an obvious problem: not one of the partners had ever lived in New South Wales. They had no local contacts to leverage new business, a great concern as Cobb & Co would be competing for passengers and mails with established firms that were well entrenched in the colony's goldfield districts. Firms such as Ford & Mylecharane and Crane & Roberts had the local knowledge and connections with stables and feed suppliers, and they already ran coaches on a number of major routes: Bathurst to Sydney, Bathurst to Forbes, Bathurst to Lambing Flat and Bathurst to Orange.

Familiarity with the colony's senior bureaucrats was crucial for winning mail contracts, and would make or break the business. The partners agreed that five of them would need to make the move north, and they sat down and devised a strategy. They would shift 150 horses and a dozen coaches north from Bendigo. Colin Robertson would branch off with perhaps two coaches to establish a new route from Goulburn. One of their best drivers, Hiram Barnes, agreed to take responsibility for Forbes, some 175 kilometres west of Bathurst, diverting two coaches there to immediately take advantage of the gold-fields traffic. That left eight coaches and two feed-wagons bound for

Bathurst. Frank Whitney would take on Orange in the central-west of the northern colony. Walter Hall would be based in Sydney, in charge of government contracts; he had the best experience and knew a little of the city as he had spent a brief period there on his arrival from England before journeying to the goldfields. James Rutherford and Walter Hall would sail up the coast to Sydney, presumably to kick-start discussion of mail contracts with the Postmasters Office. John Robertson, Colin and Alex's brother, would look after bookings from Bathurst, assisted by Rutherford, who would set up a supply chain of horses, drivers and repair works. Once business was established, Rutherford planned on rejoining Alex Robertson in Melbourne – he was hoping three months would do it. Alex Robertson and John Wagner stayed on in Victoria, both becoming hugely successful partners in the firm's Victorian business.

The fifth and newest partner, William Bradley, came up to New South Wales initially, then retreated for a period to Bendigo after falling out with James Rutherford. He was perhaps the first of the partners to feel the heat of Rutherford's temper, but he would certainly not be the last.

CHAPTER SIX

EXPANSION INTO NEW SOUTH WALES

... the triumphant entrance of a first-class equestrian troupe ...
– Bathurst Times, *1862*

The New South Wales town of Bathurst had been founded forty-seven years earlier in 1815 when, desperate for more and better land to accommodate hugely expanded sheep flocks, three explorers blazed the first route over the rugged and unforgiving mountain range to the west of Sydney.

After their discovery of a route across this Great Dividing Range, Blaxland, Wentworth and Lawson returned to Sydney to report the existence of well-grassed plains beyond the mountains. A gateway to open up the interior was just what the new colony needed, so Governor Lachlan Macquarie ordered that a road be constructed. A year later a team of just a few dozen workmen, mostly convicts, had completed the rugged, 160-kilometre route between Penrith and the banks of the Macquarie River, the most important road yet built in Australia. The colony of New South Wales was now no longer a small settlement clinging bravely to the sea.

The mountain road crossed a summit of over 1000 metres, and climbed escarpments (now called the Blue Mountains) that were higher and steeper than any terrain covered by road at that time, or indeed for another fifty years. It was a remarkable achievement, and it remains the most direct route from Australia's first European settlement into the interior. For travellers, the most difficult and terrifying part of the journey was the western descent at Mount York. The gradient here was one in four, far too steep for normal traffic to use. Drays required an extra team or two of bullocks to help them up the slope, and they dragged logs behind them to help with braking on the descent. Given the hazards, the bullock drays covered little more than 11 kilometres a day over the mountains to Sydney, and for many years only wool was worth the expense of cartage to the city.

Just three months after the road's completion, Governor Macquarie and his wife were among the first to trust their carriage to the new route, journeying over the mountains and continuing west to select a site for Bathurst. The road's relatively poor condition can be gauged from the fact that Macquarie took eight days to travel its length.

It wasn't until 1824 that a coaching firm offered a service from Sydney over the new mountain pass to Bathurst. By 1862 the journey took two days, with an overnight stop midway through the range at 'the Weatherboard' (today's Wentworth Falls). There were now something like 800 kilometres of stone-paved roads on which New South Wales' coaches and carriages could operate safely in most conditions.

At 2.30 p.m. on 3 June 1862, ten coaches were lined up and ready to depart Cobb & Co's Bendigo stables for the journey north to New South Wales. The Cobb & Co cavalcade's first leg was a short one, splashing through the mud to Bendigo's largest hotel – the Sham-

rock – where twenty or thirty grooms and stable hands were waiting to board. Around fifty paying passengers milled around, their number including lawyers, doctors and diggers eager to make the journey to the latest, most promising Mecca – the Lachlan River goldfield. In a nod to the tricks of Freeman Cobb, the firm had managed to put together two fine teams of bays, another of black horses and one of all greys. Each coach could carry fifteen to twenty-six passengers – the rough roads ahead ruled out even considering taking a larger coach north.

At the Shamrock, the firm put on two cases of champagne to toast the dozens of employees who had agreed to move to New South Wales. The men drank as if it was going to be their last. There was talk of dangerous gangs of bushrangers operating on New South Wales' roads.

The whole of Bendigo came to see off the gaily painted coaches, and by 3.30 p.m. the great caravan had departed. Rutherford rode north with the teams that first night, then returned to Bendigo to organise the last two coaches. He would then head south to ride to Melbourne in time to catch the steamer to Sydney.

The parade of coaches travelling north were in effect a huge advertising campaign for Cobb & Co, with news of their approach racing ahead of their progress. Locals came from many miles around to see the procession pass by, the coaches' huge yellow wheels a reminder of the gold towns in their sights.

Now twelve in number, the coaches carried tents and provisions, along with forty-gallon drums of water in case they met with dry stretches along the route. In camp at the end of each day's travelling, the men would gather around the campfires and sing of their great, sunlit, lonely land. Some would insist on inflicting songs with countless verses on their audience, going on for hours and hours with melodramatic intensity without any musical accompaniment. A favourite ballad of the time, 'The Wild Colonial Boy', had a chorus that was always delivered with great gusto. It never failed to elicit cheers from the men, many of whom had been involved in hold-ups by Victorian bushrangers:

> *So come away, me hearties,*
> *We'll roam the mountains high,*
> *Together we will plunder*
> *And together we will die.*
> *We'll scour along the valleys*
> *And we'll gallop o'er the plains,*
> *And scorn to live in slavery,*
> *Bound down by iron chains.*

Security was of great concern for the caravan of coaches heading north, for Cobb & Co had chosen to begin its expansion into New South Wales just as the number of armed hold-ups by bushrangers hit a new high. Sometimes ex-convicts, sometimes the wayward sons of local landowners who had become embittered by some personal injustice, these men fashioned themselves as the Robin Hoods of the colony, and indeed humble country folk often gave the outlaws a bed and a meal or lent them a fresh mount. Superb horsemen, they knew the bush far better than many of the policemen who came after them. Their chief targets were coaches carrying valuable gold and cash – exactly the business Cobb & Co was about to field.

Thirty-year-old Colin Robertson was initially in charge of the procession from Bendigo. Crossing the Murray River at Echuca, the stream of coaches caused as much excitement as a travelling circus as it passed through Deniliquin, Jerilderie, Narrandera and Cootamundra. Here, Robertson turned east for Goulburn with his two coaches. The other ten continued north to the Lachlan River at Cowra, presumably with Frank Whitney now in charge. At Cowra, Hiram Barnes peeled off with two coaches for Forbes, and the remaining eight coaches and two feed wagons moved on.

Conscious of the likelihood of attack, the front party of the column of coaches were 'armed to the teeth with rifle and revolvers' to protect their valuable consignment of horses and equipment. North of Cowra, this forward party ran into five or six armed horsemen coming towards them. One led a packhorse 'so heavily loaded as to attract attention'. At least one in Cobb & Co's lead party, a former detective, was immediately suspicious, noticing 'something so unusual in the style and outfit of the party' that he remarked to his companion he would immediately have proceeded to 'overhaul the travellers on suspicion of something wrong' if he had still been in the forces.

According to a witness, the leader of the group, a fellow with a scar under his left eye, rode up to the foremost coach but said as little as possible 'in an evidently disguised tone of voice'. He then rode on, peering into each coach carefully in turn, taking his party with him. Unwittingly, the Cobb & Co caravan had just let Frank Gardiner, Ben Hall, Dan Charters and two others pass, fresh from their robbery of the competitor coach between Forbes and Eugowra. Their seizure of gold and notes to the value of £14000 just a few days earlier on 15 June had been the hugest theft so far in Australian history. The countryside was soon crawling with policemen haplessly trying to track down these very men.

At least nine coaches would be attacked in the seven months after Cobb & Co arrived in New South Wales, most of them around the Bathurst district.

By 1862 Bathurst was a well-established town, with several banks, a School of Arts, tanneries, breweries, saddlers and bootmakers. Nevertheless, Bathurst's wide dirt streets seemed to disappear into the surrounding plains. For squatters and gold-diggers travelling to the western plains it was the last place to stock up on supplies, while miners from the diggings who might not have bathed in a week could scrub up in its local bathhouse. The town's fifty hotels and inns were often full, though many an 'inn' was merely a private home with a licence to sell liquor and perhaps a front room for drinking.

A big night in Bathurst's smoky hotel bars and brothels offered welcome respite from long weeks on the diggings. Gold fever filled the air, and those who'd struck it lucky were easy to pick – their smiles were broader, they ordered double shots at the bar and shouted the house a round. The sound of men singing along to the squeaky tune of a harmonica blended with the bleary guzzling of liquor, and especially excited newcomers declared themselves 'on their way up in the world', their shining faces soon clouded with drink. Liquor and bawdy women were the glue that held this new society together.

Bathurst had been abuzz for weeks with the excitement of the new coach company's imminent arrival. According to the local papers, the legendary Cobb & Co had the fastest coaches, the bravest drivers and the best vehicles on the roads. A recent article in the *Town and Country Journal* had promised that 'Cobb & Co's new Bathurst operations would bring thousands more gold prospectors into the district and transform the town into a centre of prosperity'. However, there was some confusion over exactly who was running the firm. The *Bathurst Free Press and Mining Journal* understood that

> *Mr Cobb, the popular coach proprietor of Melbourne, has 12 coaches and 150 horses in transition ... for the purpose of commencing business operations to and from Sydney and our Goldfields on an unprecedented scale.*

Freeman Cobb had, of course, sailed home to America six years previously.

On Sunday, 28 June 1862, an excitable crowd of townsfolk lined both sides of Bathurst's main street to welcome the coaches. Finally, there was a roar as puffs of dust turned into clouds as horses and coaches charged up the main street. Fine horses hitched mostly in teams of seven pulled a stream of black coaches decorated with gold trim, the horses' manes groomed and plaited, their brushed coats glistening with sweat. They were the smartest coaches the locals had ever seen.

James Rutherford had journeyed over the mountains from Sydney in time to meet the cavalcade outside Bathurst and drive the lead coach in. Frank Whitney manned the next coach and Hal Hamilton, one of the firm's best drivers, held the reins of the third. The *Bathurst Times* described the arrival as being

... like the triumphant entrance of a first-class equestrian troupe on a heavy scale. There were 8 comfortably covered, compact coaches, horsed by 52 high-mettled and well-trained roadsters, driven by bearded and moustached whips apparently of no mean stamp – Jehus of the first order. Six of the teams comprised respectively seven dashing animals which were handled with less seeming anxiety than one of our own towneys would manage his tandem turnout. Had a band of music preceded the line, the town would have hailed for a half-holiday.

A vital factor in running a reliable coach line was ensuring that your horses were kept well fed and healthy. If they were to canter up to 30 kilometres with a coach in tow, they needed sustenance. Hay, corn or oats were essential, but in a land of frequent drought these were often hard to come by.

When Cobb & Co arrived in New South Wales the colony was in drought. Horse feed, when it could be obtained at all, was expensive. At the company's new Bathurst headquarters, Rutherford was kept frantically busy in an uphill battle to negotiate the best deals he could on the purchase and delivery of feed to each new change station. He was a tough negotiator, insisting on only the best-quality feed, and once acquired he would pitch in to help cut hay into chaff, then load it onto drays.

While the new arrivals were settling into their surroundings, the competition was alarmed, and rightly so. Just like Cobb before him, Rutherford's strategy was to challenge his competitors' businesses by providing a better, faster service.

Cobb & Co's first flagship route in New South Wales was the Forbes to Bathurst run, already operated by the Crane & Roberts coaching company. Their service took two days, also using the new American-style coaches, with changeovers every 20 miles (32 kilometres). Hiram Barnes was on orders to slash that journey time in half. If it could be done, Cobb & Co would be bound to win business from Crane & Roberts. Rutherford's strategy was to have change stations every 10 miles, ensuring fresher, faster teams than the competitors, but the risk was high. The capital investment required for the additional horses, sets of harness, extra change stations and grooms was well beyond that of any other operator. Sure enough, with Barnes at the reins, the Cobb & Co coach arrived in Bathurst in the promised time. One of the first to try out the new service was the US consul to the colony.

No doubt annoyed at James Rutherford's famous arrogance, and determined to put a spoke in the wheels of Cobb & Co's new service, Crane & Roberts decided to play tough. Their service from Forbes ran through to Penrith, in time to pick up the train to Sydney, whereas Cobb & Co ran only to Bathurst. On the very day the Cobb coach carrying the US consul arrived in Bathurst, Crane & Roberts' driver refused to carry their competitor's passengers on their 6 a.m. coach next morning. Hiram Barnes' passengers were stranded.

James Rutherford was in a bind. He was desperate not to lose his first high-profile customer to this trickery – it would make Cobb & Co the laughing stock of the colony. If their competitors were to play this game every week, Cobb & Co's new Forbes route was doomed. Finding a coach and horses to carry his passengers onwards was the only option, though taking on the route over the mountains was a huge task.

Somehow, Rutherford calculated that he could have a coach ready by eight the next morning, and he bravely announced his plan to his testy passengers. The Crane & Roberts driver must have smirked at Rutherford's apparent lunacy: everyone knew that Cobb & Co had no fresh horses at the ready on the long mountainous road, let alone access to even one change station or groom. Seven of Cobb & Co's eight coaches in the district were already committed to routes.

On top of the long day of driving from Forbes, Hiram Barnes agreed to take the coach on to Penrith at 8 a.m. the next morning. Rutherford promised to accompany him. His plan was to make use of the recently installed telegraph lines and wire ahead to arrange stable facilities and fresh teams along the route. The story goes that one of Rutherford's loyal men overheard the conversation and volunteered to ride through the night to Tarana and on to Lithgow, Mount Victoria and Wentworth Falls. At each place, he woke the man in charge of the livery stables and, with plenty of cash in hand, secured fresh teams for the coach next day.

The Cobb & Co passengers were sceptical: Crane & Roberts' 6 a.m. departure was timed to meet the train for Sydney at Penrith, so how would they arrive in time if they left at eight?

Rutherford returned to bed but he could hear his customers angrily discussing the matter downstairs. Knowing that he could ill afford to be disturbed if his plan for the next day was to work, he grabbed a blanket from his bed, slid down a verandah post outside his window and crept around to the company's stable to bed down undisturbed in the feed room.

The Crane & Roberts coach left at 6 a.m. as scheduled. Two hours later, good to his word, Rutherford had a coach ready for his passengers. All went to plan, the Cobb & Co driver making such good time that they came in sight of the rival coach not far from Penrith.

Rutherford followed on horseback and, probably without his partners' knowledge, took the opportunity to call on his competitor's manager in Sydney. He had an offer to make for the Crane & Roberts business.

The manager must have wondered if he was hearing things when Rutherford made an offer of £16 500 for the firm's horses, change stations, coaches and harness. For almost the same amount that Freeman Cobb and his partners had received for the original Cobb & Co business, Rutherford secured eight additional mail and passenger contracts, worth over £4600 a year in government payments. On 14 July 1862, less than three weeks since Cobb & Co had arrived in Bathurst, the deal was concluded. It is hard to imagine how the company had access to this sort of money, though Rutherford was later to prove a master at buying on credit. The firm must surely have gone into huge debt to fund the purchase, and Rutherford's business partners would need nerves of steel to cope with the repayments.

There remained many small operators to contend with in rural New South Wales. One such company, Ford & Mylecharane, controlled the route from Bathurst heading west to the Lambing Flat gold-diggings (present-day Young). Through an acquaintance in the colony's police force, Cobb & Co was awarded a contract to transport twenty policemen from Sydney to Lambing Flat in the wake of recent riots at the goldfield. Law keepers were regular users of public coaches for prisoner escorts, as well as for moving between country courthouses and the goldfields, and if the police could be secured as regular customers Cobb & Co's passenger numbers would be guaranteed. Rather than pass the policemen on to Ford & Mylecharane at Bathurst, this time Rutherford played tough and refused. Instead, he had his own coach carry the men. By 1 September Ford & Mylecharane had sold their three routes to Cobb & Co rather than compete against such pig-headedness. More than £1000 was added to the firm's annual mail subsidies.

Rutherford scrutinised every competitor running coaches on Cobb & Co's routes. When they made a trip without a single passenger he would gloat in triumph. In order to grow the business rapidly, Rutherford would bribe operators who had existing government mail contracts, paying them hundreds of pounds for the right to take over their contracts and adjusting the paperwork so the government had no cause of complaint. He would then jack up passenger fares by as much as 350 per cent to cover what he had paid in bribes, knowing he had a monopoly.

Cobb & Co never attempted to compete with the railways, but tailored their services to act as feeders to the new inland railheads. This policy ensured friendly relations with the government, which was investing huge sums in railways and had no desire to encourage competitors. It was a clever strategy, helping the firm to win the lion's share of mail contracts where there was no rail service. It also meant they had to be ready to shift routes. The way to operate was to rent all the buildings you needed for a fixed time, then move on. In coaching, everything else was transportable.

CHAPTER SEVEN

HOMESICK AND LONELY

. . . I am anxious as ever, to return to my native land . . .
– James Rutherford, 1863

Cobb & Co lost no time in opening a repair shop in Bathurst, initially in the yard of the Black Bull Hotel. Four blacksmiths and wheelwrights were shipped up from the firm's Castlemaine workshop, for the aim was to build their own coaches rather than be burdened with the high costs of importing the vehicles from America. There was also a good market for traps and buggies for private use. As their routes expanded, the firm became so desperate for horses trained to pull a coach that they employed buckjump riders to break in the animals. Within a year, the Bathurst repair works stretched from the Black Bull's stables to cover an acre of ground, taking over coach houses, chaff-cutting sheds and breaking-in yards. There was sufficient shedding to store chaff for the dozens of change stations between Hartley and Forbes.

Soon afterwards they opened their own coach factory, building not only four sizes of passenger coach (the largest seating forty) but also buggies and carriages for private buyers. For short distances there were small uncovered carriages called sociables, the passengers sitting back-to-back facing the sides of the vehicle.

The Cobb & Co partners based in each town were faced with a massive task when it came to setting up new coach services. They had to decide on the best available route between towns, taking into account road conditions and terrain. Next, they had to divide their proposed route into stages of 6 to 12 miles (10 to 20 kilometres), depending on the number of hills and where they could find suitable sites for a change station. Each changeover point needed facilities to keep at least six or seven horses, as well as space for storing feed, harnesses and accommodation for a groom.

Frank Whitney was in charge of setting up the firm's route between Orange and Forbes, a distance of 110 kilometres requiring eight changes. He needed six horses per stage for the medium-sized coach, and had to ensure there were sixty-four sets of well-maintained harness (which included two spares for each team), eight grooms and victuals for animals and workers. Hiram Barnes had found a man in Forbes to manage bookings in that town, while Frank managed the bookings himself in Orange.

Two months after Cobb & Co started on the Forbes to Orange route, one of their coaches was held up a few miles out of Forbes and passengers relieved of £150, though many would-be robbers came away with much slimmer pickings. Back in 1851, bushranger William Green had complained that his robbery of the Melbourne to Port Fairy mail coach had yielded far more love letters than valuables.

By January 1863, if not before, Rutherford was keeping a diary of his daily activities. There was so much to do, he seems to have forgotten his initial plan of returning to Melbourne to work with his friend Alex Robertson. His diary entries provide an intimate picture of a man struggling to oversee a growing number of employees in an alien environment. Rutherford was nothing if not hands-on. When a coach broke down on the road or an accident required on-road repairs, it was often Rutherford who rode out to solve the matter. Cobb & Co coaches ran day and night and he was constantly on call. There was always something to attend to, whether it was ordering stables to be relocated because they lay at the base of a gully that turned to mud in the wet, or checking on the firm's many workers. Rutherford watched his employees with an eagle eye, going through their expenses and accounts fastidiously. He didn't hesitate to get rid of men if they were under-performing. Within the space of two days, just six months after the firm's triumphant arrival in Bathurst, he had engaged a solicitor to prosecute his new Forbes manager for embezzlement and fired a groom for being asleep at his change station.

Some of the drivers were cruel to their teams. James Rutherford was somewhat shocked at the tactics of a driver he nicknamed the Flying Barber when he travelled with him from Forbes to Young, writing in his diary:

> . . . if there is one man in the world qualified to get work out of worn-down horses, he is the man, for using the whip appears to be his forte. It was one continual cut and lash, interspersed with oaths, from beginning to end of the journey. It seems incredible the amount of work those poor horses had to perform.

Rutherford does not mention reprimanding the fellow. As long as the drivers met their schedules, the way they treated their teams was their own affair.

James Rutherford found the heat of Australian summers absolute torture. When he made an inspection of the firm's new routes in January 1863, severe drought meant that some of the properties he passed had no groundwater at all. Sheep and cattle were dying of starvation and thirst before his eyes. On 4 January, after an hour in the sun, his thermometer showed 137 degrees (58 degrees Celsius). The heat was so unbearable, Rutherford took to delaying his daily journeys until late in the afternoon. Despite this tactic he struggled to cope:

> *Arrived at the stopping place about 10 p.m., completely knocked up, being nearly dead with heat and thirst, not having been able to get any water for the last 17 miles. The night appeared hotter if possible than the day had been, which rendered sleep next [to] impossible.*

Rutherford wrote this on 5 January, when summer still had a long way to go. It was hard to see how he was going to last in Australia's scorching interior.

Overindulgence in rum or whisky was reaching epidemic proportions in outback towns. Even publicans were known to be continually drunk. When Rutherford brought a coach painter to Bathurst by coach he discovered he had been drinking through the whole journey and required a good day or two to dry out. He'd sometimes set up business meetings with another coaching proprietor, only to find them so intoxicated that nothing could be accomplished. In mid-April he wrote in his diary:

One great misfortune in the country is that men will get intox-
icated; it is perfectly impossible to find tradesmen who will
follow their occupation, without breaking out occasionally at
least, and unfortunately the best workmen are generally the
worst . . . but I fear that the present generation will not give
up the fiery rum and chemical brandy for the light juice of the
grape. It will not supply sufficient stimulus to satisfy their crav-
ing appetites.

Like Freeman Cobb before him, Rutherford regularly dismissed
drivers for drinking too much. He tolerated no malingering or lazi-
ness. Certainly Rutherford had a temper, but though he would fly
into a fury and turf drivers out on their ear at times, he always for-
gave those who were talented. Some men worked under him all their
lives.

In Bathurst it was John Robertson who drew cheques for purchases
and oversaw the mountains of paperwork that Rutherford hated.
Rutherford was glad of the fellow's company and trusted him completely. When Robertson was sent to Sydney to relieve Walter Hall
for two weeks, Rutherford found himself landed with piles of paperwork – nothing but bookings, invoices and orders. His mood sank
into melancholia. Lying awake at night, loneliness engulfed him – an
ache for his American family. He began to dwell on his own mortality.
Nonetheless, he forced himself to attend a Batchelor's Ball, although
he recognised none of the young ladies there. Not one for dancing, he
complained in his diary:

Having no legitimate means of making any of their acquaint-
ances, I enjoyed myself about the same a man might be expected
to do on the way to the stocks. No cards were played, nothing;
one continued round of polkas, waltzes, quadrilles, etc. I should
have been extremely glad to have left the scene of so much gai-
ety, but etiquette forbade; therefore I allowed myself to be a
martyr to the rules of decency, and took my revenge in puffing
clouds of smoke from Havanas and drinking port wine.

Those who got to know James Rutherford well must have found him
to be an odd sort of fish. Now aged thirty-six, and still a single man,
he was overworked, tired and, unsurprisingly, lonely. Since arriving
in the colonies he had worked long, long days. Waves of homesickness
overcame him, and when a colleague returned home to Germany in
late April, he was prompted to write in his diary:

I only wish that I were able to start for my native hills. How
soon would I bid adieu to this land where I have been exiled for
10 years; once more to greet the kindest best of mothers.

By June 1863, on the tenth anniversary of his arrival in the colonies,
Rutherford admitted in his diary that he was keen to return to America for good.

How long I may be forced, by circumstances, to remain in this
country, I cannot tell, but this I do know. I shall never rest sat-
isfied here, I am anxious, as ever, to return to my native land.

Rutherford had been the driving force behind Cobb & Co's aggressive expansion in New South Wales. If he were to return home, it was hard to see who else had the energy to drive the business forward.

The Australian interior was never quite as lawless as the American Wild West, mainly because the colonial authorities moved in quickly to build courthouses, police stations, and gaols as soon as there was a significant population to require them. Not one Cobb & Co driver was killed by a bushranger, but even so there was plenty of crime.

Three weeks after his private vow to return to America, on Monday, 13 July 1863, Rutherford was travelling on the firm's coach between Bowenfels (modern-day Lithgow) and Mudgee. Just before noon, Rutherford's coach passed the down coach, which carried only two passengers: Mr Kater, an accountant with the Mudgee branch of one of the colony's main banks, and a Mrs Smith, the wife of a wayside publican. Mrs Smith had £100 tucked away in the pocket of her crinoline, a year's salary for many. But there was more. Mr Kater was travelling on important bank business, carrying close to £6000 in bank notes in his carpetbag and a revolver in his pocket. It's strange that an armed escort hadn't been arranged to safeguard the carriage of this amount of money. The recent hold-ups in which police escorts had easily been overcome may have discouraged their use, as some argued that an escort merely highlighted the fact that a coach was worth robbing. Escorts tended to be made up of four to six mounted troopers, one of whom rode in front and the others abreast of the coach or just behind it. On dangerous parts of the road, a pair of troopers would ride ahead to guard against ambush. Usually troopers rode with their carbine rifles loaded at their hip.

Out of sight on the hill above Rutherford were a trio of bushrangers: Fred Lowry, Larry Cummins and Jack Foley. Fred Lowry was a wanted man – a strong and handsome fellow with a reputation as the best buckjump rider in the country, for no brumby had ever thrown him. His hatred of the authorities had hardened when they'd locked up his girlfriend, and he'd turned from horse and cattle theft to highway robbery, only to be captured and thrown in the Bathurst lock-up. Exactly four months before, he had escaped and returned to robbing coaches.

Lowry and his mates' target was not the coach Rutherford travelled on but the mail coach coming the opposite way from Mudgee to Bowenfels. Presumably, they hoped it was carrying gold from the nearby Gulgong diggings.

The bushrangers knew this route well. Sixteen miles out of Bowenfels was a steep hill, at which passengers would be asked to get out and walk to help the horses. It made a bushranger's job all the easier. Two horsemen road slowly downhill towards the coach. With gold watch-chains and black coats, they looked like wealthy squatters on their way home. Once level with the coach, Jack Foley whipped out a revolver and ordered the driver to pull up.

The bank manager reached for his revolver but Lowry had his own gun pointed at the head of Kater.

'Hands up, or I'll shoot you dead.'

The mailbags were quickly plundered, and when they discovered Kater's carpetbag he was forced to unlock it. On seeing the contents, Lowry's chuckle accelerated to laughter. Mrs Smith was left alone. 'We never touch ladies, ma'am,' said Lowry, tipping his hat.

The four Cobb & Co horses were cut loose and spooked into the bush at a gallop, leaving the driver and his passengers to stare hopelessly at each other as Lowry and his men made off. Kater eventually walked the 25 kilometres to the next town to report the embarrassing loss.

In one lucky strike, Lowry had caused the biggest sensation since Ben Hall's Eugowra hold-up a year earlier. By the time news of the heist reached Rutherford in Mudgee, at least a day had passed.

The experience taught Rutherford to be particularly wily when it came to protecting the huge sums of gold his coaches often carried. The alternative was to risk losing valuable government contracts. Some months later, Cobb & Co was entrusted to transport a large consignment from the gold-diggings at Sofala to Bathurst. Gold was often transported in sturdy bags rather than iron boxes, and as there were rumours of bushrangers in the vicinity Rutherford took some bags down to the river in Sofala and filled them with stones. The next morning he made the switch, loading the bags filled with stones onto the Cobb & Co coach and placing the gold bags in his own buggy, covering them with bags of chaff. Rutherford drove out of Sofala ahead of the coach and, sure enough, he was bailed up on a thickly timbered section of the road. The outlaws asked him the whereabouts of the mail coach, and Rutherford admitted it was only half an hour behind him.

The men let Rutherford pass, as his own freight appeared to be only feed, and he moved off slowly up the rise. At the top, Rutherford egged his horses into a gallop until his gold consignment was well beyond pursuit.

Just as Cobb & Co was carving out a reputation for itself in New South Wales, disaster struck. It was mid-July, a week after the hold-up of the Mudgee coach. James Rutherford had suffered a recent fall and was complaining of a bad back, which was making his long hours on the road agony. Within days, he stiffened up completely. He suffered stoically, but after spending five nights trapped in Bathurst, unable to move, he forced himself to see a doctor. All he wanted was to get back on the road, and by 4 p.m. the next day he was on the coach for Forbes. Not surprisingly, his injuries went from bad to worse.

As was common, the Forbes coach travelled through the bitter night. Not long after three o'clock on a Sunday morning, after having just changed coaches in Orange, they hit a huge pothole. The coach tipped over, and Rutherford was thrown underneath it, his body pinned to the ground.

Once he was pulled free, even Rutherford had to admit his injuries were serious. He spent the whole of that Sunday lying in agony in a miserable inn, as snow and rain lashed the windows of the wooden shanty. However busy the week, Rutherford usually liked to give Sundays over to rest, loving nothing better than immersing himself in a historical biography. On this particular Sunday he was in too much pain even to read. Next morning, he pushed on to Forbes, wincing with pain at the coach's continual jarring motion. He barely had the energy to write in his diary that night: 'Continually in agony; my ribs being nearly broken and my back hurt'.

Midweek, Rutherford returned to Bathurst paralysed with pain. By Sunday the slightest exertion was like a red-hot needle to his chest and ribs. He could not even get on a horse. Rutherford resigned himself to holing up in Bathurst for a few weeks. Still he refused to lie idle, and he was soon helping with the cutting of chaff and loading of bales. His bad back only worsened.

James Rutherford was homesick and lonely. On top of this, too much time spent on Australia's dreadful roads was making a cripple of the man. It was hard to envisage this impatient American lasting much longer in the driver's seat of the company's New South Wales expansion.

CHAPTER EIGHT

THE PARTNERS' WIVES

... the independence of spirit to find her own way in life ...

It was to be Frank Whitney and James Rutherford who would remain longest in the Cobb & Co partnership. They would be dependent on each other financially and emotionally for the rest of their working lives, as would their wives.

Given the long days both men put in, the girls James Rutherford and Frank Whitney were most likely to meet lived and worked in the hotels along their coaching routes. Many were brazen, tough harlots, hardly the prospective partner a respectable man thought seriously about, not that working in coaching, even if you owned the business, was seen as a gentleman's profession. Nonetheless, Frank Whitney was about to meet an extraordinary young woman.

By 1863 the firm's Bathurst staff had shifted out of their temporary quarters at the Black Bull Hotel and relocated to a booking office in William Street. The building was tiny – the grand two-storey edifice next door rather dwarfed their new shop-front – but at least it was on a main street. It was at this time that Cobb & Co began stabling some of their coaches at Mrs Rachel Leeds' White Horse Hotel instead of at the Black Bull, and it was likely here that Frank Whitney encountered

Bella Leeds, the female publican's daughter. She was a small, pretty girl, her good looks highlighted by fine alabaster skin touched with pink, though her face was a little too full and rounded to be called beautiful.

Bella was the youngest of Rachel Leeds' four surviving daughters, but older than her three brothers. She had been aged just twelve when she'd lost her father more than five years before. Rachel Leeds was a great-granddaughter of a member of the Danish royal family – King Frederick V's brother, in fact – though such a lineage counted for little in colonial Australia. Rachel had suffered the loss of three children in their infancy, and the family's plans to build their Muswellbrook sheep station into something prosperous and permanent had withered like grass with the death of her husband.

Rachel had relations in the Bathurst district, and her late husband also had family there, so she had packed up her home and journeyed there from the Hunter Valley with her family of seven children. Perhaps she'd not read the newspaper reports of just a few years before describing Bathurst as 'the worst in the colony with every third building a grog shop'. Drinking to excess was clearly the town's main recreation.

The woman quickly showed remarkable resilience, becoming publican of one of Bathurst's more prominent hotels. It was perhaps her only means of supporting her large family. The Leeds family moved into their new home, the two-storey White Horse Hotel, in January 1858. Filled with red-faced, dirty men who assumed Bella was there to serve their every whim, the hotel must have seemed a step down in the world to the young girl. She'd grown up swimming in summer waterholes, alive to the whiff of bushfires and the delicious scent of imminent rain. The bustle of a busy town and the gritty chatter of strangers were no replacement for the rhythms and beauty of nature, although it wasn't that Bathurst lacked excitement. In her first year in the town, an attraction billed in the paper as 'the Wonderful Nondescript Great Sea Monster' toured Bathurst – a living animal from the sea with its own keeper – but to Bella Leeds it was far less interesting than the wide open spaces.

Five years spent running a busy Bathurst hotel while bringing up seven children on her own was killing Bella's mother. By 1863 she was confined to her bedroom, too weak to take a walk or do up the bodice on her dress. On the second day of winter, she took her last shallow breath.

Bella Leeds was now an orphan, but she was to reveal the independence of spirit to find her own way in life.

It was not only Frank Whitney who was falling for a lass from a public house. James Rutherford had also met the woman he would marry, Ada Nicholson. Ada's English mother – also a widow – was the publican at the hotel in Taradale, outside Melbourne, which Cobb & Co used as a change station. Ada could surely not have failed to have noticed Rutherford a few years earlier, when he had lost his temper and bashed the groom in her mother's stables, and then been arraigned in front of the local magistrate.

Five years after her own husband's death, Mrs Nicholson had found herself destitute, having invested most of her husband's savings in England's new railways. They had proved to be a financial black hole. With the little money that was left, she had gathered up three of her daughters and abandoned her native Essex. At the age of ten, Ada

Nicholson found herself travelling to a strange land by sailing ship, a journey which took three months. Ada's ship sailed through Port Phillip Heads on Christmas Eve, 1851. Sixty-six years later she could still recall the day.

> We dined on porpoise steak, it was very good after living on bully-beef, salt pork and tinned potatoes for so long. The first news of the gold find was just announced and in the morning, not a man was left on board but the Captain and his son. The men did not return and we had great difficulty in getting ashore.

Ada's mother initially found employment in Melbourne in the hat trade. Her father and late husband had worked in the trade, and it was the only business she knew. She toiled away miserably for a few years, hating it, before shifting to the goldfields north of Melbourne. In the nine years since 1854, Ada's mother had become Taradale's best-known publican.

James and Ada had begun courting by 1862, though they had perhaps seen each other only once in the eighteen months since Rutherford had left Victoria and they now lived close to 800 kilometres apart. Frank Whitney would likewise have had little time to spend courting, as he was busy setting up routes for much of the year in Orange. Nevertheless, by the spring of 1863 it's likely that both men had proposed. The two girls accepted: for both of them, it was a way out of lives spent cleaning up after drunken hotel patrons.

Bella was intent on a real country wedding at Nanima, the property owned by one of her maternal uncles in the newly settled

Wellington district. It was one of the best and largest properties in the district, with a beautiful homestead on good flat river country. Bella's uncle, Joseph Aarons, had purchased the property's 16 000 acres for the ridiculously low sum of just over £7000 from an early settler, a Jew by the name of Montefiores. The settlement of Montefiores, across the Macquarie River from Wellington, was named after the pioneer. Bella's brother Arthur worked for Uncle Joseph, managing the property while Joseph Aarons bought and sold land for his clients.

On 7 November 1863, Bella and Frank were married in the newly constructed wooden church in the Montefiores township, and a reception was held at the Nanima homestead. Relatives and townsfolk gathered to witness the union of the wily Canadian to this short but striking, some would say intense, girl. Beneath her smooth-skinned good looks there was a sturdiness of character about the now-orphaned Bella Leeds. She was a sensible choice for a man intent on making his mark.

The guests were mostly Bella's relatives and friends, for Frank of course had no local family of his own. Rutherford arrived nine hours after the ceremony, seemingly by chance. Unconcerned, he made his way to the remains of the reception, having eaten nothing since breakfast, and soon polished off the leftovers from Frank and Bella's wedding banquet.

In early December 1863, just six months after he had admitted in his diary how keen he was to abandon Australia, James Rutherford travelled south to Taradale outside Melbourne to wed tiny Ada Nicholson. Rutherford's arrival set in train a frantic few days as Ada's wedding dress was yet to be finished and his bride needed to have her bags packed for Bathurst a day after the wedding. Rutherford could stay only two or three days in Taradale, as he was anxious to get back to his mountain of work in Bathurst. Frank Whitney did not attend the wedding, as it is unlikely he could be spared from the business.

After the ceremony, the newlyweds took the steamer from Melbourne to Sydney, where Rutherford procured a buggy to drive his wife out to Bathurst. In Blackheath, just a few miles before they were to descend the Blue Mountains to the great plain below, they stopped briefly to give the horses a drink from a trough. A breeze caught Ada's treasured new hat – white straw with cherries on it, bought in Melbourne especially for the wedding – and it settled in the drinking trough. This was a time when neither ladies nor men would appear in public without a hat. Ada cried out as James geed up the horses, imploring him to stop and fetch it, but Rutherford refused. The hat was done for, in her husband's opinion, and they couldn't afford to dilly-dally. He promised to buy her a new one once they reached Bathurst, but when their buggy clattered into town they were met by hundreds of townsfolk turning out to welcome them. Ada was mortified to be presented, hatless, as the new wife of the town's most talked-about businessman.

James and Ada Rutherford settled into a new house at the top of William Street, just down the road from the firm's booking office. It was a newly built, spacious brick cottage with four large rooms opening off a central hallway, verandahs at the front and rear, and a lean-to kitchen on one side of the building. Behind the home lay stables large enough for two horses, a coach house and a small room for a coachman. Not until their sixth child came eleven years later was the tiny cottage enlarged; ten of their eleven children would be born here.

In the eighteen months since Rutherford had arrived in the town, Bathurst had become the largest town west of the Blue Mountains and Cobb & Co the business to watch. One fed off the other, as the firm demanded a growing number of workers to supply the raw materials for its coach construction and countless artisans to build and finish each vehicle. Then there were the accountants, booking agents, grooms and suppliers of horse feed and saddlery whom the firm kept busy.

Meanwhile, the rapid demise of the town that had sprung up around the Forbes diggings was typical of the rise and fall of dozens of towns that sprang up around gold-diggings – Ophir, Sofala, Hill End and Gulgong all went the same way. Shortly before his wedding, James Rutherford had been shocked to find Forbes looking wretched and all but abandoned, when just weeks before it had been the firm's busiest destination. Forbes was indeed a sad sight. The surrounding bushland had been cleared of trees for firewood and temporary shanties, and the abandoned buildings dotting the scarred landscape looked like a swarm of locusts had been through them. The population of 20 000 had been decimated to one-tenth of that number, and first-class hotels were on the market for a tiny fraction of their value six months prior.

The exodus had at first been good news for Cobb & Co's passenger numbers, but Rutherford was reminded of a deserted soldiers' camp. The situation was not unexpected, for Cobb & Co had witnessed the same boom-and-bust pattern in Victoria and were well prepared to adjust their timetables and routes to follow the market. Fortunately, there was a constant demand for new routes to carry the public to shanty towns springing up around remote creeks that promised an undiscovered fortune.

By late 1864, with the drought behind them, Cobb & Co's New South Wales and Victorian coaching businesses were looking healthy. Having successfully harnessed local talent in the manufacture of coaches and saddlery, the partners began looking at further ways to reduce costs. The answer was livestock. If the firm was to breed and train its own horses, rather than buying them in, the potential savings could be huge. In addition, British colonial India had become a profitable market for exporting sturdy, broken-in horses as cavalry mounts for its large army since breeders in New South Wales had come up with a horse that was well suited to the Indian climate. What Cobb & Co needed was land where the company could breed its own horses, which would have the added advantage of being a source of hay for their coaching teams, for Cobb & Co was continually buying in huge amounts of feed from local growers.

Rutherford had his eyes on a huge station called Buckiinguy on the Macquarie River, east of present-day Nyngan. Considering the opportunities starting to emerge in outback Queensland, the property was well placed. It's unclear just what level of consultation Rutherford had with the other Cobb & Co partners, but Rutherford moved fast when he heard the property was for sale. Two days after Christmas 1864, he was reputedly waiting in Sydney at the land agent's office when his doors opened for business. Rutherford wrote out a cheque for £24 000 to purchase the massive 450 000-acre run, an acquisition that was to be immensely significant for the future of Cobb & Co. The company soon diversified from breeding horses into raising cattle and sheep. Buckiinguy marked the beginning of a property empire that would outlast the firm's coaching interests.

However, there was a problem. Although he had lived in the colonies some eleven years by now, James Rutherford was an American by birth and was therefore ineligible to purchase property in the Australian colonies. Frank Whitney and Walter Hall faced no such obstacles, being Canadian and English respectively. Their Australian citizenship was automatic, but strangely neither of them stepped in to put their name on the sales contract. Instead, it was Rutherford's friend Alex Robertson from Melbourne who put his name on the Buckiinguy documents. By May 1865 Rutherford been naturalised, removing that particular barrier to further land deals. Around the same time, the firm purchased another large station, Yanda, 40 kilometres south of what is now Bourke, on the Darling River. William Bradley, one of the partners, ran it for a time.

Someone was now needed to manage the new Buckiinguy venture. Frank Whitney had settled into life with Bella in Orange, coordinating the firm's three main routes heading west to Forbes, north to Wellington and east to Bathurst and Sydney from Hanrahan's Hotel in Orange's main street. Rutherford's son George claims that his father pushed Frank Whitney into shifting up from Orange to manage Buckiinguy. Perhaps it was an easy sell, given Whitney's love of animals.

It was no secret that Buckiinguy's last owners had been beaten by its isolation and harsh conditions. Although Frank had never seen the property, he must have been well aware of the risks involved in moving to the outback. Plenty of fine men went bad in the bush, becoming toughened and coarse, no different from station hands, and often taking Aboriginal girls from the camps to ease their loneliness. But Frank had Bella, and although it would be impossible for a woman at the beginning, a few years would give him time to build a comfortable homestead. He was perhaps relieved that Bella was not yet pregnant.

Cobb & Co also purchased a much smaller 6500-acre station on the Victorian border at around this time, on which to also breed horses. The property was called Pericoota, and a grand two-storey homestead and stables were built over the next few years, both of which still stand proud on the banks of the Murray River today. Decades after its purchase, the property was sold to the famous Falkiner sheep-breeding family for the enormous sum of £225 000.

Bella Whitney joined her husband at Buckiinguy about a year later. When the bullock dray arrived to collect Bella and her baggage, there would have been a sea of chests to load. The typical frontier settler needed to pack all kinds of equipment and supplies: a butter churn, kitchenware, nails, garden tools and six months' supplies of dry goods, including flour, sugar, tea, tapioca, corned beef, salt and vegetable seeds.

It was the bullock dray that made the journey to Buckiinguy so slow; if you travelled the same road by light buggy it might take just six days, but by bullock dray it took several weeks. Apart from wondrous changes in its tint, the view was incessantly the same, and travellers had nothing but flies and the flat mallee-dotted scrub to entertain them. Bella was not accustomed to long journeys, and her thighs would have blistered and ached from the interminable movement as the bullock dray's wheels rumbled and squeaked.

By now Frank had built a rough slab cottage 'homestead'. It was perched just above a large waterhole on Mara Creek. The men's quarters lay a hundred metres through the bush, just discernible through the grey ghost gums. What madness had made twenty-year-old Bella Whitney give up the comforts of town life for this?

Frank's responsibility was to breed not only horses but also cattle. In later years, fencing would take up months of his time. White workers were scarce and high wages had to be paid to keep them. It was more common to employ local aboriginal stockmen and shepherds, sawyers and bush carpenters. A station manager was put on to supervise over 10 000 sheep and the day-to-day running of Buckiinguy. Meanwhile Frank broke-in horses so they were ready to pull a coach. Bella had a cook for company, who travelled with the men when Frank and his stockmen rode off to look after the branding, mustering and sorting of stock. Bella must have felt a gaping solitude during the long weeks they were away. There was the continual laundry to keep her busy, scrubbing the clothes on a washboard, and keeping the house clean. The summers were infernally hot, but the winters could be so cold the men had to break the ice on the creek's waterhole to fill their kettles. According to the blackfellas, the severe cold signified a major drought.

Most of the run was black-soil plains. Soft rich alluvium soil, which, with a run of water, melted away like sugar. It carried saltbush and cotton bush, with the less common red-soil areas studded with belts of box, belah, budda and yarran trees. Big well-grassed swamps watered the lower end of the run, and the beautiful open myall and whitewood plains were ideal country for stock. There were Aboriginal camps on Buckiinguy, shifting unpredictably from season to season, but the smoke of their fires invariably gave away their location. The major fear for many frontier settlers was not drought but trouble with the local Aboriginal tribes.

Cobb & Co's land was criss-crossed by the Macquarie River, as well as by the Mara and Crooked creeks. The house was only a few metres from the Mara Creek, which never seemed to dry up, so filling the house tank was no effort. As Bella was soon to discover, however, the mud and dust posed an unusual problem. The geography of the local river system meant that huge tracts of the run were under a sea of water for months every year. The stock might vanish for weeks at a time in the reed-filled marshes.

Bella's staple pantry items would have been tea, sugar, jam, flour, baking soda, cream of tartar, salt and pepper, corned beef and potatoes. If she was resourceful, she might have boiled the tops of young stinging nettles to make a dish something like spinach, or substituted pigweed cooked in fresh water and eaten with sugar for rhubarb. Outback settlers often shot pigeons or rock wallabies for the cook to prepare as a change from the dreary diet of salted beef week after week.

Travelling pedlars would come by the station every six months or so, spreading out their wares on the homestead's front verandah. There would be books, dress materials and ribbons for Bella, boots and tobacco for the men. Every few months, drovers came through Buckiinguy with a mob of horses or cattle and there were always stories to hear from the south. Occasionally, Rutherford arrived at the property at a trot in his sulky, covered in two weeks of dust or mud, depending on the season. He would stay for only a day to rest his mares, chewing quickly over the latest horse prices or land deals with Frank. There might be a good buy up on the Diamantina River, a drought on the Darling that was pushing land prices down and cattle prices up, or he might advise that he'd just purchased a new mob of cattle or sheep. Bella, however, would have had little to do with Rutherford.

By the winter of 1866, Bella was expecting her first child. She had toughened to the harsh isolation but was looking forward to returning to Montefiores – not only to see her favourite brother Arthur, but also to give birth.

Around 10 per cent of infants born in New South Wales died in their first year at this time. When Bella Whitney gave birth to her tenth child in 1882, this statistic had worsened to twelve in every hundred babies. The risk of infection was greater in the city, so babies had a better chance if they were born in the country. Today's infant mortality in New South Wales is closer to half of 1 per cent.

By today's standards, pre- and post-natal care was primitive, sanitation was far poorer, unplanned pregnancies were many and no techniques were available to deal with premature birth. Having your baby in a hospital was an uncommon event; most women, particularly if they were well-to-do, delivered at home, attended not by a doctor but a midwife. Bella was to bear her child at her uncle's Nanima homestead.

The midwife's skill (or lack of it) could dramatically affect the child's and mother's chance of survival. If the birth became complicated, the midwife could send for the doctor, but in some areas relations were strained between local midwives and the medical profession. The midwife felt it was a poor reflection on her competence to send for a doctor, while the doctor often arrived on his horse or buggy too late to save either child or mother.

Bella's journey south to her uncle's homestead was a slow, two-week ordeal by bullocky. It's probable that she arrived there seven months pregnant, her body aching from the long journey; it is unclear whether Frank accompanied her. There were no complications and she bore a healthy girl they christened Rachel, in memory of Bella's mother. When Bella was strong enough, mother and daughter made the long journey back to remote Buckiinguy to begin life as a family.

Meanwhile, in their little Bathurst cottage, Ada Rutherford had by now borne her husband a girl, Ada Catherine, and a boy they christened James after his father. In contrast to what was to come, both families' lives would for a period be blessed by a purity of purpose that came from hard work and the will to succeed.

Part Two

The Boom Years: 1865–1882

CHAPTER NINE

EXPANSION INTO QUEENSLAND

The well-known character of Cobb's coaches will be a guarantee that . . . speed and certainty of conveyance will be assured.

The rapid rise and even faster decline of the gold-mining settlements had shown Rutherford that you always needed to look further afield. Fierce competition from established coaching operators in both New South Wales and Victoria had also taught him the advantage of being early to market. One part of the new country was particularly ripe for the arrival of an established coaching operator: the new colony of Queensland. The distances, and therefore profits on transport, were potentially as huge as the colony itself. Best of all, Queensland was just finding its legs, and well-resourced competitors were nonexistent.

Having successfully managed Cobb & Co's Forbes route, Hiram Barnes had been transferred to Orange when Frank Whitney had moved to Buckiinguy. Now, in late August 1865, he was dispatched north to Toowoomba with instructions to examine the market and investigate mail contracts.

The district between Toowoomba and Brisbane was the main axis of Queensland's settlement. Even before Queensland had separated from New South Wales as a new colony in 1859, operators had been carrying mail and passengers from Brisbane to Ipswich, Toowoomba and Drayton (then the capital of the Darling Downs). These early operators' two-wheel drays and four-wheel spring carts were uncomfortable and difficult to manoeuvre, and certainly nowhere near as sophisticated as the coaches being used in the southern colonies. Most of the operators ran on an erratic schedule and their businesses were accordingly short-lived. Joseph Booth had commenced the first of these mail-cart runs in 1858, before being taken over by Joseph Cook two years later. A more successful service had been initiated by William Fraser in August 1864, though schedules remained inconvenient. Passengers would pre-pay their fares and then have to wait until all the seats were sold before a departure time was announced, which could take several days. The £2 fare from Toowoomba to Ipswich was exorbitant, costing a skilled worker more than a week's pay.

Soon after Barnes' arrival in Toowoomba the *Darling Downs Gazette* signalled the locals' approval of Cobb & Co's potential expansion into Queensland:

The well-known character of Cobb's coaches will be a guarantee that, should the firm commence in this colony, speed and certainty of conveyance will be assured.

In early September, Barnes travelled to Brisbane to negotiate a mail contract with the Postmaster General. Barnes must have been quite a salesman, for six weeks later, on 21 October, the *Brisbane Courier* announced:

It is satisfactory to know that the tender of Messrs Cobb and Co has been accepted for the conveyance of mails between Ipswich and Toowoomba. Their contract will commence on the 1st January next.

The government mail contract between Brisbane and Ipswich had already been secured by John Nolan; no doubt Barnes talked to him also. Barnes returned to Bathurst to report his success, and plans were hurriedly made to take on the Queensland market. Cobb & Co had to move fast, as they had not a single coach in the colony. Neither Frank Whitney nor Walter Hall was prepared to invest in the company's expansion into Queensland, so Rutherford set up a separate company for the new operation. Frank Whitney was probably more comfortable with Cobb & Co's investment in land, rather than dealing with the logistical problems of an expanded coaching empire. Frank was something of a homebody, and the idea of spending weeks on the road managing routes could not have held great appeal. Instead, Rutherford took a half share in the new business, Hiram Barnes a quarter and John Robertson another quarter. James Rutherford was now the only partner with a share in the Cobb & Co business in each of the three colonies.

On 23 November 1865, two American ten-passenger coaches and twenty horses arrived by ship in Brisbane. Four horses were immediately harnessed to each coach and driven off to the city's Royal Hotel. Two days after Christmas, another two larger coaches, seating 30 passengers each, arrived in Brisbane.

Hiram Barnes opened the firm's Brisbane headquarters in Albert Street, before setting off in search of new coaching routes, and a general manager was appointed to oversee the rapidly expanding business. Cobb & Co slashed the fare between Brisbane and Ipswich from eight shillings to six, forcing out their competitor, John Nolan, and presumably winning the mails on that leg also. In its first eighteen months in Queensland, Cobb & Co carried passengers on just three short routes – Brisbane to Ipswich, Grandchester to Toowoomba and Toowoomba to Dalby – each no longer than 100 kilometres. The colony was experiencing a drought and was economically depressed, but despite these setbacks Cobb & Co delivered on its promised departure times with great reliability. Making money on the busy route to Toowoomba was going to be a race against time, however, for the railways were advancing rapidly. Little more than fifteen months after starting up their Queensland operations, Cobb & Co's new routes were halved when steam trains began to run between Toowoomba and Ipswich.

By 1867 Hiram Barnes had set up routes to Warwick, Dalby, Roma and Condamine, following the pastoralists who were taking up land far from Brisbane. Important change stations were located at Mount Gravatt, Eight Mile Plains, Waterford, Loganholme, Beenleigh, Yatala, Coomera and Nerang – nowadays all large residential suburbs outside Brisbane.

When a new coach route was first opened, there was usually nothing in the way of a made road to follow. On steep descents, drivers would attach small trees or huge branches (and later logs) to the back of the coach as a kind of drag device to prevent it tumbling over on the sheer, uneven track as it travelled downhill. The skill of these intrepid coach drivers was respected and admired by travellers as famous as the English writer Anthony Trollope, who journeyed extensively around Australia in 1871. Trollope had ridden in English, European and American coaches, and described his Cobb & Co journey from Maryborough to Brisbane via Gympie in glowing terms:

> *The wonder of the journey was in the badness of the roads and the goodness of the coachmanship. I have been called upon by the work of my life to see much coaching, having been concerned for more than 30 years with the expedition of mails . . . I have now travelled over the Gympie road and I feel certain that not one of my old friends of the box seat – and I had many such friends – would, on being shown the road, have considered it possible that a vehicle with four horses could have been made to travel over it.*
>
> *There is often no road and the coach is taken at random through the forest. Not infrequently a fallen tree blocks up the track and the coach is squeezed through some siding which makes it necessary for the leader to be going one way and the coach another. But the great miracle is in the sudden patches, looking as though they were almost perpendicular, down which the coach is taken – and then the equally sharp ascents – not straight, but at a sharp angle, up and round which the coach is whirled.*
>
> *The art of driving on such rounds depends very much on the foot. The vehicle is supplied with very strong machinery for dragging the hind wheels so as almost altogether to stop their rotation, and this the coachman manages with his right foot.*
>
> *I here pronounce my opinion that the man who drove me from Cobbs Camp to Brisbane was the best driver of four horses I ever saw. Had he been a little less uncouth in his manners, I should have told him what I thought of him.*

Hiram Barnes went on to extend the firm's routes south across the New South Wales border to Tenterfield and Armidale, a district which soon boomed with the discovery of large quantities of tin. Cobb & Co's Queensland lines would eventually stretch west to Charleville and north to the Gulf of Carpentaria.

Such growth was not without pain, however, particularly when a fire destroyed the firm's first coaching centre in Brisbane. It was replaced with a new headquarters of large offices, stables and a coach-building factory at Petrie Bight, opposite the ferry crossing over the Brisbane River. Two well-respected tradesmen – Edward Jolliffe, a coach-builder, and Ludwig Uhl, a saddler – also established businesses at Petrie Bight. Strong links would be forged between these three firms, and both men would go on to become large shareholders in Queensland's Cobb & Co.

Gold fever struck Queensland in October 1867, when goldfields were discovered at Gympie, just 170 kilometres north of Brisbane. Today, a tilt-train delivers you there in two and a half hours; in 1868, Hiram Barnes took two days and nights to drive a four-horse passenger coach over the almost impassable road. The road workers had taken much longer than planned to cut the road through the bush, partly because whenever word came through of a good gold find up at Gympie, the road workers took off, state-issued pick and shovel on their shoulders, to try their luck.

As Hiram Barnes and his coach appeared at the edge of the shanty town for the first time, the diggers were so excited by Cobb & Co's arrival in Gympie that they all came out cheering, pulling Barnes from the driver's seat, onto their shoulders and into Gympie's North-umberland Hotel. For lonely diggers, Cobb & Co's service heralded a reliable link with friends and family. In those days of heady euphoria, the goodwill and kudos the firm's first coach to Gympie gave to the Cobb & Co name was a marketer's dream.

The coaches also provided links with law and order, although their very presence was a temptation to some. Regional newspapers in districts served by coaches reported dozens of incidents involving bushrangers, and an outrage would be mentioned in at least one of the country's papers on a weekly basis. Horses were sometimes shot and killed when a coach driver attempted to outrun the bushrangers, and when spooked on a mountain road the animals could miss their footing and end up hurtling off the road into steep gullies, pulling their passengers and coach with them.

Most bushrangers experienced no opposition at all from the pas-sengers or driver when they held up a coach, hoping for a large haul, so it must have come as some surprise for the two bushrangers who held up Cobb & Co's Gympie to Brisbane coach in the early morning of 6 January 1869 to find the tables turned on them. The hero of this hold-up – bank manager Mr Selwyn King – was to bear a son who, thirty-six years later, would marry Frank and Bella Whitney's sec-ond-youngest daughter.

Selwyn King had come up from Sydney to manage the Bank of New South Wales branch at the Kilkivan goldfield. The prospectors had now moved on, and King was shifting back to the bank's Sydney head office, taking the balance of deposits with him – £2000 in gold and cash.

The coach that left Gympie's Foo's Hotel with King on board

carried five other passengers. On the box seat were a storekeeper and a young fellow; inside with Mr King were a miner called Walker and a Mr Freeston. The last passenger to board was noisy and boisterous, having been drinking heavily all night.

Five miles south of Gympie, two men came from behind an ironbark tree and ordered the driver to stop or they would shoot. The taller bushranger was slightly built, his face covered by a black cloth, and in his hands was a double-barrelled shotgun. The shorter bushranger held a revolver, his face hidden behind green oilcloth.

When King heard the shouts outside the vehicle, he drew his Tranter revolver and, leaning in front of Walker, fired. In response, one of the pair immediately fell back, firing two shots, followed by a third when he was safely behind a tree. The first shot passed through the wrist of poor Mr Walker; the second went so close to King's nose that he could smell the gunpowder; the third embedded itself in the woodwork of the coach. King's drunken fellow traveller hiccupped and giggled, then scolded King for not being a better shot.

The taller bushranger pointed his shotgun at King inside the coach, and seeing the odds were against him, the bank manager sat down. The young lad up on the box seat was told to hold the heads of the lead horses while the five other passengers were ordered out at gunpoint and forced to stand in a row on the other side of a log. The coach driver also dismounted, but was ignored – the usual etiquette among bushrangers. The passengers were told to strip off their coats and waistcoats, and throw their money and watches on the ground.

As Mr Freeston disembarked, he threw up his arms, blabbering and terrified, and repeatedly cried: 'It was not me who fired. I have no revolver. It was him inside,' pointing to Selwyn King, still seated inside the coach. With much swearing from the bushrangers, King was ordered to get out of the vehicle. The bank manager had returned his revolver to its holster, and had pulled his shirt out of his trousers to conceal the weapon. As he disembarked, King threw off his coat and waistcoat, and once he had joined the other passengers he removed his shirt and dropped it to the ground – the revolver inside it.

Having emptied their pockets of money and surrendered their watches and jewellery, the passengers were now ordered to lie flat on the ground. King ignored the order. At that moment the drunkard suddenly staggered to his feet and grabbed his coat. Distracted, the taller bushranger pointed his gun at the fellow. Seeing his chance, King stooped to pick up his revolver. The other bushranger shouted a warning to his mate but too late, for King fired three shots in quick succession at him before darting away into the bush. His target, in the act of turning to aim, staggered back, his gun slipping through his hands.

The shorter bushranger swore at King but did not attempt to chase him. Instead, he scooped up all the watches and money from the ground and with his injured mate took off into the open scrub, located their horses and cantered off towards Gympie. Their take totalled just £24 and a few watches. The bank's £2000 and the all-important mail was safe.

King emerged from the bush at a nearby change station, and hours later was welcomed into the bank at Gympie with loud cheering. The bank manager had stood alone and unsupported against two armed bushrangers, protecting the mail and his bank's money. Hailed a hero, he received £100 from the bank, some of which was to be spent on an engraved gold watch and the rest given to him as sovereigns.

While the Queensland firm was establishing itself, and going from strength to strength, back in Bathurst the company was facing public scrutiny on several fronts. Local business people relied on Cobb & Co's coaches for the delivery and receipt of all their correspondence with Sydney. Since June 1867 many had been complaining that not only were they getting the Sydney papers a day late, they had no time to receive and read the mail from the 11 a.m. coach, then pen a reply by 12.30 p.m., when the same coach departed for Sydney. They blamed Cobb & Co's coaches for being too slow, and the *Bathurst Times* printed a petition from a vocal part of the community asking for shorter travel times.

James Rutherford was furious, for he had staked his reputation on providing reliable mail deliveries. He wrote a vituperative letter to the paper:

> *Had you, before publishing this document, taken the trouble to fully consider the subject, and not have put down mere ascertains [sic] as facts, you would have found that our present rate of travelling is even faster than that the memorial asks for.*

Rutherford went on to inform the paper's readers that there were nine post offices on the route between Bathurst and the Weatherboard (Wentworth Falls), each requiring a fifteen-minute stop to enable the postmaster to receive and deliver mails. An additional fifteen minutes was allowed at Lithgow. By this stage in his letter, Rutherford had a calculation to impart to his readers:

> *The contract time for performance of the journey is fourteen*
> *hours. Deducting from this two hours and a half for stoppages*
> *at the different post offices, thirty minutes for changing horses*
> *(six changes) and thirty minutes for passengers to take supper*
> *and breakfast, will leave ten hours and a half for travelling sev-*
> *enty miles. The average of the present rate is therefore nearly*
> *seven miles an hour, over a road, which, though the words of*
> *the petition imply to the contrary, is a disgrace to the colony. I*
> *assert without fear of contradiction, that the pace we now drive*
> *is as fast as is consistent with the safety of the passengers, and*
> *mails, and that an increase would be attended with great risk,*
> *not to mention discomfort to everyone travelling . . .*

Rutherford justifiably pointed out that even the train journey between Sydney and Wentworth Falls, some 96 kilometres, took more than four and a half hours. The government railway operators eventually came up with a solution by altering their own timetable, so the train at Wentworth Falls met the coach much earlier in the evening.

Other vicissitudes clouded this otherwise prosperous period for Cobb & Co. The company suffered the tragic loss of one of its best drivers on the last day of May 1868. Hal Hamilton had been part of the Cobb & Co cavalcade that had entered Bathurst just six years earlier. Since then, he had been driving the firm's Bathurst to Lithgow run, which took in the steep descent at Frying Pan Hill, now Yetholme, midway along the route.

This road was now well used, so Hamilton no longer relied on a drag device to slow his descent. Just as his team was starting its run downhill, Hamilton realised that his brakes were not working. His was a small coach, but it was full – eight passengers inside and four on top – and Hamilton well knew that the situation was dangerous. If his coach careered headlong into the back of its own team, it would bowl the animals over with its weight, before tumbling over a mass of kicking horseflesh.

For an experienced driver there was only one option. Hamilton whipped his horses into an ever-increasing gallop to keep them ahead of his accelerating coach, and so began a terrifying downhill plunge. Hamilton knew there was a sharp bend to the left towards the bottom of the Frying Pan Hill descent. He turned in his seat and yelled at his terrified passengers to throw their body weight to the inside of the bend, but his words were drowned out by screams and the pounding of hooves. Sure enough, the momentum of the turning horses lurched the coach to the right. Something snapped and the coach was suddenly tumbling down the side of a gully. Horses, tangled in their harnesses, shrieked as they were pulled backwards over the gully on top of the coach. Hamilton was thrown from the coach, his head hitting a boulder as he tumbled down the gully. He was dead on impact.

Just six years after his arrival in Bathurst, Rutherford was persuaded by the Church of England to become one of its trustees. After declining an earlier nomination, Rutherford also accepted the position of mayor of Bathurst in February 1868. Not long into his term, he presided over one of the most extraordinary community meetings the district had yet seen.

The 1868 visit of Prince Alfred, Queen Victoria's second son, was the first time a member of the British Royal family had set foot in Australia. This inaugural Royal tour – taking in Adelaide, Melbourne, Sydney and Brisbane – produced an outpouring of national exultation that the Australian colonies were at last to be inspected by a son of their queen. However, the celebratory mood was cut cruelly short. On 12 March 1868, during a picnic at pretty Clontarf Beach on Sydney's Middle Harbour, a madman attempted to murder Australia's royal hero. Prince Alfred was shot in the back, just to the right of his spine, by Irishman Henry James O'Farrell, who was arrested on the spot.

One writer described the scene at Clontarf beach as 'terrible beyond everything – Women and men fainted and sobbed and the criminal was nearly torn to pieces on the spot and with difficulty saved from Lynch law'.

The Prince made a quick recovery, and was able to leave Australia by early April. O'Farrell's conviction was rushed through the courts, and he was hanged less than seven weeks after the attack.

The damage to the standing of Irish Australians, particularly in country areas, was immense. Having little faith in his own, mostly Irish police force, the New South Wales premier, Henry Parkes, had carried out his own investigation against O'Farrell, searching the fellow's hotel room. Parkes' theory was that O'Farrell was a member of the Fenians, an Irish secret society intent on ending British domination in Ireland. Parkes used the shooting to gain public support for his personal prejudice against the Irish and Catholics, whom he dismissed as 'jabbering baboons and disruptive troublemakers'.

Most Australians felt that the scandal had shamed them in the eyes of the world, which were turned upon them because of the Royal tour.

Sorrow, shame and rage swept through the colonies. Spontaneous public 'indignation' meetings were held around the country, with around 20 000 people attending one in Sydney the day after the attack. A day later, new mayor James Rutherford had to face a crowd of two thousand locals in the Bathurst town square – a frightening proposition for a man who hated large gatherings. The Bathurst townspeople raised motion after motion of sympathy, condolence, horror and loyalty, which they insisted Rutherford pass on to the Queen's representative.

Perhaps this ordeal was a catalyst in making Rutherford realise he was not cut out for such a public role, and was better suited to concentrating his energy on forces he could control. Given the increasing scale of his business interests, being mayor was always going to be problematic. Sure enough, Rutherford resigned a few months later, after just six months in the role.

Rutherford was more effective and comfortable in the large number of small committees in which he was involved. To allow Cobb & Co to take best advantage of the ever-present railways, he ensured he was elected a member of the Bathurst railway committee. Although the rail line was fast approaching Bathurst, Cobb & Co, while losing some routes, remained crucial in providing services that fanned out from railway towns. The timing of line completion and the new railway timetables were important to the firm, as their routes fed passengers into the railway network. By 1868 travel time across the mountains had improved to the extent that Cobb & Co could ensure passengers arrived in Sydney by nightfall. The only hitch was the departure time from Bathurst at the ungodly hour of four in the morning in order to connect with the Sydney rail service.

One of the toughest jobs in the firm was that of managing clerk at Cobb & Co's Bathurst headquarters. In the 1870s a man called Septimus Pryce filled this role, running what amounted to a central help desk for passengers using the firm's main terminus. Tired and groggy men, women and children were channelled into Bathurst from Sydney, usually arriving after midnight. Pryce required every ounce of good humour he could muster to sort passengers onto coaches fanning onward to twenty different destinations. His challenge was to keep a smile and good temper in the face of the crankiest of travellers – an almost impossible task, especially during busy spells.

One of these demanding, but also profitable, periods occurred in 1870, when an intercolonial exhibition of Australian produce and industry was held at Sydney's Prince Alfred Park, commemorating Captain Cook's landing in New South Wales a century earlier. The Great Western railway line now reached Rydal, only 50 kilometres east of Bathurst, so the capital was much more accessible to the huge population now living west of the Blue Mountains, attracted to the region by the pastoral and mining boom, and the wealth of employment these industries generated. It seemed everyone wanted to travel to Sydney to see the exhibition, for Cobb & Co's offices were overwhelmed with bookings. The firm put on three of their largest coaches a day to shuttle travellers from Bathurst to Rydal, each packed inside and out, but even so they could shift only one hundred travellers a day.

Cobb & Co was licensed to carry a certain number of passengers in coaches of a particular size, with the number of passengers painted on the side of the coach, similar to buses today. However, drivers often ignored the rules and packed passengers aboard, rather than making them wait another day. In the crush of passengers trying to get to the train at Rydal there was inevitably an accident and an inquiry in which Mr Brown, the firm's factory manager, was called into the witness box. In a letter to the editor of the *Bathurst Times*, one writer revealed just what passengers had to contend with:

About Coaches

Sir,

This is what I want to know, and what your well-known courtesy to us all will perhaps induce you to tell us.

First: Who licences coaches; or, rather, who determines the number of people they carry when full? We are all puzzled over here as to what Mr Brown, of Cobb & Co, means in what he says . . . First of all, he says there were too many on the coach; then, no more than it was licensed to carry; next, not more than it could carry; and winds up by saying there were more than forty people on it!

Secondly: If I book a seat, can I insist on a seat, other than lying along the roof of the coach (with undesirable people) packed like red herrings in a tin?

And thirdly: Can I be forced to get out at every little rise because 'too many people are on the coach' and walk two-thirds of the distance between here and Rydal as Mr Madden says he and his friends did, when I think I'm going to get a ride?

I'm just as game at walking as any of my sex; but I'd like to know about it first.

Yours

Jemima

Kelso, 20 September

Coach travellers in the 1870s were not restricted to those willing to pay high fares. As the gold rushes faded, so demand and hence fares had fallen considerably, opening up coach travel to passengers from all walks of life. Those who ten years before had had no viable means of transport but their own two feet or a horse, if they were lucky, could now afford to take a coach. There were children making the long journey home from boarding school, newly appointed police-men, squatters returning from a city visit to their bank manager, and young people about to start their first job on a country property as governesses, domestic help, station hands and shearers. The most regular coach users were commercial salesmen with order books and catalogues of their wares, who often made sales trips of over a thousand miles by coach. 'Snaggers' were also frequent coach users. These men were employed to use bullocks and hand winches to drag dangerous logs and branches from major waterways such as the Mur-ray, Murrumbidgee and Darling, keeping them clear for steamers carting wool and supplies to and from the coast.

In 1871 Cobb & Co's unwieldy New South Wales and Victorian coach-ing business split. Rutherford was preoccupied by the Queensland and New South Wales operations, and any funds he received in set-tlement would have been sorely needed to fund the firm's expansion. Alex Robertson and John Wagner bought out the Victorian Cobb & Co business, retaining the name and becoming the sole beneficiaries of profits in that colony. While some Victorian routes had been lost to the railways, there remained many inland mail contracts feeding mail and passengers from the railway to outlying towns. By 1872

the Victorian firm had won a massive 85 per cent of these contracts – worth $5.6 million in today's terms. Two years later their
income from the mails had skyrocketed to the equivalent of more
than $7.7 million, and they had won every mail contract available.

Robertson and Wagner did not operate Cobb & Co coaches
solely in Victoria. In the 1880s, when rich gold deposits were
discovered at remote Mount Browne, near Milparinka in the far
north-west corner of New South Wales, along with silver deposits in nearby districts, they extended their coach routes and mail
contracts from Deniliquin north through Hay, Booligal, Ivanhoe
and Wilcannia, and right up to Tibooburra in the far north-west of
the colony (now known as the Cobb Highway). Their vast routes in
outer New South Wales transported settlers and diggers over more
than 1000 kilometres in each direction. In times of drought, such
as the one that occurred in April 1882, there might be no water
sources in the most remote sections for more than 50 kilometres
at a time. It was then that Robertson and Wagner would switch to
employing an Afghan camel driver and some of his beasts for up
to a month at a time. The mail would be strapped to one camel, with
the others carrying essential supplies for the remote settlements.
These caravans could cover 80 kilometres a day. Robertson and
Wagner paid off a competitor firm, just as Rutherford had done, to
ensure they had a monopoly over the remote Mount Browne goldfields route, although their service was not without criticism from
the local press:

> *From the time this bargain, so unfortunate for the public, was*
> *struck, the former efficient conduct of the line has week by week*

declined, until now when the distance which used to be covered
on a couple of days often takes a couple of weeks.

Robertson and Wagner also refused to provide sufficient camels to carry the bulky newspapers so beloved of diggers in the outback, so they received further barbed criticism from the local press for their stinginess.

To avoid wasting time on unsuccessful tenders, Robertson and Wagner made a deal with other coach operators providing services in Victoria, splitting up the spoils a little. They agreed to tender for mail contracts from Melbourne into Central Victoria only, leaving the northern mining areas, the Western District lines and the Beechworth and North East lines to three other firms, all running under the Cobb & Co name. The four separate and unrelated Cobb & Co firms dominated Victoria's coaching until the end of the century.

It was not only in Victoria that Cobb & Co entities were run by separate operators. By late 1872, quite independent parties had launched Cobb & Co lines of coaches in South Australia, Western Australia and New Zealand, and Freeman Cobb had established the brand in South Africa. If the company had been a franchise, Freeman Cobb would have been an immensely wealthy man.

Meanwhile, Rutherford was finding the battle for New South Wales mail contracts much tougher. There were close to 300 mail routes throughout the colony, covering more than 20 000 kilometres. However, due to the sparseness of settlement, four in every five were still serviced by single horsemen. Only thirty or so contracts were up for grabs by coach and Rutherford managed to win just ten of them. Admittedly, Cobb & Co's wins included some of the busiest routes,

which meant the firm received more than half the colony's mail subsidies, but the resulting income of £8380 (equating to $1.1 million in
modern terms) was a drop in the ocean compared to the booming
Victorian mail business.

In 1874, in a popular move to grab votes, the New South Wales
government removed the one-penny charge on sending newspapers
through the mail, having reversed its policy on this issue on average every ten years since mail had first been introduced. For Cobb
& Co, this was a major headache: it meant that people would send
friends and family old newspapers – thousands and thousands of
them – with letters scrawled in the margins. It saved on both postage
and letter-writing paper, and cost the public nothing.

Some of Cobb & Co's New South Wales mail contracts still had
two years to run when the decision to remove the penny charge was
made. Faced with the prospect of carrying tonnes of extra weight the
firm had not budgeted for, Rutherford refused to carry mail after a
certain date unless the government increased its contract payments
to Cobb & Co. The Postmaster General stood firm, and instead called
for fresh tenders. Cobb & Co reapplied for all their New South Wales
routes, winning back seven contracts. For the government it was a
costly means of winning votes: Rutherford's seven re-costed tenders
alone extracted an extra £6500 from public funds.

CHAPTER TEN

DIVERSIFICATION

... We regret that this gentleman is preparing to leave the colony ...

In the years after 1865, when Cobb & Co bought the Buckiinguy property, the firm tried its hand at a multitude of business pursuits, some of them strategic, some of them wild flights of fancy, and all of them involving an element of risk. Rutherford and his partners injected capital and passion into huge pastoral stations, the iron industry, gold and copper mines, the railways, coach and buggy-building, general stores and donkey breeding. Never before in colonial Australia had a single partnership taken on such high levels of risk in such diverse fields.

Business growth was put on hold for a period when James Rutherford, the backbone of the New South Wales business, sailed home to America, undeterred by the fact that Ada had given birth to twin girls only a month before his departure. Their brood now numbered eight, and all of them were under eleven years of age. Rutherford was making a business trip to buy some choice animals, and he would be accompanied by the firm's Goulburn partner, Colin Robertson, and his wife, Jane. The local press, however, seemed to be concerned that Rutherford might not return. On 8 May 1875 the *Bathurst Times* alerted its readers:

We regret that this gentleman is preparing to leave the colony. It is not requisite to say one word of Mr Rutherford's useful career since he came to reside among us at Bathurst. His name, and his public acts, are as 'Household Words'; besides it is not so easy to speak of one's friends, whilst they are present with us; and Mr Rutherford is about the last man to desire anything of the kind. It will, however, make itself prominently and gratefully felt that, with every public institution, and every public movement of the town and district, through which it was designed the common good should be promoted, our esteemed townsman has always connected himself; and has ever been one of the most forward and generous in practically assisting them . . . We are given to understand that the arrangements for Mr Rutherford's departure from Bathurst are likely to be completed by the end of the present month, and we are informed that it is in contemplation to initiate a movement of public recognition of the untiring efforts he has made to improve and give character to the city.

A farewell dinner was hurriedly organised in Rutherford's honour at Bathurst's School of Arts, presided over by the Police Magistrate. The town band was to play, and the *Bathurst Times* reported that tickets had been sold to more than sixty gentlemen; such serious affairs were not suitable for women. The next day, 4 June 1875, Rutherford left by train for Sydney to meet the steamer for America.

Steamer services had developed rapidly since the 1850s, with regular fortnightly services established by P&O across the Indian Ocean to Galle in Ceylon (Sri Lanka), from where one could take another ship on to India and through the Suez Canal to Europe. At the same time, the Pacific Royal Mail Line set up a service across the Pacific via New Zealand to Panama, from where passengers such as Rutherford and the Robertsons crossed the isthmus on the Panama Railroad, the world's first and shortest transcontinental railway. Connecting ships at Colón, on the Caribbean coast, transported passengers and mail to US east-coast ports and Europe.

Frank Whitney and his Sydney colleague Walter Hall were left holding the reins of the New South Wales business; it's likely that John Robertson oversaw Cobb & Co's busy coach factory and accounts in Bathurst during Rutherford's absence. Walter Hall had manned the firm's Sydney booking office since the move to New South Wales in 1862, looking after the government mail contracts and the much-tested relationships with Cobb & Co's bankers. There was seldom a need for Hall to leave Sydney, but with Rutherford out of the country he would now have to take on more responsibilities, including a good deal of travelling to keep an eye on Queensland operations.

Although childless, Walter Hall and his wife, Eliza, had purchased a grand site on the tip of Potts Point, and in 1874 had completed a fine two-storey brick mansion on the site they called Wildfell, whose gardens ran down to the harbour's edge. Eliza was a classicist at heart and she collected beautiful things for their home. Lovely sculpture and European paintings adorned the mansion's many rooms, hand-carved rosettes embroidered their ceilings, a stained-glass dome floated magnificently above the hand-carved cedar staircase and each fireplace was framed by an Italian marble mantelpiece. Eliza kept a pet macaw in the hallway, along with a more chatty cockatoo that loved to pass disdainful comment on the macaw's behaviour. Tiled verandahs encircled the house, and together with the garden's huge fig trees they shaded the downstairs rooms from the sun that sparkled off the deep blue of the harbour below. James Rutherford surely called in to inspect his friend's luxurious new home before leaving for America.

The first leg of Rutherford's sea journey took him to Auckland on a mail steamship that was dangerously overloaded with coal. The vessel hit choppy seas and sat so low in the water that her decks were continually washed by the swell. As he watched livestock being swept overboard, quickly drowning in the huge seas, Rutherford was reminded of his disastrous attempt to ship horseflesh to Sydney. The boat was damaged, and limped into Auckland four days behind schedule. Rutherford felt lucky to be alive.

To occupy himself on the long onward journey via the Sandwich Isles (Hawaii) to San Francisco, Rutherford wrote vivid accounts of the ports he visited and mailed them back to the *Bathurst Times* for publication. Once in San Francisco, he took in the sights, taking care to record his observations for the townsfolk at home:

> *Horses are about the same price as with us in Bathurst until their travelling qualities begin to be developed, when according as the pace increases, the price runs up from $3000 to $10 000 for smart buggy pairs, while the fastest bring fabulous prices. A gentleman in New York paid the high price of $30 000 for a buggy horse.*

He then travelled a further 4800 kilometres by rail, east to Kentucky. His improbable destination was specifically chosen. Rutherford had thought long and hard about the kind of draught animals that would be of most value in pulling the firm's coaches into the future. He was looking for an animal that combined the power of a horse, the sure-footedness over rough ground of a bullock and the camel's tolerance of dry conditions. Kentucky was home to the country's premier breeding stud for Rutherford's dream animal: American donkeys.

While in the US, Rutherford also discovered the superb quality of Hill & Co's harnesses, quickly judging them to be far superior to those his teams were using in Australia. Not one to do things by halves, he placed an order for two thousand sets. The harness-maker took down the order carefully, then dismissed it as the dreamings of a madman. Not until his bank manager informed him months later that a full cash payment had been made did the American harness-maker realise Rutherford meant business.

After spending just seven months away, James Rutherford took a steamer back to Sydney in January 1876. In the steamer's hold were his purchases: four trotting horses and six well-bred donkeys (two jackasses and four females). One of the male donkeys was enormous, seventeen hands high; the other much smaller animal came with the rather grand title of Napoleon III. On their arrival in Bathurst, these males were pronounced by the colonial press as 'beautifully ugly'. Despite the derision, Rutherford proudly announced that they'd been hand-picked from the stud of the most celebrated breeder in Kentucky so Cobb & Co could begin breeding their own donkeys and mules to pull coaches on the rougher, steeper routes.

In the event, Rutherford's dream of a first-class Cobb & Co donkey team died an embarrassing death. The two jackasses expired after several years of services, supposedly while mating in a boggy paddock, before they were able to sire more than a few replacements. The

Bathurst townsfolk took great delight in the donkey debacle, and as Rutherford's sons passed through the local school system each was nicknamed 'Donkey' in reference to their father's grand plan.

Colin Robertson also returned from America, but he was a changed man. His speech began to slur and his short-term memory was poor. These symptoms were soon followed by paralysis down his left side. Nursing was carried out by the women at home in the nineteenth century. Hospitalisation was rare, as the risk of picking up a nasty infection when surrounded by other sick people was high. After months spent nursing her husband, Jane Robertson was at her wit's end. Colin had become another person, dangerous and violent, even towards his wife. The doctor's diagnosis was 'general paralysis of the insane' – today known to be caused by end-stage syphilis. Colin and Jane had already lost their three children as babies; two of them lived just fifteen months, their third child survived only three months. Untreated syphilis at conception is now recognised as a cause of early infant death, and Colin had unwittingly infected his three children. With his hands and feet bound to prevent him doing harm, he was transferred to Cooks River Private Mental Asylum in Sydney. Just a month after his admission, he died. It was Christmas Eve 1876.

Based on Colin's share of the New South Wales Cobb & Co business, Jane Robertson was left a rich widow, with an annuity of £1500 a year. Little more than a year later she married a prominent Sydney surgeon. She remained childless.

The tragedy left just three partners in the New South Wales business: James Rutherford, Frank Whitney and Walter Hall. William Bradley had exited in 1875 from the coaching side of the business, buying out Yanda Station from the firm, to focus on pastoral interests.

The railway line from Sydney now reached Bathurst. Nonetheless, Cobb & Co's New South Wales operation was kept busy running coaches from outlying towns to meet the railway, and there remained a booming market for private carriages and sulkies in the country. The firm had established coach-repair works at Goulburn, Hay and Bourke, and in 1877 they moved their Bathurst coach and buggy factory from the Black Bull Hotel site to a larger space and showroom in lower William Street, opposite the old police station. Cobb & Co was now the largest coach-builder in the colony.

The factory was a constant buzz of activity, with its furnaces roaring, steam hammer pounding, tyre bending and setting machines whirring, timber mill and body shop in which immense coaches, smaller traps, carts and wagons were constructed. Sparks and sawdust shot up and mingled in the air, before floating down to be swept away by grease-black boys with huge brooms. At its peak, one hundred staff were employed here. Rutherford took pride in being able to source nearly all the raw materials required for coach construction from the local area – quality timber, iron and especially leather (according to some, Bathurst tanneries were equal to any in the world) were all available in the district. Only the glass for the coaches' lamps had to be imported by the Bathurst factory. Coaches now carried three large kerosene lamps, which lit the road a little better than the candle lamps of earlier times. One lamp was set on each side of the box seat and another towered high above the driver.

In the paint works and trimming shop, master craftsmen tenderly applied the finer detail to each coach. Men ground coloured powders to mix colours – Chinese vermilion for the body and gold leaf for the Cobb & Co lettering on the door panels. In the 1880s, Rutherford's youngest son George, playing at repelling imaginary bushrang- ers from the box seat of coaches, remembered being amazed at the extravagant application of gold leaf, perhaps forgetting that Bathurst had been a gold-mining centre.

The Bathurst factory soon developed a distinctively Australian coach: lower, squarer and more open than the American stagecoach on which it had been based, since Australia did not suffer the severe cold of American winters. Cobb & Co's coach-builders had also found a combination of braces and springs that gave the best ride, and, as in so much else in Australia, the ideal design was a compromise between British and North American notions, with a few colonial innovations thrown in.

Cobb & Co's driving force found it impossible to slow down. James Rutherford was usually up well before dawn and in the saddle before sunrise on his way to inspect stock, station overseers, water levels or coach-booking agents, navigating the dusty back roads hunched over his sulky's reins. He liked to arrive without warning if he was checking up on staff or property. He might be away from his wife for three months at a stretch, particularly in later years as the business expanded, with little idea where he could be found from one week to another.

The Buckiinguy purchase had whetted Rutherford's appetite for property, and he was developing a habit of snapping up huge land parcels that took his fancy, regardless of whether they were within the firm's financial reach. His expansionist tendencies coincided with his elevated moods, and had no connection at all with the firm's cash

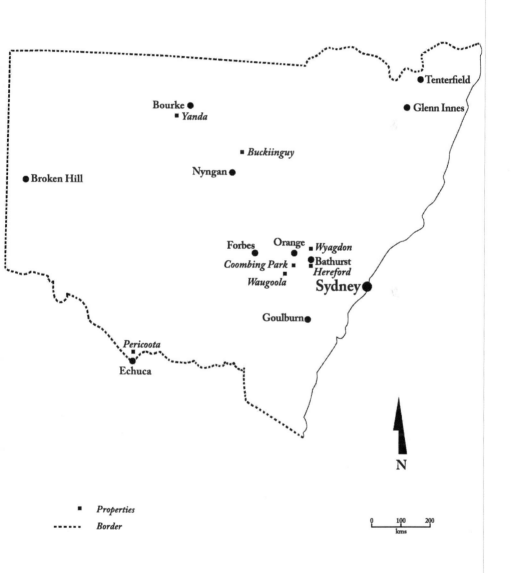

Cobb & Co's New South Wales properties

● Tenterfield

Bourke ●
■ *Yanda*

● Glenn Innes

■ *Buckiinguy*

Nyngan ●

● Broken Hill

Forbes   Orange
●   ●   ■ *Wyagdon*
Coombing Park ■   ●Bathurst
                    Hereford
        Waugoola ■
                        Sydney ●

Goulburn●

Pericoota
■
Echuca

N

■   *Properties*
- - - -   *Border*

0   100   200
            kms

flow; drought and recession were minor irritations. Cobb & Co's expansion into Queensland meant that Rutherford was often among the first to view huge expanses of virgin farming land, and he was quick to recognise opportunities. Sheep- and cattle-breeding were booming industries, and the place to invest capital.

Back in 1867, Frank Whitney, Walter Hall and Rutherford had purchased a huge station called Cunnamulla on the Warrego River, more than 200 kilometres north of Bourke in remote south-western Queensland. The property was bought on Cobb & Co's behalf with borrowed capital, the aim being to take advantage of the extraordinary profits to be made in sheep. The station was soon renamed Burrenbilla, and eventually sprawled over 1000 square kilometres of flat grazing country. To service the many new settlers passing through, the partners opened a store that became the nucleus of the modern-day town of Cunnamulla. Claverton, another vast acreage a few hundred kilometres south of Cunnamulla, was added to the New South Wales partners' Queensland holdings in 1875 in order to expand the firm's sheep- and cattle-breeding capacity, along with providing feed for their coaching teams. Similarly huge, at 1200 square kilometres, it became such a landmark that it would one day have its own government railway siding.

Income from wool, sheep and cattle sales, horse-breeding and pasture rental were to become an increasingly important income stream, justifying further expansion and ever-increasing bank loans. The Cobb & Co that James Rutherford, Walter Hall and Frank Whitney ran from New South Wales was now clearly far more than a transport enterprise.

By the 1870s, Frank Whitney was earning the equivalent of more than $154 000 a year in personal dividends from the New South Wales coaching business, and three times this amount from sheep, cattle and horse breeding. Rutherford was earning double the amount from coaching in New South Wales, given he held two shares to Frank's one, as well as half the profits from the Queensland coaching business. Both men had begun to dabble in local speculative gold mines when an opportunity to channel profits into another area emerged: iron production.

The government had continued its investment in railway lines that were built to impress, with fine stations and two parallel tracks where one would have sufficed. Rutherford and Whitney were well aware that the government was committed to railways for years to come, and iron for tracks was surely going to continue to be in demand. Each of them agreed to invest £10 000 in a Lithgow iron mine they called Eskbank. For good measure, they also purchased 800 acres of a nearby coalfield to give the business a cheap source of fuel. They put on a manager, and between them simply signed the cheques.

Their investment was to lead to years of headaches and financial losses, as there were constant problems. The major issue was the fact that the business was competing against cheaper imported iron, which the colonial government refused to tax. Over ten years, Whitney and Rutherford worked though another £10 000 in capital and landed themselves £29 000 in debt. With so many other business affairs competing for their attention, the debt spiralled out of control until they owed a massive £130 000. Copious injections of capital were required over the decades.

Whitney and Rutherford were saved from bankruptcy by the ongoing profits generated by Cobb & Co's coaching and property enterprises. In just a few more years, their half-yearly profits from property were equivalent to $5.6 million in today's currency, and by 1879 the profits from coaching were nearly as great. They could afford to make the occasional mistake.

Not long after Rutherford's return from his American trip in 1876, Rutherford had been in his sulky again, inspecting the remote Channel Country of far western Queensland. Just fifteen years earlier, Burke and Wills had travelled through this same land with a team of six camels, one horse and two other men. Their well-funded expedition to find a route to the Gulf of Carpentaria was to end in disaster – both Burke and Wills perished and just one of their party was eventually rescued, close to starvation.

The landscape, while remote, was famous for its magical lagoons, the wet-season run-off from a maze of river channels fed by the Georgina, Diamantina and Thomson Rivers making it perfect cattle country. These rivers confused many by flowing not towards the sea but inland to the great mysterious sinkhole that was Lake Eyre – a salt lake covering the area of a small nation. Sixteen metres below sea level, it sat like the plughole of a great bath in the continent's desert centre.

The Channel Country's haunting beauty must have mesmerised James Rutherford, for he was quick to invest Cobb & Co funds in purchasing a huge portion of this remote slice of the outback – a swathe of vast floodplains and sand hills called Davenport Downs. Covering over 7700 square kilometres, the station was soon merged with a neighbouring station to become as vast in size as modern-day Lebanon.

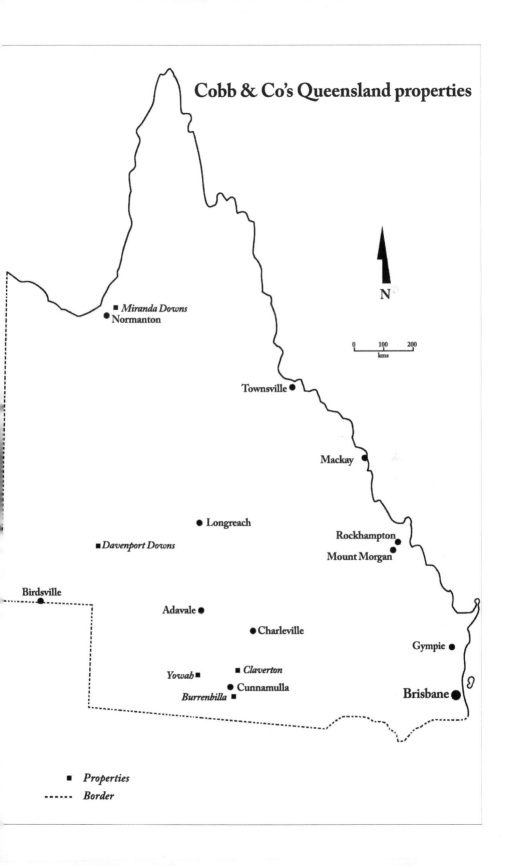

Cobb & Co's Queensland properties

N

0   100   200
      kms

■ *Miranda Downs*
● Normanton

Townsville ●

Mackay ●

● Longreach

■ *Davenport Downs*

Rockhampton ●
Mount Morgan ●

Birdsville ●

Adavale ●

● Charleville

Gympie ●

Yowah ■   ■ *Claverton*

● Cunnamulla

Burrenbilla ■

Brisbane ●

■   *Properties*
----   *Border*

As a youngster back in 1851, amid great excitement, Ada Rutherford had attended the world's first International Exhibition with her mother in London, just prior to migrating to Australia. The exhibition brought together a menagerie of unrelated industries, and Dublin had jumped on the bandwagon to host the event after London, followed by cities that fancied themselves as leading world traders: New York, Paris and Vienna. London and Paris must have been popular for each hosted a second exhibition in later years. Melbourne put on a very modest affair in 1875, followed by Philadelphia the next year.

Impatient to have its own time in the sun, and keen to push its own industries and wares, Sydney was to host the event in 1879. The city felt the need for a major new building. The site for this architectural contribution would be the Royal Botanic Gardens, and plans were drawn up for a building of an epic scale, to be called the Garden Palace. At 352 500 square feet (almost 33 000 square metres), it was to be just one-third the size of London's exhibition space, but it far surpassed Melbourne's recent efforts, and that was the important thing.

Australian and international producers, small and large, were encouraged to show their wares, and James Rutherford was carried along by the colony's enthusiasm for the event, though it was not the type of show in which you could enter a transport business. Instead, the obvious choice was the firm's best four-in-hand team, but Rutherford couldn't resist entering his magnificent and costly ass Napoleon III as well, along with the trotting stallion he had also brought back from his Kentucky trip a few years earlier. Caught up in the mineral fever that still gripped the nation, he even prepared a collection of gold specimens and gold-bearing quartz to put on display.

Invitations to participate were dispatched to thirty-four countries and their colonies, and 800 men began working on the construction of the massive Garden Palace in January 1879. Sydney had given itself just eight months to prepare for the exhibition, and the building works were immense. Four months in, it was clear that time was running out. More men were put on, and a new invention – electric light – was introduced so tradesmen could work through the night. By May, nearly three thousand men were employed on the project, nearly a quarter of them carpenters. A tram line to ferry workers was built from the city's southern outskirts to the exhibition site.

In early July, guests crowded the city's Botanic Gardens to witness the last of the twelve ribs of the Garden Palace's great glass dome being hoisted into position. The dome towered above the tiny figures below, and the building beneath it boasted four great entrance towers, eight grand staircases and massive cellars to showcase wines, beers and spirits. On its eastern front, looking out over the glorious harbour, wide balconies stretched 75 metres from end to end.

Sydney's *Daily Telegraph* promised its readers that careful provision had been made throughout the building for the extinction of fire. It assured them that water mains piped into the building had hoses attached at strategic points and that a body of fireman would always be in attendance, ready for any emergency.

The London High Commissioner offered to lend a collection of British pictures to the event, valued at a massive £150 000. In a colony of ex-convicts, ensuring their safekeeping would be essential. The organisers were embarrassed to find that the walls of the Garden Palace building had not been designed to hang art, lacking the surface area and having inadequate wall lighting. The problem sent everyone into a panic, especially as some of the works had been lent by Queen

Victoria and the Prince of Wales. In the end, an exhibition space of iron and wood was built specifically to house the artworks. It would cost another £5000 but Sydneysiders were oblivious, drunk with the city's coming fame. For months, the impending exhibition was all anybody could talk about.

In the face of continuous heavy rain and gale-force winds, exhibits from around the world began arriving, and in September 1879 the International Exhibition finally opened. The thousands who put on their best clothes and queued every weekend to see the wonders of manufacturing were treated to the latest in fancy saddles, stock-rider's saddles, ladies' riding habits and enamelled kangaroo-hide boots. Europe was well represented, with firms from Great Britain and Ireland exhibiting, along with manufacturers from France, Austria, Germany, Italy and Belgium. Canada and the United States took space, as did India, Japan and even tiny Fiji and Ceylon.

Exhibits ranged from mouth-watering confectionery displays of 'conversation' lozenges and Tom Thumb drops through to homely samples of preserved fruits, jellies and sauces. Visitors would nod approvingly at the familiar tobacco brands of the day – Hubble Bubble, IXL, Goldbar and Baby's Toe – then marvel at the exotic cigar cases spun from the outer shell of a silkworm's cocoon. In one aisle, Miss Ada Wilshire's collection of beetles and butterflies, shells and mineral specimens catered to the collector, while in another the American firm Abbott, Downing & Co's wagonettes, light carriages, single-hooded and box buggies demonstrated why Cobb & Co's Bathurst warehouse stocked these popular models as well as its own.

The exhibition was a celebration of progress, invention and the wonders of an increasingly global market. Through his regular dealings in the US, and his sharp eye for quality, Rutherford was one busi-nessman who already appreciated the value of such events. Sydney's Garden Palace Exhibition was an occasion to inspire improvements to the services Cobb & Co offered its customers. Given the money he had spent on his Kentucky asses, Rutherford must have been satisfied that Napoleon III came away with first prize. His four-in-hand team took only a second place, while the gold and quartz entries turned out to be a disaster, as most of the minerals went missing during the journey down from Bathurst.

Glorious monuments can be ephemeral. At 5.45 a.m. on a spring morning in late September 1882, little more than two years after the Royal Exhibition had farewelled its thousands of guests, smoke was reported coming from the Garden Palace. Within minutes, the whole central dome was ablaze – witnesses barely had time to call the fire brigade. The heat was so intense that the glass windows of Macquarie Street residences 100 metres away cracked. By the time Sydney's office workers were at their desks three hours later, all that was left of the great edifice was a pile of smouldering ruins and ash.

CHAPTER ELEVEN

MOVING UP IN LIFE

*Except for the four-poster wrought-iron bed they slept
in . . . everything belonged to the company . . .*

After eleven years at Buckiinguy, the property had become home
to the Whitneys – it was certainly roughshod, but home nonetheless. Bella had been stoic in the face of hardship. After the birth of
their daughter Rachel, two sons had come in quick succession. Frank
and Bella called their first boy born at Buckiinguy Glassford, Frank's
mother's maiden name. Their third child, Walter, died at just six
months; Bella was heavy with her fourth baby at the time. Walter's
neglected grave still stands near the banks of Mara Creek.

Bella was just twenty-four years of age when she lost her son. She
must have hated the world for continuing to produce sunrises and
sunsets in the face of her loss. Life and the routine of child-rearing
left little room for dwelling on grief. The daily chores involved in car-
ing for such a young family were hard and grimy, and there was no
school, nurse or local store in the vicinity, but at least the children
took away from her loneliness. Whenever Bella heard the ground
start to vibrate around her with the rhythm of faraway hooves, she
knew her man was not far from home. She was now vastly changed

from the pale-skinned girl Frank had married, her flesh burnished a darker tone from hours spent outdoors every day. Bella bore another girl, Thirza, in 1871, and another boy, Arthur William, in 1873, bringing the family to six.

It was at Buckiinguy that Bella began to understand cattle – what caused them to thrive and what was their downfall. Sheep, too, had become an important part of the business. It was all in a month's work for stockmen to drove seven thousand sheep south down the Darling River to Robertson and Wagner's Pericoota station on the Victorian border. From there, the stock would eventually shuffle onwards to the Melbourne saleyards.

When Rutherford had taken off for America in 1875, with an uncertain date of return, Frank and Bella Whitney had been forced to shift back to civilisation, so Frank could keep a closer eye on business operations and sign cheques. The Whitneys chose to return to Orange, the town where they had begun their life together. Rachel was aged nine, Glassford eight, Thirza four and Arthur – whom everyone called Billy – was two. Perhaps Bella was relieved to leave the property. Her children had no chance of receiving proper schooling at Buckiinguy, and there were no opportunities for socialising. The move also presented an opening for her brother Arthur. For the past five years Cobb & Co had employed Arthur to drove cattle from Buckiinguy to the Victorian border, so he knew the country well. Arthur Leeds was quiet and reserved – certainly not a braggart – but he was more than ready to take over the management of Buckiinguy. His skills as a manager of stock and men would become integral to the future of the firm.

Orange was a pretty town, handsomely laid out with fine parks and public works. It was also a busy regional centre of two to three thousand people, boasting a number of brick houses, three banks, three flour mills, a brewery, stores and hotels, a large gaol and several churches. In 1877, when it became the western railway terminus, the town's status would increase. Already, the wide streets of Orange were lined with young European trees – elms, oaks and hedges of privet. Each road crossed the next at neat right angles, with the distances from one block to the next perfectly equal. The wide open spaces of Buckiinguy must have seemed an eternity away from this ordered place.

Orange was at the centre of a rich agricultural area, the local farms growing wheat, barley, oats, hay and potatoes. The district had once been thickly timbered, but now much of the surrounding land had been cleared. This was a time when a man's acreage defined his future. The average settler stretched himself to purchase as many acres as was legal, and was often left with no capital to work his plot or to make his home comfortable. Typically, he could not afford hired labour or the money to buy sufficient stock to graze his land. Sad, roughly finished homesteads surrounded by scattered cultivation and fences of logs and brush dotted the landscape.

Positioned high on a plateau, Orange served up winters that were extremely cold. The snow that cloaked the town and every garden in the Whitneys' first winter must have caused huge excitement among the family, but as time wore on the novelty faded. Bitter frosts wreaked havoc on one's vegetable garden.

The family moved into what must have seemed a luxurious house at 106 Moulder Street, close to the centre of Orange. Eight months later, Bella bore another girl – Katie. The family continued to grow with another boy, Harold, born three years later.

Harold was nearly two when he sickened with pneumonia. There was little anyone could do but watch him worsen. As the pneumonia took its course, there followed long days of waiting, broken only by the clip-clop of street traffic and the child's crying. It was May 1880, five years since the Whitneys had left Buckiinguy for Orange, when little Harold took his final breath. Bella was seven months pregnant.

When infection had plagued a house, pillows and mattresses were slashed open, exposing the feathers within. A nurse would scrub down the nursery with soft soap, carbolic acid and water, then burn the infant's clothes. A dish would then be suspended over a tub of water in the child's bedroom, the windows and chimney flue closed, and a little sulphur and saltpetre measured into the dish. Lit with a candle and the door tightly shut, all evidence of infection was sucked from the room. Bella might have wished the same could be done with her grief.

Still mourning Harold's death, Bella Whitney bore another boy – Sidney. The infant survived barely five weeks before his tiny lungs slowly collapsed with the same wheezing gasps as his brother. Bella had now lost three children, and her eldest boy, Glassford, was not quite right in the head. Of the eight children Bella had borne, only four were still living and robust. In contrast, her friend Ada Rutherford had just borne her eleventh child and all were in good health. It could not have seemed fair to Bella Whitney.

After five years in Orange, Frank and Bella Whitney had come to enjoy living in the district. To Frank, used to the freezing temperatures of the Canadian Great Lakes, the cool climate must have been far preferable to the heat of Buckiinguy. However, their eldest boy, now thirteen years of age, was showing increasing signs of oddity, and neighbours were nosy in a country town. A pastoral property would give the family more privacy, so the hunt was on for a station not too far from Orange. It was not an opportune time to be buying, as land prices were spiralling upwards due to the profits being made in sheep and cattle.

Over in Bathurst, Ada and James Rutherford had outgrown their William Street townhouse, despite having extended it some years earlier. In 1878 they purchased Hereford, a stately property situated on a low hill with a magnificent view of Bathurst and the river flats below. It was choice land – over 3000 acres – originally granted to William Cox as a thank you from the government for constructing the first road over the Blue Mountains. After the uncertainty regarding Rutherford's trip to America a few years earlier, the local community felt it was surely a sign that he and his family would stay in the area for good.

The old homestead was pulled down in 1879, and Rutherford had an impressive two-storey brick residence built in its place, as Walter Hall had done in Sydney. Like most of their properties, it was paid for with Cobb & Co money and listed as an asset of the firm. The family moved into the new house early in 1880, when Ada was pregnant with her eleventh child. Their oldest child was fifteen, the youngest, Florence, just a few months old. Ada must have been relieved to have the extra space the huge homestead provided.

Marble had been shipped from Italy to create an opulent tiled floor in the mansion's entrance hall, and two spacious hallways flanked by Corinthian columns provided access to thirteen rooms. Like all wealthy settlers, Rutherford had insisted on cedar throughout. Cedar doors led off to the drawing room and library, and a circular cedar staircase wound up to the bedrooms. Every room had a mantelpiece of marble. A large kitchen, maids rooms, stables and dairy had been constructed away from the house.

Rutherford was financially prosperous, but at fifty-three years of age his once-fit body was not what it had been. In June 1880 he was mounting a colt in Cobb & Co's coach factory courtyard in William Street, Bathurst, when he found himself being bucked violently. The animal had not been ridden a great deal and Rutherford was thrown with force. His foot became entangled in the stirrup and he was dragged around the yard once or twice, the horse smashing him into a gatepost. When his foot finally separated from the stirrup, the colt kicked him hard in the stomach and ribs. Rutherford was carried home to recover, too sore and bruised even to undergo a doctor's examination.

The risk of calamity was by no means restricted to men in rural Australia. Five months later, shortly after the birth of her eleventh child, tiny Ada Rutherford came close to losing her own life while crossing a river between Bathurst and the Hereford property. Ada was perhaps unused to reading the river, having spent only a few months in the new house, for she failed to notice that the water was flowing deeper and faster than usual over the ford. Halfway across, her horse and buggy were pulled downstream and Ada was swept into the water. As she flailed her arms, trying to stay afloat, the weight of her heavy petticoats dragged her under. Ada watched with horror as both her horse and buggy became entangled in the willows downstream. Her mare's head was trapped under the surface, her hind hooves lashing out for over a minute before she was still, drowned.

Ada too was carried underwater, but she managed to struggle to the surface. Gasping for breath, she instead gulped in water. Half-choked, she reached for a willow branch, but twigs broke away in her hands. Now desperate, she seized a stronger branch and managed to raise her head above the fast current. Summoning all her strength, Ada clung on until help arrived. Three local brothers, seeing her in trouble, threw her a rope from the bank and hauled her to safety. It is likely that neither Ada nor the men who saved her could swim. With eleven children and a husband to look after, Ada Rutherford had come terribly close to drowning.

Another prestigious station was added to Cobb & Co's portfolio when Frank and Bella Whitney came across Coombing Park, just 80 kilometres east of the firm's Bathurst headquarters. It would be Cobb & Co's eighth station. The purchase of Hereford and Coombing Park – two icons of the district's history – was a turning point for the company. It cemented their move away from the business of coaching to the far more respectable occupation of sheep and cattle breeding.

Bella was perhaps relieved to be leaving Orange; the family needed a fresh environment after the sadness of losing two infants in one year. An attraction for Frank was that nearby Carcoar, like Orange, had a race club. Frank found time on one or two Sundays a month to indulge himself in one of his favourite pursuits – betting on good horseflesh. There were races at the Carcoar track once a month and in the surrounding district every other week. To spend a few hours betting and discussing the merits of this or that mare was pure bliss for Frank, a passion he shared with his colleague Walter Hall.

Frank would have been thrilled when he learned that Coombing

Park had produced not only fine cavalry chargers, police horses and station hacks, but some of the colony's most famous early racehorses. The colony's first thoroughbred mare, Manto, and sire, Sir Hercules, had been imported to Australia in 1825 by Coombing Park's owner, Thomas Icely. Sir Hercules had sired The Barb, winner of the 1866 Melbourne Cup.

In early January 1881, Cobb & Co officially acquired not only Coombing Park but also the title to every house in the town of Mandurama. Icely's eldest son had fallen on hard times and his holdings had been repeatedly mortgaged, so there was a good deal of debt thrown into the purchase agreement. Built on land belonging to Coombing, Mandurama came with a debt of £16 000. Whitney and Rutherford agreed to take on the debt, and every house, cottage and store in the town was now theirs. The area was predominantly populated by English and Irish emigrants, elderly freed convicts and their families. Carcoar, the first town in the district after Bathurst, had grown up around the sizable workforce that Thomas Icely had imported to help create his grand estate. Indeed, during the 1830s and '40s it was Coombing Park rather than Carcoar that housed most of the district's population. The government had assigned Icely dozens of convicts to construct his station buildings, fire his bricks and shoe his horses; leg irons hung on the walls of a solitary-confinement cell near the stables.

Thomas Icely had been a man with connections and capital. He had accumulated enormous wealth through a series of dubious, yet very large land grants and acquisitions, as well as taking early advantage of the captive Sydney market by importing English goods. Gracing the Coombing homestead were cedar tallboys with scrolled legs, oak glass-fronted bookcases, French chaise longues and Belgian tapestries. Merely occupying the homestead raised its inhabitants to a higher echelon of society.

Coombing Park had been the centrepiece of the district since white settlement began. Once the sole source of civilisation in the district, it was known for its garden parties, thoroughbred horses and merino sheep breeding, and had played host to governors of the colony as well as famous artists and writers; both Anthony Trollope and Conrad Martens had been guests. Just seven years earlier, Trollope had published *Australia and New Zealand*, a book whose vivid descriptions of Australian coach journeys and Cobb & Co drivers had already enhanced the firm's reputation. So popular was the book that three editions were published in three years in London, and it was serialised in the *Australasian*.

Like Frank Whitney, Thomas Icely had grown up in an era of gold fever. In 1846, five years before E. H. Hargraves made headlines with the official discovery of gold in the district, Icely had sent quartz that glittered with streaks of dirty yellow to a well-known geologist in Sydney for analysis. He received back a positive assay. A word of this to anyone, and he knew his land would be overrun. In Icely's mind, his family risked having their throats cut in a deluge of gold hunters, and the last thing he needed was for his hundred-odd workers to be spending all their time in the creeks fossicking for gold. He would keep quiet about his find and concentrate on copper instead. The geologists had assured him that his copper and iron deposits were rich.

A few years passed, and no throats had been sliced open in the night, so Icely could not help boasting to a few friends in high

places – the Colonial Secretary, in fact – of his discovery. It was perhaps not surprising that the Colonial Secretary happened to mention
to a certain Mr E. H. Hargraves, the famous prospector fresh out from
the Californian goldfields, that he should talk to Icely in his search for
a commercially viable goldfield in the promising colony.

Hargreaves was met with silence when he raised the subject with
Icely, but the prospector had no difficulty finding significant gold
deposits in other parts of the district. And so the gold rush, and its
influx of prospectors and services to meet their needs, began.

Coombing Park was purchased not in Frank and Bella Whitney's
name, but by Cobb & Co. The property was sold on a walk-out,
walk-in basis, so even the household contents belonged to Cobb & Co
rather than Frank and Bella. Only the four-poster wrought-iron bed
they slept in (a wedding present) was theirs, everything else belonged
to the company – the crockery and cutlery settings for twenty guests,
the English oak furniture, the French tapestries and hall clocks, the
works of art and the library of illustrated books. Such an arrangement
was common at the time, and was similar to a multinational firm of
today buying houses for its key executives around the world, then
leasing them to directors at a nominal rent.

The long drive that led up to Coombing Park's homestead was
littered with pine cones fallen from the forty-year-old trees lining
the avenue, the surrounding landscape was beautiful – gently sloping
green and rocky hills seemed to ripple outwards in every direction.
For a family of seven, at first sight the main house didn't appear to
be overly large. In the late 1820s it had been the first refined dwell-

ing built in the district – an elegant English cottage built on a knoll, surrounded by a rambling garden. Icely's gardeners had created a beautiful flower garden bordered by fruit trees and vines, crowded with rhododendrons, rose bushes, elms and oaks with creepers tumbling down their trunks. Large crows and brightly coloured lorikeets shared the garden with cockatoos and little peewits.

The wide front verandah and elegant proportions of the house exuded a sense of permanence. From the verandah a view through shrubs to the creek and rolling hills beyond drew one's gaze to the foothills of Mount Macquarie. Coombing Creek's gully running deep just past the garden had been cracked by drought and eroded by sudden rains. It resembled the long-neglected moat of a castle, dividing the home paddock from the house.

Inside, the cottage was in fact deceptively large. Imperious portraits glared down from the walls of the hallway; a door to the left led into the station office, the one on the right led into a ladies' sitting room or parlour, unmistakably feminine with its flowered wallpaper and petite, low armchairs. There was a piano and behind it a large fireplace, with a painting of a snow scene suspended above the mantelpiece. Lacquered vases, bronze statues and an oil reading lamp sat at eye level. The parlour was also crowded with high cane chairs with deep cushions, an imported French-upholstered chaise longue, dainty occasional tables and fine china.

In the dining room the oak dining table, chairs and silver dinner service were of the finest quality, imported from England. The room was only just large enough for the table. A fine French clock punctuated the mantelpiece in the drawing room, in a celebration of continental wealth. More European painted vases decorated every surface, and dark oak bookcases were squeezed against the left-hand wall. It would be hard to imagine Bella's five children fitting into this cluttered space.

The kitchen and staff quarters were separate from the main house, and hidden behind it so that guests wouldn't see the buildings when approaching up the circular drive. Coombing was mainly a sheep property, and the station buildings were extensive, solid affairs far enough away from the homestead to give the family privacy. The workmen, their wives and children lived in whitewashed cottages on a rise among solid farm buildings, also gleaming white. In the stables sat a grand private carriage with its leather-upholstered cushions and retractable hood, the Icely name engraved on the body.

In the 1830s there had been a large village of families on the place – overseers, shepherds, grooms, house servants, cooks, superintendents of convicts, carpenters, gardeners, bricklayers, coachmen, miners and boundary riders were all listed in the station's payment books. The original property had its own blacksmith, butcher and bakery.

Back in the 1870s, Hall, Rutherford and Whitney had invested in at least one gold mine in the Carcoar district. Now, Frank Whitney began pumping serious amounts of his own money into a copper mine that Icely had started at Coombing Park. Over ten years, the mine became a major operation, employing over two dozen men. It must have yielded good profits to justify the enormous capital expenses and sizable workforce Frank employed.

Frank Whitney would often outlay £800 a month on the operation. He had to build accommodation for his mine workers. Then there were the ore dressers, labourers, carpenters, firemen, shaft sinkers, whip drivers and blacksmiths to pay and house. To build mine tunnels, gunpowder, gelatine and timber needed to be purchased; horses, drays and men were needed to haul the ore, bricks and timber. Once the timber had arrived, there were men employed just to stack it. The ore needed to be smelted, and this also required its own team. Bricks were made on site to make ovens and bracing for the mines. Tools constantly needed to be replaced.

Whitney was constantly being reminded of the investment possibilities that lay elsewhere, and it was hard to say no to every share offer that passed his desk. In the years to come, he would buy thousands of shares in two other copper mines and four new gold mines. None of them seemed to be a real winner.

Frank's peers – the now wealthy Alex Robertson, Rutherford and Wagner – were all sending their sons away to be privately schooled at Geelong Grammar, 75 kilometres south-west of Melbourne. An education at such a school ensured that their lads mixed with good Church of England boys and made the right connections before returning to the land, going up to university or heading off to England. Geelong was a long way from Coombing Park for Glassford, especially with Bella and Frank's concerns about his mental disposition. Instead, the Whitneys chose a closer option, the King's School at Parramatta, perhaps so they could better oversee their son's progress. Glassford began boarding at the school before the family shifted to Coombing Park.

A boarding school education was not common for the daughters of wealthy pastoralists, and Bella's and Ada's daughters were instead taught by governesses at home. The most that daughters from respectable families might expect was to take a final year at a 'finishing school' in the city or away in Europe. The partners' daughters spent their time sewing, perfecting their side-saddle riding technique, being schooled and writing letters. Whereas once these girls might have made their own butter, brought in the milk pail or cleaned out the stables, there were now numerous staff to perform such tasks.

In their new homes, Ada and Bella busied themselves getting their houses in order, training new maids and cooks to prepare food and serve at table, and writing to employment agencies to find good governesses for their girls.

James Rutherford and Frank Whitney's perseverance had brought their families a long way up in the world. For Rutherford the contrast was vast since the time, twenty-five years earlier, he'd been forced to sneak aboard the boat between Geelong and Melbourne, a broke and desperate horse-trader. Now it was others who came begging, asking the Cobb & Co partners to give their son a job or to sit on some hospital committee or board.

CHAPTER TWELVE

ROADS, ROUTES AND PASSENGERS

*... the firm was the Qantas of nineteenth-century
Australia – powerful, complex and highly respected by the
average Australian.*

Imperialism was at its peak in the 1870s, with European nations
scrambling for a share of Africa, Southeast Asia and the Pacific.
The massive land grab was made possible by a capital-rich Europe
looking for highly profitable and secure investments, and the United
Kingdom was to make off with the lion's share. Australian and other
colonies were popular places to invest because they offered government guarantees. Capital raised mostly in London was invested in
railways – the modern and civilising new form of transport – leading
to a frenzy of construction, not just in Australia but also in India,
Canada and Argentina.

Given the huge distances and small population, Australia became
perhaps the most impressive railway builder in the world. By the mid-
1880s investment had gained alarming momentum, and by the early
1890s about £100 million had been poured into their construction.

Policy-makers in New South Wales and Victoria had a clear plan
to radiate routes from the coastal capitals of Sydney and Melbourne,

as both colonies' politics were dominated by a well-off urban merchant class. In New South Wales, railway building had been limited to a simple system of three main lines – the Great Western, Great Southern and Great Northern – fanning out south-west, west and north-west from Sydney. The many coastal towns north and south of Sydney were more cheaply serviced by steamer ship. Victoria had gone over the top with its railway construction, building a complex web of routes that reached even the smallest of settlements. Many of its lines would soon become white elephants.

Railway policy in Queensland was dominated by pastoral interests. Rather than branching out from Brisbane, separate railway routes fed livestock and grain from the hinterland direct to the nearest coastal port, spread along a huge coastline. All the colony's railways were built to lower engineering standards and to a narrower gauge than in New South Wales and Victoria. At one time there were eleven small, lightly constructed and unconnected lines in Queensland, compared to one system in Victoria and two or three in New South Wales. By the end of the century, Queensland's railways reached into once-remote centres, from Charleville to Cunnamulla, Winton to Hughenden. There would even be a railway stretching up the Atherton Tableland from Cairns. However, the continent's 16 000 kilometres of railway track had been poorly planned, and many of the routes did not link up. Coach travel was still needed to plug the gaps.

With its excessive reliance on railways, Victoria had seen its roads deteriorate to become some of the worst in Australia, despite the colony's density of population. The difference between roads in Victoria and New South Wales was obvious at border crossings on the Murray River, where the construction of bridges was split between the two colonies. On the New South Wales bank of the Murray, the government built well-engineered approaches. In contrast, untrained contractors employed by local councils were left to do the job on the Victorian side. Some new bridges opened without any road leading off on the Victorian side whatsoever.

By limiting its railways to just three main lines, New South Wales had been forced to spend money on good roads and bridges. In the 1870s and '80s, the colony was building better roads and bridges than any other Australian colony. Bridges in particular were important, as New South Wales had so many large coastal and inland rivers, as well as thousands of substantial creeks.

Before 1906, only a tenth of New South Wales was under local government control, so road and bridge building fell to the colonial government's Public Works Department. Fortuitously for taxpayers and coach operators like Cobb & Co, this well-funded department boasted a large and professional drafting office and was committed to quality. New South Wales had plentiful supplies of ironbark and turpentine, just about the best bridge-building timbers in the world. The result was the design and construction over three quarters of a century of 422 timber-truss road bridges, a feat probably unequalled in the world for number or quality. Eighty-two of these bridges still stand.

Large steel-truss and iron-girder bridges were also built. A road connecting remote Glen Innes to Grafton, for example, intended basically for bullock wagons of wool to reach the coast, boasted such engineering feats as a tunnel cut through sheer rock and a lattice iron-girder bridge over the local river. No other colony would even contemplate wasting such high-quality infrastructure on remote

Railways and Cobb & Co routes
in New South Wales, 1883

Stanthorpe

Hungerford   Barringun   Warialda   Tenterfield

Bourke   Brewarinna   Inverell

Louth   Walgett

Wilcannia   Gongolgon   Boggabri   Armidale

Cobar   Nyngan   Coonabarabran   Tamworth
          Warren   Werris Creek

Nymagee   Nevertire   Coolah
          Dubbo   Merriwa   Muswellbrook

          Wellington   Mudgee

Eubalong   Condoblin   Parkes   Molong   Sofala   Rylstone
                    Orange   Capertee   Newcastle

Forbes   Blayney   Bathurst
          Grenfell   Trunkey   Gosford

Hay   Temora   Sydney

Narrandera   Cootamundra   Murrumburrah
          Urana   Tumblong   Gundagai   Goulburn

Deniliquin   Jerilderie   Tumut   Kiama
          Culcairn   Rosewood

Echuca   Albury

          Cooma

N

—————— Railways
············· Coach routes
------ Border

0   100   200
        kms

roads. In 1879 the government built a huge steel-truss bridge across the Shoalhaven River at Nowra that still carries the heaviest highway traffic more than 125 years later. By 1888, even Bathurst could boast of an enormous single-span iron-truss bridge to take road traffic over its railway yard.

New South Wales may have been in the midst of a railway-building boom in the late nineteenth century, but significantly more was spent on the colony's roads, harbour and river transport. Cobb & Co took full advantage of these new roads. In the ten years up to 1880, the firm had tripled its share of New South Wales mail routes to over 3680 kilometres and more than tripled its income from mail contracts.

Cobb & Co's advertising in local newspapers was straightforward to the point of being banal, simply mentioning routes, fares and perhaps timetables. Coach travel was a staple, like milk or bread. There were no fancy claims made about customer comfort or punctuality, for the proprietors knew that comfort was not their strong point. On many outback routes, especially in remote Queensland, there was little or no competition, so there was no need to promise a dream journey. Punctuality depended on the state of roads that were usually nothing more than dirt tracks – whether they were in Victoria, New South Wales or Queensland. Two days' rain could turn them into a muddy bog. Everybody knew that no two journeys were ever the same – it was part of the adventure.

The company was now paying drivers according to the distance they drove. Fares had come down, and the threat of bushrangers had vanished, so the average driver's wages were just a quarter of what they had been in the heady gold-rush days. They now made only £10 or £12 per month, with tips adding another one or two pounds, and they were obliged to cover 12 to 16 kilometres an hour to meet the requirements of government mail contracts.

Each Cobb & Co driver had his own teams, and his local road manager held him responsible for their condition. Horses were allocated to particular stages along the route, according to their suitability for the local conditions. Being habituated to certain country meant a horse used to working on the open plains tended to become 'moonblind' if put on stages that passed through timbered country at night. Unused to the changing shadows, such horses would imagine they saw something on the road, take fright and try to tear out of their harness. In the same way, coaching horses working Queensland's black-soil plains did so without shoes, so they were not suitable for use in stony country.

Most of the firm's horses were stabled at change stations along the routes, though some were held in reserve on the company's stations; for example, those managed by Arthur Leeds in Queensland. Station owners who wanted their own horses broken-in to pull private carriages would sometimes loan them to the firm, though in return their horses had to pull Cobb & Co coaches for at least a year.

The company's diverse routes traversed Queensland's tropical rainforests, rattled past gum trees heavy with snow high in the Australian alps, wound through the gullies and low ridges of the gold country, and travelled in mind-numbing straight lines across the inland plains. The most comfortable journey for a passenger was over grassy paddocks, avoiding the rutted, often boggy tracks. The coaches would swish through long grass as rotten branches crumpled underneath their wheels. Such untrammelled ground was only found on what drivers called 'natural roads' – routes picked out by the driver through open unfenced country. Many routes were cut through bushland, and drivers would swing their teams one way and another to avoid tree stumps and fallen trees blocking their journey. Overhanging tree limbs would groan and crack as the blinkered teams pushed past urgently.

Red gravel country was also popular with drivers and passengers, as such terrain stayed firm even after heavy rain. Clay soils were dust traps in summer and turned to deep mud in winter, while gravel tracks in mountainous terrain were often washed out down to the bare rock, making it hard on the horses' hooves and rough for passengers. However, it was the black-soil plains of north-western New South Wales and western Queensland that could be a traveller and driver's worst nightmare. The travelling was smooth and easy when dry, but with just a little rain these plains became a black spongy glue, clinging to the coach wheels until they were slowed to a crawl. The heavier the rain, the deeper the coaches would sink into the mud, until finally the wheels and axles were buried a metre deep, the body of the vehicle resting on the boggy ground. In order to get the all-important mails through the black-soil plains after rain, passengers might be unloaded and the coach lifted off the front axle. The driver would sit on this axle, strap the mail bags to it and plough onwards on two wheels behind his team of horses, leaving his passengers and coach stranded in the mud. Queensland's Clermont to Aramac run had perhaps the worst of these black-soil plains. The Normanton to Croydon route in the Gulf of Carpentaria was the firm's most difficult track, however, closed entirely in the wet season as the landscape turned into boggy lakes, while the Cooktown to Palmer run was notorious for the scores of hostile natives. It wasn't a route on which you felt comfortable taking long stops.

Many routes passed through sheep and cattle stations, and as the squatters fenced their runs an increasing number of gates appeared across the tracks. Opening and shutting these gates was tedious, the job falling to the male passengers who arranged watches between themselves. On some routes an accompanying gate boy was paid to do the job or a 'sundowner' – an itinerant unemployed fellow – was given a free ride for doing the task (though this was officially against company rules). If a Chinese or Aboriginal man was aboard, the gate-keeping often fell to him.

Constance Ellis was one among thousands of Cobb & Co's customers. Her experiences illustrate the day-to-day realities of coach travel. In May 1889 Constance made a journey from Toowoomba, heading 1000 kilometres west to a property past Adavale in a coach that lumbered over the flat, unending plains like a giant, piled high with packages of beef, tinned meat and hams, whisky, clothing and flatirons – indispensable items to families in rural Australia. Passengers were allowed just 21 pounds (9.5 kilograms) of luggage – less than half the allowance one is permitted today on a commercial Dash 8 flight into a country town. Early on in Constance's journey the roads had been so boggy that the driver had insisted she abandon much of her luggage mid-route, to be picked up later and carried on by bullocky. She did not see her forfeited belongings for four months.

Often coaches departed heavily laden with stores that would be dropped off along the way. On the early part of her journey, Constance would likely have found herself fighting for room with bags of flour and sides of bacon on the seats next to her. For the young Englishwoman there were also the flies to get used to – a solid mass of them, thick on a person's back, rising in a loud buzzing cloud as you moved. Then there were the distances. Normally one might complete such a journey in five long days and nights of travelling, but Ms Ellis missed a connecting coach in Adavale, and with wet weather and blocked routes she had to wait eight days before being able to continue her journey.

Adavale was a remote town of 100 people in the black-soil floodplains not so far from Rutherford's Davenport Downs. The nearest doctor and dentist were 200 kilometres away at Charleville. Constance was alarmed to discover that the men of the district spent every evening drinking in one of the town's six hotels. It was hard to see how so many bars survived until one witnessed the weekend pilgrimage of station hands, shearers and managers. It was a crowd seemingly bent on drinking until they passed out.

Roasted goat was a common dish served up by innkeepers for dinner, as the animals were cheap and easy to look after, though the lady of the house might pretend her meat was somewhat choicer. Ms Ellis reported:

> I was asked whether I would have lamb or venison. I chose the latter, and very tasty and tender I found it. Afterwards I found that both joints were just plain goat.

The fare paid for a Cobb & Co coach journey may have included meals but it came with no guarantee that a passenger would not have to walk or even swim some of the way. In its race to make a profit on routes well before the railways took over, the firm's coaches often travelled over country where there were no bridges, and rivers or creeks simply had to be forded. The company ensured there was a barge moored at deeper river crossings, but coaches often had to cross shallower river beds. After good rains a shallow stream could swell enormously, making crossings a major operation. Cobb & Co's regulations forbade drivers from entering water that might rise above the horses' saddle flaps, but it was often difficult to judge the depth from the riverbank. Sometimes a rider would go ahead to scout the water levels, but even so, many drivers underestimated the depth, and the strength of the current. Constance Ellis described how passengers, mail, coach and horses were brought across a flooded river on her journey west of Brisbane in the pouring rain:

A man swam across with a rope, our end being fastened to the coach which was then hauled across, endless chain fashion, then the mails and luggage were loaded into washing tubs and ferried over. Meanwhile the four horses were swum across and harnessed. The male passengers went farther up, stripped and swam over. Then Delia and I were packed into the tubs and pulled over. I didn't feel too safe but as everyone took things as a matter of course I did the same. By this time it was dark and the rain much heavier.

Despite the hardships, many travellers saw such experiences as pure adventure and laughed them off. The indefatigable Constance Ellis was more than resilient:

The night got blacker and the rain heavier and the road worse. We frequently stuck and then all had to get out and walk till a better patch of road was met. The Bulloo manager was most kind to me; we walked arm in arm for miles that night in the blackness, and talked as cheerfully as we would have on a sunny day.

With the huge distances and flat plains, change stations in Queensland did not need to follow the 10- to 20-mile formula that Freeman Cobb had devised. If conditions were bad and horses became exhausted from pulling a coach out of ditches and the boggy black soil, the driver might have to rest them wherever they happened to be, setting up camp for the night, which forced the passengers to sleep on the ground or in the coach. A fire would be lit, tea made and someone would usually produce something worth cooking.

Some routes were only viable for one or two years until the railways came through, in which case there was no point investing in a solid building. Instead, the company often relied on using a settler's remote homestead facilities or outstation huts as change stations, rather than going to the expense of setting up their own. The amount of traffic did not justify the establishment of an inn, and some change stations were as simple as a tent and a bough shed.

Passengers had to stay overnight in these rough dwellings. The man in charge, often an Aboriginal, might have his own simple bed – four posts driven into the ground and joined by saplings, with more saplings laid across. His mattress would be a sack filled with leaves. Constance described one of these change stations:

Such a tumble down place – slab walls and bark roof – an ant bed floor, worn into deep holes in places – tabletop of packing case wood, legs driven into the earth, the seat a board, also with permanent legs; no tablecloth; but everything spotless.

James Rutherford regularly went out on the road to inspect the quality of change stations and traveller facilities, but with a business as big as Cobb & Co, total quality control was impossible, and the company's passengers were not always guaranteed their own bed at night. Constance Ellis arrived at one whitewashed clay-brick homestead during her journey west – and to her horror had to share a bed with the squatter's three daughters.

As the passenger loads diminished on the more remote routes, smaller coaches were used. West of Adavale, where Constance Ellis was headed, her ticket entitled her to ride in a simple 'buckboard' cart – a square box on wheels that city grocers used to carry fruit.

In the decade to 1880, Cobb & Co's Queensland operations had doubled the total distance of routes to more than 2200 kilometres. The coaching dividends were a massive £16 500 in 1880, half that amount going directly to James Rutherford.

By 1881, the Queensland coaching business had become so large that it needed a more formal structure and more capital. The partnership between Barnes, Robertson and Rutherford was dissolved and a new public company was formed. Rutherford took a third of the shares and Walter Hall, always keen to get in on a profitable concern, stepped in to take up 30 per cent of the business himself. The remaining shares were bought up by Tom Gallagher, soon to be general manager; Ludwig Uhl, the saddle-maker from Brisbane who had by now made his fortune from Cobb & Co work; Mr Coyle, a long-time road manager; and a Mr Fred Shaw.

In response to huge tracts of back country being opened up to farming and mining, the firm added another 2700 kilometres of routes over the next three years. It is unlikely that Ada Rutherford saw much of her husband as he busied himself taking advantage of the booming Queensland market. Cobb & Co was harnessing three thousand horses to pull its Queensland coaches, and by 1883 the firm's combined Queensland and New South Wales routes covered over 9600 kilometres.

It was by no means just passengers, mail contracts and coach and buggy building that ratcheted up the value of the Cobb & Co business. The New South Wales Cobb & Co partners now owned close to 11 000 square kilometres of pastoral land in New South Wales and Queensland – nine stations that collectively sprawled over an area more than three-quarters the size of Northern Ireland. Bella's brother Arthur Leeds had become the firm's lieutenant in this area and had shifted from Buckiinguy to Burrenbilla station, where he oversaw the three monster stations among their holdings.

Frank was a natural horse breeder, but he had come to work well with his brother-in-law Arthur Leeds on the sheep and cattle side of the business. Arthur had developed into a fine manager, and he now had two sons to help him run the Queensland stations. He never spent a pound of company money without documenting it: every lamb, sheep and heifer was carefully tracked and accounted for in his meticulously kept stockbooks. Leeds was a godsend to the firm, and seemed to expect little by way of reward for his efforts.

Burrenbilla and Claverton stocked well over 70 000 sheep each, and Claverton and Davenport Downs, 320 kilometres south-west of Winton, ran over 20 000 cattle apiece. Each property was reaping enormous returns through wool and livestock sales. In good years, the profits were far higher than from the New South Wales coaching business. In 1877, for example, the partners' stations netted over £77 500 in profits, compared to £11 500 from coaching. Buckiinguy and other stations were also breeding hundreds of horses each year for both the coaching business and export. With its expanding web of investments, the firm was the Qantas of nineteenth-century Australia – powerful, complex and highly respected by the average Australian.

PART THREE

A CERTAIN STATION IN LIFE: 1883–1895

CHAPTER THIRTEEN

OPPORTUNITY SOURED

*The fate of the black man and the marsupial will, one plainly
sees, be the fate of Cobb: He will be improved out of existence.*
– Australian Pictures, *1886*

By the mid-1860s it was possible to travel by a Cobb & Co-branded
coach from Normanton on the Gulf of Carpentaria or Port Douglas
on the Coral Sea down to northern Victoria and on into South Australia. The total mileage of Cobb & Co's routes in the three eastern
seaboard states made up perhaps the most extensive coaching network in the world, covering distances greater than Wells Fargo's huge
American coaching business.

By 1886, however, Queensland had the most significant demand
for passenger coaches. The colony's drier inland routes, stretching
beyond the reach of the railways, made up the bulk of the firm's activity. At the turn of the century, the combined distance of the firm's
Queensland routes peaked at over 7200 kilometres, almost twice the
distance from Sydney to Perth. Cobb & Co opened and closed more
than eighty Queensland routes over nearly sixty years. Some were as
short as ferrying passengers from a railway depot the mile or two into
the nearest town. Others, such as the Cloncurry to Normanton route,

Railways and Cobb & Co routes in Queensland, 1885

N

| 0 | 100 | 200 |

kms

Cooktown

Maytown

Port Douglas

Thornborough

Normanton

Townsville

Charters Towers

Cloncurry

Richmond

Hughenden

Winton

Muttaburra

Aramac

Clermont

Barcaldine

Jericho

Emerald

Rockhampton

Isisford

Alpha

Springsure

Blackall

Tambo

Windorah

Adavale

Charleville

Mitchell

Yeulba

Gympie

Morven

Surat

Thargomindah

Eulo

Bollon

Cunnamulla

St George

Toowoomba

Brisbane

Warwick

Southport

Hungerford

Barringun

— Railways
.... Coach Routes
- - - - Border

were over vast distances requiring four to five days of travel. Profits in the Queensland coaching business fluctuated wildly, depending on whether the country was in drought and thus horse feed expensive. The year 1883 was the peak year for Queensland Cobb & Co's revenue, with more than £50 000 in mail subsidies and fares flowing in. Net profits were close to £20 000. A year later, however, there was a net loss of £8000. Wages remained a huge outgoing.

The situation was very different in New South Wales, where the encroaching railways were increasingly making Cobb & Co's coach routes redundant. Here, it was the railway contractors rather than the coaching firms who were making huge profits. Not surprisingly, Rutherford, Whitney and Hall wanted a slice of the action, and in 1882 they made a bid for one of the railway-building contracts to advance the Great Northern Railway from Tamworth to Tenterfield. Cobb & Co tendered for the final 90-kilometre section of the route, from Glen Innes to Tenterfield along the ridge of the Great Dividing Range, some of the most forbidding country in the colony. Great granite boulders and outcrops shared the landscape with deep ravines and impenetrable, craggy mountains. The railway would need to navigate a tortuous descent to the valley below.

It took a Cobb & Co coach two days and nights to cover the 320 rugged kilometres between Tamworth and Tenterfield, thirty-seven hours on the road and perhaps ten hours of rest and meals. After a few hours' sleep at an inn, passengers might be woken at 4 a.m. for breakfast, and an hour later they would be on the road, only to be ordered out on steep sections to walk or to give the coach a push to help the horses up a precipitous or muddy track. The ordeal would cost £8 or more, including meals. Once the railway line was built, the same journey cost little more than a pound – second class – and slashed travel time from forty-eight to just nine hours. Today, the same route can be covered in three hours by car.

The government's line surveys had forecast average construction costs of £10 706 per mile. How Cobb & Co estimated their own costs when they had not a day's experience of railways construction is not clear, but they successfully bid a little lower per mile than their five competitors – just short of £618 800 all up – despite this being the most difficult terrain of the entire route. Given their lack of experience and the fact that neither Hall, Rutherford nor Whitney was going to be actively involved in managing the work, they were taking an enormous risk. They had just thirty months, until 30 June 1885, to complete the work.

Construction began in early 1883, with much of their workforce based in a purpose-built bush camp next to the tiny town of Bolivia, high in the Great Dividing Range, 30 kilometres south of Tenterfield. Bolivia, named after a pioneer's nearby property, was a settlement Cobb & Co already knew well. Their coach passengers travelling en route to Tenterfield had taken meals and rest at the Bolivia Hotel for over thirteen years.

To oversee the project, Cobb & Co dispatched their trusted accountant Mr Trout, along with a Mr Mason as manager and Mr Simons as deputy manager. It is unlikely that any of the three were experienced in managing railway contractors. Advertisements for workers soon appeared in the regional newspapers, offering eight shillings a day. There would eventually be 400 workers, storekeepers and tradesmen and their families living in the Bolivia camp, along with hundreds of others based in smaller camps along the line. It was a rocky and barren district, with no prospect of permanent settlement, so the firm had to offer incentives beyond wages to attract the workforce they would need for three years. Cobb & Co constructed offices, workshops, stables and a post telegraph office in their main camp at the top of Bolivia Hill. They then spent enormous sums building a weatherboard school large enough for 100 children, complete with a fireplace and attached toilets, all 'out of reach of rocks thrown up during blasting operations'. In their letter to the Education Department, Cobb & Co requested a teacher, furniture and schoolbooks, and attached a list of the seventy-seven children they intended to enrol. The Department was convinced of the need for at least temporary funding and leased the school back from the firm for the next three and a half years.

There is now little evidence of the Cobb & Co employees who lived and died building that line. Every homemade wooden cross that once marked the hard lives of railway workers and their families has long since rotted away. The Bolivia railway platform is overgrown with weeds, and no passenger trains have interrupted the silence since the early 1970s. The station building has long vanished, with only a signal box remaining.

The railway navigator (shortened to 'navvy' and now known as a fettler) was the unsung hero of railways construction. Their forebears were the thousands of itinerant labourers who had dug the canals of eighteenth-century Britain. As the canal era declined, these workers transferred their expertise to railway cuttings. They were itinerant men, paid by the hour. In Australia, they often worked a twelve-hour day of tough manual labour, six or seven days a week in all weather, with no protection from the harsh elements. Some of the men brought along wives, children or lovers to the rough and transitory bush camps; others left families at home, sometimes for years. Those wives who accompanied their husbands had to put up with drunken brawls in the camps, mistreatment, children who ran wild and mail that could be months arriving. Sanitation in the camps was poor, and many children sickened and died from infectious diseases.

The navvies used gunpowder and dynamite to blast railway cuttings through rock with minimal safety precautions. Blasting tended to take place at noon, when the men had knocked off for lunch, and at five in the afternoon, when they had finished for the day. It meant no time was lost interrupting work to clear the blast area, but serious injuries following tunnel collapses and rock-blasting were common nevertheless. Management simply recruited replacements to take the place of the injured workers.

Tobacco and alcohol were a navvy's great supports. The most notorious drinkers in the Bolivia camp would work a month, then take a month off to drink away their earnings. It was the nomadic shopkeepers and liquor merchants who profited most, charging exorbitant prices for both grog and necessities to a captive market. These merchants followed the railway teams from camp to camp, setting up temporary grog shanties that they could take with them when they moved on to another site. According to a Sydney reporter who visited in 1883, Bolivia was soon home to not only two hotels but

> . . . half a dozen stores, two butchers, two bakers, a blacksmith, a bootmaker, a cordial factory, tobacconist, a saddler and a barber of coloured extraction whose shopfront sign advertised 'Hairdrasin'. A couple of boarding houses completed the camp,

which was surrounded by scores of canvas and bark humpies,
giving the barest of shelter and comfort to the navvies and their
families.

The invasion must have been a rude shock to the tiny Bolivia community. Such ramshackle shanties and grog houses had previously been limited to the region's goldfields.

In the mid-winter of 1883, six months into construction, things started to go wrong. The process of laying rails required hundreds of men to dig and blast long cuttings and embankments using picks, shovels and wheelbarrows. Cobb & Co could not find enough men. In desperation they turned to Queensland, advertising in the country papers for 'two hundred pick and shovel hands and hammer and drill men'.

The project was making progress once again when the firm, perhaps sensing losses ahead, decided to cut wages. The navvies' daily pay was cut by sixpence, while the fee to see a doctor was raised from sixpence to ninepence. In response, by early 1884 the Cobb & Co workers had coordinated a full-scale strike up and down the line. Over five hundred strikers gathered in Bolivia. Accompanied by a band playing 'The Girl I Left Behind Me', they marched off along the railway in the direction of Glen Innes, demanding that their prior pay rates be restored, as well as the right to smoke on the job. For several weeks there was no progress, neither side giving ground. Cobb & Co was now well behind in its time commitments, and in desperation they sub-contracted the 10 northern-most miles of construction to help speed up completion. On the part of the line they retained, many of their workers were forced to return to work on the lower pay rate or be unemployed.

The 30 June 1885 deadline passed, and the line had not been completed. Typhoid fever decimated the squalid Bolivia work camp, claiming many children and adults, and then in August 1885 several thousand sleepers and much of the timber reserved for the construction of culverts and bridges were condemned as rotten, unfit to be used. A month was lost finding new timber at huge expense. The project was losing Frank Whitney, James Rutherford and Walter Hall money on a massive scale but their contract was binding – the firm had no choice but to continue.

Fourteen months behind schedule, Cobb & Co's navvies laid the last track. The bitter winter of 1886 had just ended. The next day, 1 September, the first train chugged into Tenterfield. The *Tenterfield Star* printed a poignant statement from Cobb & Co announcing its last coach between Glen Innes and Tenterfield. It was reported that the firm's loss on the railway-construction contract was £80 000 – a major wound to their pride. Never again would Cobb & Co touch the railways.

Earlier, during the final days of 1885, when the railways project had been bleeding money, Whitney and Rutherford had suffered another setback. Walter Hall had had enough of managing Cobb & Co's government contracts in New South Wales, and he was ready to exit the coaching partnership. The disastrous Tenterfield railway contract and the increasing reach of those same railways is likely to have blown his confidence in the coaching side of the Cobb & Co business.

Rutherford and Whitney could not afford to pay Hall out – in fact, they were desperate to hold on to his capital. They begged Walter to leave a massive £63 000 in the company as a loan (more than $7 million in current values), and they must have been mightily relieved when he agreed. On paper at least, Frank Whitney now held a third of the firm and Rutherford two-thirds. Regardless, they were in serious debt. It was hard to see how they could afford to pay their interest bills.

The issue of public recognition highlighted a key difference between James Rutherford and his partner Frank Whitney. The Carcoar district held Frank Whitney in general high respect, his judgement lending weight to any dispute. However, Frank purposefully kept well away from local politics, preferring to spend time with his family. Both Rutherford and Whitney had been gazetted as magistrates in their adopted colony years before, although it is unlikely that the authorities were aware that Rutherford had previously been prosecuted in Victoria for violent behaviour. Rutherford had accepted the appointment of magistrate in 1870 but Whitney, not one to court public honours, declined the honour more than once.

Rutherford could be irritable at times, displaying an overly inflated sense of self-esteem that often landed him in trouble. In 1884 Rutherford found himself in front of the Bathurst court, not as magistrate but as a defendant once again, charged with a violent attack. He objected to the entire district using the river flats on his Hereford property as a short cut to town. The time-honoured route led diagonally across his rectangular paddocks, so Rutherford fenced them, at first leaving gaps at either end, but not for long. Henry Bruce, a former manager of Hereford, was outraged, and simply cut down the fence and continued using the short cut. Rutherford repaired the fence and warned Bruce that he'd be horsewhipped if he trespassed a second time. Bruce ignored the 'mad American', as Rutherford was known to many, and pulled the fence down once again. Furious, on 2 June 1884 Rutherford carried out his threat and was charged for assault.

Rutherford's case was heard in Sydney. Embarrassed to see a fellow public officer so charged, a magistrate quickly dismissed the case, fining Rutherford just £10. That was until a senior judge stepped in to cry foul play, demanding that magistrates should set a public example. The case went to trial and the jury awarded £600 damages to Henry Bruce. Infuriated, and not used to losing, Rutherford appealed to the Full Court in Sydney, claiming that the damages were excessive. His appeal was thrown out.

Rutherford was also sued by at least one small landholder in his capacity as majority shareholder of a gold mine in the Carcoar area. The sluicing from his mines had ruined the farmer's pasture, fouled his creek and killed off stock that became bogged in the sludge. The poor farmer had saved for years to be able to afford to take his case to court. Rutherford was found guilty, and he again insisted on a retrial. The second jury, this time with at least one colleague of Rutherford's on board, overturned the guilty verdict, despite the judge asserting that their verdict was improper.

Cobb & Co's reputation in New South Wales was also becoming tarnished. The Bathurst factory manager was increasingly being criticised for producing coaches and buggies in which the timber was not properly cured. Complaints from customers were being received, and the firm's own newer coaches were repeatedly in for repairs.

For many years Cobb & Co's coaches had been built of timber sourced from the wetter coastal forests. Such wood had to be properly treated in order to prevent it from drying out and shrinking in the continent's dry interior. The Bathurst coach-builders had taken shortcuts when executing the drying-out processes. As the coaching business was now concentrated in Queensland, the firm decided to shift the coach- and buggy-building operations from both Bathurst and Brisbane to Charleville in central Queensland's dry interior, 800 kilometres from Brisbane. The government had flagged Charleville as a railway terminus, so it seemed a sensible location.

Within five years the new factory was the largest of its kind in Australia. The Charleville factory built sulkies, wagons and more than 120 types of buggies and coaches, their standard models being an eight-seater and a fourteen-seater coach. Like the Bathurst operation, there was a public showroom for the display of buggies and sociables. Most of the coaches Freeman Cobb had imported to Victoria had been painted a golden yellow, but soon after moving to New South Wales a dark red had begun to be used, with a cream undercarriage. When the Charleville factory opened in 1886, the new policy was to paint each coach white with red lettering, a colour scheme that then remained unchanged. The firm's Queensland coach-builders came up with a few improvements for passengers in the more expensive but more exposed box seats: a folding hood to protect from the searing summer heat and a canvas that could be pulled over the legs when it was wet and cold.

For both Frank Whitney and James Rutherford, pressure was mounting. Rutherford in particular found that the demands on his time were enormous. He had now committed himself to properties and massive coaching operations in both Queensland and New South Wales, mines, coach- and buggy-building and stockbreeding. If Rutherford was on a high, and the horses were fresh at the change stations, he would happily spend twelve or more hours in his buggy, covering up to 190 kilometres a day. He was a man who needed little sleep, and people marvelled at his stamina and energy. He would pop up at the most unpredictable times to check on the firm's stables, stock, staff and property. The man's thoughts raced forward ahead of his buggy, already rearranging horse-feed contracts, networking with hotel owners and drivers, scrounging for titbits of information that might lead to a desirable postal contract or purchase of new land. A hundred little details of the business would obsess him.

Throughout his life Rutherford endured periods of increased talkativeness, racing thoughts and an inability to stop working. Like a crazed coach-driver who whipped his team to achieve faster and faster times, Rutherford seemed unwilling to rein in the pace of the firm's growth. Ironically, it was this manic energy that helped Rutherford achieve so much on Cobb & Co's behalf.

Ada spent long periods without her husband. In fact, Hereford was more a home for herself and her children than for James, who was awkward around the house, too used to his swag and the rough cots at the coaching inns. He could relax at a coaching inn in a way that was impossible in the cluttered finery of his home. Rutherford would come home late at night, heavy with the smell of horse and mud, and next morning be gone before dawn. Three hours or three weeks away – he was as unknowable as the timing of good rain.

At some point in 1886 James Rutherford became severely depressed. Perhaps his depression was triggered by Walter Hall's exit from the coaching business, the shift of the coach factory to Charleville and the huge losses incurred by the firm's railway construction. He remained upstairs in his bedroom at the Hereford homestead, wandering aimlessly about the room and muttering that he and his family were ruined. In his mind, the future was so bleak, so hopeless, that he was inconsolable. Ada gave up telling him to lie down and rest, as all this achieved was a repeated 'too late, too late' from her husband. He began to claim that the food she brought him was poisoned. It is unclear exactly how the attempt was made, but during this period James Rutherford tried to kill himself.

His family and close confidants could see the man was in no state to continue directing Cobb & Co. Three of the Rutherfords' sons, the youngest just twelve, were hurried out of the colony to begin boarding at Geelong Grammar in Victoria, shielded from their father's suffering. A daughter was shipped across Bass Strait to a school in Hobart. It was agreed that Rutherford, accompanied by one of his daughters, should take another voyage back to San Francisco to give him an enforced break, safe from the prying eyes of the hundreds of staff who depended on him for their livelihood. Ada was left with just two young daughters to care for in the Hereford mansion.

James Rutherford's suicide attempt was never discussed beyond the family's intimate circle. It is possible that Frank Whitney wasn't even told. Rutherford and his daughter sailed to America in May 1886, and once again Frank was left in charge of the New South Wales operations. By the time Frank arrived in Bathurst to meet with their accountant, Rutherford was gone.

While Rutherford was recuperating abroad, Walter Hall came to Frank Whitney with a mining investment proposal from his brother Thomas, a bank manager in Rockhampton. Investment in speculative mines had been extremely popular since the gold rushes of the 1850s, and Frank Whitney had invested in many mining ventures, often with his own money. Thomas Hall was recommending that they buy into a gold-mining venture in northern Queensland, at a place called Mount Morgan. Thomas had invested in the mine six years previously with Fred, Tom and Ned Morgan. The Morgan boys had sold out their shares very profitably two years earlier, believing they had extracted the best of the lode.

Thomas Hall had recently installed another of his brothers – Wesley – as general manager of the mine, so the pair seemed ideally placed to judge the mine's ongoing potential. They believed it was worth digging deeper, and were looking for friends to put up capital for a more structured company.

Walter Hall approached not only Frank Whitney with the proposition but also Alex Robertson and John Wagner, among others. Walter Hall was able to raise £125 000 to buy a 12.5 per cent share, partly by calling in £30 000 of the loan he had left in Cobb & Co after his recent departure. His old Victorian colleagues Robertson and Wagner together took up a 6 per cent share. Their gamble would soon make millionaires of each of them.

Frank Whitney's hands were tied, however. Along with Rutherford, he had just invested further funds in the Lithgow ironworks, in the continued hope that profits could be made selling iron and coal to the expanding government railways, and he hadn't a single pound to spare.

Rutherford returned from America in late August 1886, restored to his usual energetic self, and he soon heard of Walter Hall's and his Victorian colleagues' investment. True to form, he was furious at the missed opportunity. The actual extent of the gold find quickly became clear and the Mount Morgan company went public, its share price soaring. Almost overnight, Walter Hall became one of the colony's wealthiest men.

Mount Morgan would become one of the world's richest mines, yielding huge quantities of gold, silver and copper. One hundred years later, Mount Morgan's open-cut mine, dug out to 320 metres below its original summit and nearly a kilometre in length, was still the deepest man-made cutting in the country. At its peak, the town ballooned to 16 000 inhabitants and eight villages. The fact that one suburb still bears the name of Walterhall hints at the high esteem placed on a man who so believed in the town's riches.

The mine is now closed, the streets quiet, and it is in the cemetery that the heart of Mount Morgan lies. A hillside of graves stretches far into the distance, the mine accidents, infectious diseases and hardship that killed its inhabitants now a vague memory. Today, Mount Morgan is one of the poorest towns in Australia, with unemployment rates among the highest in the nation.

The Mount Morgan drama was perhaps the first sign of a rift between James Rutherford and Walter Hall. Rutherford contended that Hall's shares, having been bought with money Hall had lent to Cobb & Co, automatically became an asset of the partnership, just as the purchase of a sheep or cattle station with undivided profits had always been treated as an addition to Cobb & Co's investments. Litigious as ever, Rutherford lost no time in calling in his solicitors to prepare a case, and was looking forward to orchestrating a fine battle. His hopes were dashed when his solicitor advised there was no case to be made. Rutherford seethed with helpless fury, convinced that Walter Hall had bribed his lawyers to drop the case. Nonetheless, he knew he needed to tread carefully. Hall's friendship and loyalty were valuable commodities.

When Rutherford needed to purchase a new station, equipment or stock, and his banks refused further credit, there was always Walter Hall to rely on. However, Hall was now talking about taking his remaining loan out of Whitney and Rutherford's huge property portfolio. The firm's insatiable appetite for new ventures meant borrowings were always stretched to capacity, and Rutherford needed to shore up support from Frank Whitney to stop Walter Hall from calling in his loan. Undeterred by his unsuccessful claim on Hall's windfall, Rutherford had another plan. He knew the childless Walter Hall remained very fond of Frank, Bella and their children. The Whitneys were keen to build a bigger house at Coombing Park; since shifting there, Bella had borne two more girls, bringing the family to nine. Walter Hall and his wife Eliza's grand harbourside mansion Wildfell had fine fittings, gaslights and elegant French doors, while Bella's kitchen and bathrooms were falling apart. Surely Walter Hall could justify a loan to the business to rebuild the homestead.

Rutherford asked Hall to dig out the old Coombing homestead

valuation and discuss it with Frank Whitney, who was due in Sydney in a few days' time. Rutherford was already in town when Frank received an urgent letter from his partner, suggesting a little emotional blackmail.

Dear Whitney

. . . I think as you are coming down, you may as well come on Monday night. Hall will show you the valuation – you can object to it and say that it is too high by at least £20 000. Say . . . that the house is no good and that you will not live in it.

I have told him that you want to build or leave and go to Orange to live and that you will not build at your own cost. Tell him that he ought to give us at least what he got of Mount Morgan . . .

Now do not make any mistake about destroying this. You're sure to have. I shall be back in time to have a day with Hall before he goes to Melbourne on Thursday night.

You can make some excuse for being in town – want to take a house at Manly – or any other you like. He wants to take his investment out of stations and still remain in coaching but that will not answer all. Remember you and I are in this together.

J. Rutherford Esq.

It is unknown how Walter Hall responded to the request for funds. If he did contribute any money it certainly did not go towards building a new house, as nothing was done about fixing up the run-down Coombing homestead. Bella and Frank must have been annoyed that both Rutherford and Hall lived in fine new houses, built with company funds, while they were squeezed into a dilapidated six-ty-year-old homestead.

CHAPTER FOURTEEN

STATUS AND POWER

I know I carry the whole burden and you live in peace and comfort at home . . .

With Walter Hall now a silent partner in the property side of the business, Frank Whitney and James Rutherford were growing increasingly testy in their dealings with each other. While Rutherford concentrated on the coaching aspects of the business, at Coombing Park Frank was more concerned with managing the firm's horse, cattle and sheep breeding, concentrating on getting the most out of the stock and land they purchased. There was some overlap, as Frank was regularly required to travel to Bathurst to sign this cheque or solve that problem, especially as Rutherford was so seldom in Bathurst himself.

The towns radiating from Orange still required coach connections and Frank remained involved in managing some of these routes, as it was a district he knew well. He had recently made a few unwise decisions about fares on the Forbes–Orange route, and his partner was quick to remind him of any shortcomings. Rutherford hated to delegate anything, and for Frank his partner's constant suggestions about how their properties should be stocked and managed were wearing very thin.

Meanwhile, despite purchasing six routes out of Bourke from the Morrison brothers in 1885, the firm's New South Wales mail contracts were drying up. In 1886 Rutherford and Whitney won just 14 per cent of available contracts. A year later, a mere 7 per cent was theirs. Not since Cobb & Co had started out in New South Wales had their mail contracts been so low. By the late 1880s, single operators were tendering for government mail contracts at ridiculously low sums – too low to make it worthwhile for large operators like Cobb & Co to run coaches. As a result, the firm had dozens of coaches laid up in Bathurst, Bourke and a dozen other country towns that looked like they would never see another passenger. The partners' decision to leave far-western New South Wales to their Victorian colleagues Robertson and Wagner had cost them dearly. It was hard to see railways ever threatening Robertson and Wagner's 1000-kilometre stretch of outback routes between Deniliquin and Tibooburra, and the minerals boom in these districts ensured they remained busy.

On 5 July 1889, Rutherford approached Walter Hall for another loan. This time he needed £50 000, and quickly. There was little evidence that Cobb & Co could repay such a debt, but Rutherford was desperate for more funds. He promised to mortgage the entire contents of Coombing Park and the neighbouring Waugoola property to Hall, including 40 000 sheep as well as cattle and horses. It was not enough, so he threw in the stations' entire collection of 'wagons, carts, carriages, machines, tools', as well as a mortgage over the progeny of every animal and every future wool clip.

For the mild-mannered Frank Whitney, the threat of losing the beloved Coombing Park, home to his family, was perhaps the last straw. He decided it was time he and Rutherford divided their properties and dissolved the New South Wales Cobb & Co business. His partner was caught unawares, but quickly went on the attack.

Cobb & Co

7 Aug 1889

Dear Whitney,

You today broached the subject of dissolution. I had not thought of it before at least to take place for some time but that is remiss of me. We each have our own families to make the best provision possible for and to do this we must have each his own property under his own control. I think it a time to think most seriously about, with a view of dissolving at an early date.

You are very restive under my suggestions and of course like every other member of the firm consider that the whole thing is on our own shoulders, while I know I carry the whole burden and you live in peace and comfort at home.

I have complained and still do because you have not done what you might and ought to have done. You practically forced the Forbes-based opposition upon us and have run it, if I may say so, in the interest of that opposition. I have repeatedly told you that you were only playing into the hands of the op by tripling your fare at 5/- more than the mail, yet it is kept up because you know more than I do about it. I know I pointed out how it could be at the start and what I then saw is owing now to you I think. We are lagging at the rate of £3000 per annum where we might at least have paid our way.

J. W. Rutherford

The remaining two Cobb & Co partners in the New South Wales business seemed ready to part company. In the end, however, nothing came of Frank Whitney's suggestion that they sell up the business. Perhaps Rutherford talked Whitney out of the idea, for it was always going to be a hugely complex issue to untangle their web of assets. Instead, two days after Christmas 1889, Frank Whitney found himself signing a document for Coombing Park and neighbouring Waugoola that mortgaged every farming tool and every one of his stock, not to mention their progeny and the profits from future wool clips on 40 000 sheep, in exchange for Hall's £50 000 loan. The interest was to be 5.5 per cent, payable quarterly. Walter Hall had Whitney and Rutherford's Cobb & Co by the balls.

Rutherford had a new project up his sleeve. All the trouble he and Frank had weathered over the disastrous Lithgow colliery investment, with cheaper imported steel killing their contracts, had made him realise that the Protectionist cause needed a voice. He invested his own money in the establishment of a second newspaper for Bathurst, the *National Advocate*, which he would use as a mouthpiece to lobby for the placement of tariffs on imports to protect Australian manufacturers.

Meanwhile, Billy Whitney and Rutherford's son Laurie were becoming the best of friends. In May 1888 Billy Whitney had been withdrawn from the King's School, Parramatta, and dispatched to Geelong Grammar for his final three years of schooling. The school was more than 800 kilometres south of Coombing, but the Rutherfords, Robertsons and Wagners were all sending their sons there. Graduation from the college was seen as a rite of passage for the well-to-do, especially for boys from wealthy pastoral families. The school's

1886 *Quarterly* magazine had run an editorial outlining the institution's perceived role in nurturing good practical values in the ruling classes of Australia:

> *... they must be men of whom all can feel that they are trustworthy, honourable gentlemen, courteous to all, and holding their money, if they have any, not as a selfish instrument of their own pleasure, but as a gift bestowed on them for good purposes ... if the lads of this school can leave it with ingrained habits of self-respect, of moderation, of courtesy to all men and women, they will be more truly educated than many a learned pedant.*

Schooling at Geelong Grammar was a necessary stepping stone for Billy, who might well be the only son to carry on the family name. Such an education would cement the Whitney family's status among the great pastoral families of the colonies.

Frank's second son was a born sportsman and his three 'R's were not reading, writing and 'rithmetic but rifle shooting, rugby and rowing. Billy Whitney led the school teams in each of these sports, and Geelong Grammar convinced him to stay on an extra year as Captain of Boats. Billy, and Laurie and Arthur Rutherford were members of their school's First Four rowing crew in 1890.

Billy's uncle, Arthur Leeds, continued to live the life of a remote station manager. However, the wealthy Whitneys and Rutherfords, like many successful pastoralists, were certainly no longer interested in living so far from civilised society.

Arthur Leeds' base, Burrenbilla, was typical of a large station of the day: a huddle of buildings resembling a small village and a comfortable house for the station manager, usually low-set with wide verandahs. There was a store, a blacksmith's shop, a bakery and a butcher; a cluster of smaller houses and huts to accommodate staff – cooks, gardeners, servants, a book-keeper and the overseers; and scattered over the property, shacks for the boundary riders to live in. A few miles downwind of the homestead were the woolshed and quarters to accommodate shearers, shed hands and wool classers during the shearing season. Cobb & Co's Burrenbilla, Claverton and Coombing Park stations all had a layout such as this.

Before the days of road freight and fencing, cattle had to be watched at all hours, particularly when they were being mustered over unfamiliar country. The young stockmen would be up before dawn, eating their breakfast by starlight before spending perhaps fourteen hours a day in the saddle. They might have to drove the cattle all day, then take turns at the night watch, getting up in the icy cold to sit on their horses for two to five hours. These night shifts on horseback were difficult, as it was so hard to keep awake. The worst fear was that something would spook the cattle, causing them to stampede in the dark. Hours would be lost chasing the mob, rounding them up and quietening the mass of beasts.

Meals were prepared by a cook, but they tended to be horribly monotonous. There was always beef of some description – salted, hot, cold, boiled, stewed, curried or minced. If they were lucky it might be disguised in a pie. A meal might come with sour bread or damper, treacle, jam, doughboys, brownies and, of course, plenty of tea.

Like many managers, Arthur Leeds ran Cobb & Co's Claverton as a bachelor station. The men could earn good money in a short period by enduring the long hours of stock work, but the art was in keeping what they earned. With much of the week spent in rough camps, and few opportunities to drink more than lukewarm spirits, Saturday night in town meant spending huge amounts of money on binge drinking, despite the best intentions. Downing twenty drinks at a sitting was not uncommon. The country publicans took full advantage, charging wildly inflated prices. A jackeroo would often spend half his week's earnings on grog in a single night.

Barcroft Boake was a 23-year-old who worked for Arthur Leeds as a cattle hand on a number of the firm's Queensland runs. He had trained as a surveyor in Sydney but, disillusioned with city life and the hopeless inactivity of his fellow clerks, he'd turned to the romance of life in the saddle. Boake was a dutiful writer to his family and his letters home paint a vivid picture of outback station life.

Burrenbilla
21 Oct 1889

Dear Father,
We are out at the Yowah now very busy mustering and hope to be away next week sometime. They had to knock off today to shoe horses as they are nearly all too footsore from the stones. It is very rough country here, nothing but stones and scrub. A bit different to the Diamantina where it was nothing but plains. The cattle here are wild as hawks and we are galloping all day long.

The first day we went out to camp about ten miles away

*we just took pack horses and as it was very hot weather only a
blanket apiece. In the middle of the night it started to rain hard
and I laid in two inches of water till morning. We had a job to
light a fire and it was infernally cold.*

*Every day brings something new – no two are alike. There
is a charm about this life always in the saddle only those can
appreciate who have lived it.*

Bartie

In a letter dated November 1889 that rang out with resentment of
worker against rich pastoralist, the young stockman had written:

*. . . some man will come yet who will be able to grasp the
romance of Western Queensland . . . for there is a romance
though a grim one – a story of drought and flood, fever and
famine, murder and suicide; courage and endurance. And who
reaps the benefit? Not the poor bushman, but Messrs So and So,
merchants of Sydney or Melbourne or the Mutual Consolidated
cut-down-the-drovers-wages Co Ltd or some other capitalist.*

*I wonder if a day will come when these men will rise up,
when the wealthy man . . . shall see pass before him a band of
men . . . whose unhallowed graves dot his run . . . burnt unrec-
ognisably in bushfires, struck down by sunstroke, ripped up by
cattle, dashed against some tree by their horse, killed in a dozen
different ways and what for? A few shillings a week and these
are begrudged them; while their employer travels the continent
and lives in all the luxury his wealth can command.*

Just such an uprising was to occur among Queensland shearers in a few years hence, making this sensitive young man's musings all the more powerful.

The 1890s brought social upheaval and a severe financial downturn compared to the heady days of the 1880s. In the rush to invest during the '80s, money had been injected into purely speculative businesses, mostly in real estate. Hundreds of such businesses had been created, attracting not only British monies but millions of pounds invested by Australian families. The Australian colonies had done too good a job at selling themselves at events such as Sydney's International Exhibition of 1879.

Over-investment meant that city land prices were forced up far beyond their value, the new owners knocking down two- and three-storey buildings to replace them with eight- to twelve-storey confections of 'gilded shoddy grandeur', hoping to recoup the money spent by charging high rentals. Large agricultural areas bordering Sydney and Melbourne were cut up into suburban blocks and offered for auction by land companies. Further money was then raised to build transport links to these new areas, without a thought as to who would live there. Capital and labour were thus diverted away from the nation's primary industries, and exports fell dramatically.

In November 1890 a huge financial scare was triggered in London by the default of an Argentine loan and the subsequent collapse of the Baring Brothers Bank. The spending spree was over. Borrowings for both public and private purposes were frozen in Australia, as British investors pulled their money from the colonies' banks like scared rabbits. Eastern Australia's long railway boom came to a screeching halt, construction having exceeded what was economically viable. Some lines built during the late 1880s had very dubious financial or social benefits, particularly in Victoria.

With so many railways criss-crossing Victoria, coaching routes had almost disappeared in the colony. In 1890 Robertson and Wagner closed the doors of their Melbourne booking office for the last time. Both were now immensely wealthy men, having made additional investments in mines and property.

The financial scare caused land values to plummet. A third of the new companies that had formed in Victoria filed for bankruptcy (the actual proportion of collapsed businesses was far higher) – building societies, land investment firms, a regional bank and mortgage companies were all among the casualties. Over £9 million of shareholder monies vanished, equating to more than $1 billion at current values. The financial downslide was aggravated by a general fall in prices of Australia's main exports – wool and wheat – caused by the appreciation of gold and increased overseas competition. Employment nose-dived, and there was a glut of unemployed clerks, agents and unskilled workers. The press published accounts of prominent businessmen committing suicide 'in the coolest and most deliberate manner' rather than weather the ignominy of the bankruptcy court.

Bartie Boake's father was one Australian who lost all his savings in the financial collapse. Bartie arrived back in Sydney at the end of 1891, carrying a small Gladstone bag, the lash of his favourite stockwhip and a swag fashioned from a possum skin. Bartie had published a few poems in a local newspaper, and had been discovered by

A. G. Stephens, the literary critic and Red Page Editor for Australia's leading magazine of social commentary, *The Bulletin*. The magazine began publishing his work alongside that of Banjo Paterson and Henry Lawson, and over the next sixteen months he became a regular contributor. Of Bartie, Banjo Paterson wrote: 'to very few of us is it given to express their feelings in such words as came with the poetic inspiration of Barcroft Boake'.

Bartie's father wished fervently that his son had stayed in the countryside. Barcroft senior's photographic business was failing, and he was heavily in debt. With the economy in trouble, nobody was indulging in photographic mementos. He wrote:

> . . . *my welcome to him was dashed with bitterness and however I strove to conceal it, my depression made itself apparent. I felt that he was coming full of spirits to a home of gloom and I feared the effect of my own despondency upon his sensitive nature.*

The oppression of his father's dark mood gradually dragged Bartie down. He tried to find work, but in the depressed economy there was nothing available. Bartie's mood darkened further when he received a letter telling him that his 'best girl', the daughter of the Monaro family who had hosted him when he'd worked as a surveyor, was going to be married. His father wrote:

> *In his state of mind there could not have been selected for him a worse companion than myself at that time. The sight of him was a pain to me and I suppose my presence was the same to him*

and our deep mental affection made it worse. He used to come in to my office daily the last fortnight to assist me in any small way but I had really nothing for him to do.

At breakfast on 2 May, Barcroft senior glanced at his son, in the hope of seeing some change. Bartie raised his head and, after months of avoidance, their eyes met. His father recalled 'there was some meaning in his glance even though he himself may not have intended it. I now know it was his farewell'. Bartie left the house and did not return that night or the next. As the days passed, his father knew his son was dead.

His grandma and I used to discuss his absence on these lines only disagreeing as to how. She said his body would be found in the harbour. I said no for he was a swimmer and such do not generally drown themselves. On the other hand my revolver was in its place and he had none I knew.

Eight days later Bartie Boake's body was found hanging by the lash of his stockwhip from the limb of a tree on the shores of Sydney Harbour. Barcroft senior was able to identify his son by the initials F.E.B., his mother's, tattooed on his arm.

The Bulletin's literary critic believed that had Boake lived even seven years longer, he might have won recognition as Australia's foremost poet.

The lives of the Whitney and Rutherford families were now far removed from those of cattle hands such as Bartie Boake. Their lifestyles were reined in by neither the Melbourne real-estate crash nor falling wool prices. For their wives and children, wealth brought with it the finer things in life.

The Hotel Australia in Sydney had a style and elegance that almost hypnotised the visitor. In 1891 it was the most exciting building to open in Sydney since the ill-fated Garden Palace exhibition building, and was to become popular with the wealthy grazier class. Bella Whitney always insisted that the family stay at the Australia when in Sydney. 'Meet me at the Australia at three', she would write to a friend. She meant the hotel's grand central court, from where Bella would adjourn with her friends to one of the fine dining rooms to take tea and cake. When Bella discovered that the hotel's architect had been one George Allan Mansfield, she promised herself one day she would commission the fellow to design her a home of equal beauty at Coombing.

The Hotel Australia paid tribute to the great buildings of Europe, its seven floors dominating tiny Rowe Street, just south of today's Martin Place. Only nine years before, an illustrated Sydney guide had described Rowe Street as 'foreigners quarters where hurdy-gurdy artists, street musicians and others congregate who obtain an uncertain living by such means'. The street had been transformed by the hotel's construction. J. C. Williamson, the American theatre producer, would have appreciated the Australia's proximity to the Theatre Royal across the road when he stayed at the new hotel a few months after its opening. With the addition of the popular society nightclubs Princes and Romano's, that part of the city was dubbed 'the golden half mile'.

The hotel's flagstaff fluttered high above the city, and the building's lights welcomed ships entering the harbour and coaches approaching from afar. Its grand entrance was a flight of marble steps between great red granite columns, flanked by two bronze figures holding the latest wonder of a civilised city – electric lights. A small army of porters and bellboys rushed to assist the hotel's first guest, the famed French actress Sarah Bernhardt, and all who followed her. Beyond the hotel's heavy stained-glass doors, the atmosphere was one of comfortable but cosmopolitan wealth. In style and grandeur it far outstripped Sydney's existing hotels, the Royal and Petty's, for the discerning traveller. Finally, Sydney had an establishment on a par with the Savoy in London.

What struck guests such as Bella and Frank Whitney was the vast Moorish vestibule, complete with rounded arches, carved latticed screens and Persian rugs that suggested the luxury and exoticism of Granada's Alhambra Palace. Guests gazed up at the huge glass roof framed in wrought iron towering two storeys above the elaborate vestibule and its intricately tiled floor. Subtle motifs of Australian flora flowed from the ironwork of the light fixtures. The huge central court was punctuated with a fountain and aquarium tanks, and furnished with a swathe of comfortable buffalo-hide lounges.

From the foyer, seven hydraulic-powered lifts could transport 450 guests each hour up into a world of further comforts. Alternatively, a marble staircase – white Sicilian for the steps, Belgian deep rouge and fawn for the handrails and balusters – swept upstairs and into a massive corridor almost 5 metres wide, lined with Doric columns and lit by stained-glass windows. From here, Bella Whitney would have entered the main dining room many times, where there were more columns – Corinthian this time – and mirrors fitted with sprays of electric light lining the walls. A large iron electrolier hanging from the centre of the dining room ceiling dripped with flowers and foliage in hammered copper. Intricate lyrebird escutcheons in oxidised silver and groups of waratahs bursting from smaller electroliers continued the Australian native theme.

The bedrooms were elegantly papered, and featured asbestos fires and – an unexpected luxury – basins with unlimited hot and cold running water. A male social writer with *The Bulletin* seemed unimpressed, however, that the hotel had seen fit to provide a private breakfast room for ladies:

> *Fancy, oh women! The rapture of camping in a palace where the management sets apart a private room for ladies who are too lazy (the courteous violet-eyed manager said, 'Indisposed') to rise and dress for the general breakfast . . .*

Poised on Louis XVI-style furniture, Bella would have written her letters in the sanctity of the ladies' drawing room, while next door the gentlemen drank port and whisky on lounges upholstered in Moroccan leather or read the daily papers in the Jacobean-style reading room with its elaborately carved fireplace. This was an environment where one came to enjoy the spoils of success with others from the wealthy propertied classes.

The hotel's daily tariff was not cheap. Sixteen shillings was charged for a single room or around thirty shillings for a double. However, to dine at the hotel and use all its facilities added an extra twelve shillings and sixpence to the bill. A shearer would need to shell out almost half a week's earnings for one night in a single room with board. From 7.30 p.m. to midnight, supper was offered at no extra charge to guests, who could choose from great tables laden with turkey, chicken and ham.

The new establishment soon became an Easter headquarters for country families down for the races and the show, Billy Whitney being among the first of the graziers to register. At just twenty years of age, Bella and Frank's son was already developing a reputation as a hard-drinking carouser and gambler.

In the 1890s, the bottom end of Pitt Street, next to Circular Quay on Sydney Harbour, was the thoroughfare of a great port. The street was jammed with the offices of shipping companies, ships' providores and seamen's outfitters, and the rigging of tall ships could be heard clanking above the noise of the city. Sailors of all nationalities filled the wine shops and pubs, exchanging incredible tales of adventure, love and escape from death at sea.

Across Bridge Street, heading south, was the Stock Exchange, where the offices of the wealthy insurance firms and global indent agents could be found. Further south again, Pitt Street became a more mundane shopping block. Beyond Bathurst Street, the thoroughfare took on an old-world atmosphere, lined with private semi-detached homes shut off from the street by high stone walls. Further down, Pitt Street became a little disreputable, ending in a section of Chinatown.

When Hall, Rutherford and Whitney had business to discuss they would usually meet in one of Sydney's gentlemen's clubs. In 1890 a reporter from the London *Temple Bar* magazine had pronounced that 'Sydney is a clubbable place and clubland there is yearly widening its borders and strengthening its powers'. The London writer was surprised to note the apparent absence of pressure in the daily lives of the city's club members. It was indeed common to find doctors, lawyers, merchants and journalists at their club at two, three or even four o'clock on a weekday afternoon, engaged in a leisurely game of dominoes or billiards.

Commercial and professional men in Australia work hard and faithfully, yet they seem to possess a genius of resting by the dusty wayside of life, which reminds one of the temperament of Southern Europe rather than Britain.

All of these busy gentlemen's clubs were within a short walk of each other. Apart perhaps from the Athenaeum, members were almost entirely men in business or a profession. The Union Club was the largest and most luxurious, patronised by wealthy merchants and rich commercial men. The Australian Club was the oldest and it still reckoned itself the most select. The *Temple Bar* magazine labelled it 'of quite classical antiquity. There is no other Australian club probably where the wine and the wit are so old'. The Warrigal was a squatters' club, the Athenaeum the meeting place of the literati, journalists, artists and musical people. The Reform Club was almost entirely a political club.

James Rutherford was a member of the Union and Reform clubs. He would host lunch guests such as Frank Whitney in the Reform Club's archaically named Strangers Room, and the leather armchairs of the club's drawing room were a fine place to sip sherry or rattle ice cubes in a whisky highball. Club members were expected to conduct themselves in a manner appropriate to their station in society or risk expulsion. The Reform's rule book warned, for instance, that if a member failed to pay his subscription within thirty days after it was due, his name was to be placed over the mantelpiece of the dining room and remain there for thirty days or until the subscription was paid. Members with unpaid house bills exceeding £5 suffered the same fate.

Walter Hall's office was at the southern end of Pitt Street, the view from his office a serene vista of blue harbour and green trees suspended like a bright tapestry framed by sandstone. At sixty, Walter was older than both Frank Whitney and James Rutherford, although with his pale, unlined English skin it was hard to tell. He lived his days under the muted light of green-shaded desk lamps while Rutherford's and Whitney's burnished and wrinkled faces spoke of their time under the harsh Australian sun.

Hall's life was far removed from that of his former partners. He held senior director's positions with a number of large Australian businesses, including Mercantile Mutual Insurance. Despite his vast wealth and affable nature, Walter was a very private man – some called him mean – and he seldom entertained even close friends at home. However, his reputation for generosity with the staff at Mount Morgan and with his own nieces was legendary.

Walter Hall was also on the committee at the Sydney racecourse and he had diverted some of his wealth to the purchase of thoroughbreds. He mixed with the likes of wealthy department store proprietor Sam Hordern, who had recently developed an interest in the track. Hall could often be found at Zetland Lodge, the old-fashioned Randwick stables, watching his trainer exercise his racehorses. With its belltower and clock overgrown with ivy, the training yard had a distinctly English feel.

Back in 1884 one of Walter Hall's horses had scored a huge win at Randwick's Easter races. In the last decade of the century, Hall purchased at least three more fine thoroughbreds, which between them won six big Sydney races, including Randwick's coveted Doncaster Handicap. He even shipped his best horse to race in Melbourne, and gained a second place in the 1893 Caulfield Cup.

Privately, James Rutherford considered Walter Hall to be leading too soft a life, and he was sure he would outlast his city colleague. True enough, Hall was now rotund, his wavy hair swept back smartly from a receding hairline, his shirt of crisp thick white cotton embellished with a discreet tie of the finest silk. He wore a rather distinguished handlebar moustache of a salt and pepper hue that shook like a forest in the wind whenever he spoke.

It was the fashion at this time for wealthy Australian families to provide their children with an education in Europe. Alex Robertson in Melbourne had sent his daughters to a Paris finishing school and a son to Cambridge University. In 1886 Bella Whitney had married off her eldest daughter to a doctor, William Kelty, but she still had six unmarried children to care for, the youngest only six. She was happy at Coombing, and satisfied with the occasional trip to Sydney with Frank to stay at her favourite hotel.

Ada Rutherford, however, had her sights on a goal far beyond Sydney's Australia Hotel. She was preparing for an extended round-the-world trip with her ten youngest children, aged from eleven to twenty-seven – without her husband. It was impossible for Rutherford to get away, and the family were perhaps relieved to have some respite from his domineering and unpredictable behaviour. Their final destination was to be Scotland, presumably to rediscover and connect with the Rutherford ancestral roots. James had dreamed of studying there himself when he was young. Now he could give his children that chance, and he took three of his boys out of Geelong Grammar to finish their schooling in Europe.

In 1891 the family sailed to California, from where they travelled to Iowa to visit their father's brother Robert. Ada's second-oldest boy Norman stayed on to study engineering in California, where another uncle worked as a banker. Norman eventually settled in America, secretly marrying a girl called Bella without consulting his difficult father. In a letter to his brother he alluded to a mysterious 'disagreement' as a reason for his silence, and complained that his father was 'too domineering for anyone to be really independent and successful while under his management'.

For Ada and the remaining nine children, New York followed and then England. The six girls and their mother toured Athens, Venice, Heidelberg and Copenhagen, while one of the boys was enrolled into Edinburgh's medical school. The other two boys were studying German in England, in preparation for their attendance at a fashionable new British-run school in Heidelberg. They were also to spend time at one of Scotland's best resourced and exclusive private schools, Blairlodge near Glasgow.

It would be more than a year before Ada and her two eldest daughters returned to Bathurst, leaving her four youngest daughters to complete their education at an exclusive Edinburgh school. Most of the Rutherford children did not return to the Hereford mansion for at least five years.

Rutherford kept himself busy developing a stream of entrepreneurial ideas while his family were in Europe. The ongoing drought and collapsed wool market meant sheep were literally rotting in the paddocks around him, a disaster that was affecting not just Cobb & Co's properties but much of Queensland and New South Wales as well. Ever the opportunist, Rutherford had a boiling-down works for sheep constructed at Hereford, allowing him to turn a profit from his starving sheep and those of his neighbours by buying them for next to nothing, boiling their wretched bodies down until the organs congealed to fat and on-selling the product as candle wax and soap. It was fortunate his wife and children were abroad, and so spared the overpowering stench emitted by the process.

Rutherford was also busying himself with a new sheep-dip mechanism he had been formulating. His time-saving invention dealt with thirty sheep at a time, herded into a pen positioned over his new dip. Rutherford would pull a hidden lever to open multiple trapdoors, dropping all thirty sheep into the dip. The trapdoors would then swing back into place, forming a floor once again.

Rutherford and Whitney now had many thousands of pounds tied up in their sheep and cattle stations. The Warrego district, named after the river running through Charleville, was one of the richest pastoral districts in Queensland. Milo station, a few hundred miles west near Adavale, ran 375 000 sheep; the second biggest, Thurulgoonia, south of Burrenbilla and stretching to the New South Wales border, carried a third of a million. Cobb & Co's Burrenbilla station, one of the fifty largest in Australia, carried close to 114 000 sheep, a fairly average number for a big sheep station.

Shearing was done in winter when the sheep's coats were thicker and there was less risk of ewes developing pregnancy toxaemia with the stress of mustering and shearing. The job had to be finished before the grass seeds ripened in spring or the wool would be full of burrs. With such huge flocks, the average shed took seven to eight weeks to 'cut out', and as the shearing season lasted only four or five months, shearers could work just two or three sheds per year. The typical shearing shed on a big Queensland run had stands for thirty to eighty shearers; some had up to one hundred stands.

Australian shearers of the 1880s were a smart and generally prosperous group. When off duty they often wore black coats and gold chains, and in towns and cities they would dress up in a starched collar, a dark felt hat and dark trousers. A competent shearer could shear eighty to ninety sheep per day, earning more than a coach driver – £3 10s a week, after deducting a pound for food and five shillings for blades.

Bartie Boake's ponderings about shearers rising up as a united force were about to become a reality. In 1891, Queensland's shearers were provoked to revolt against their employers, an action that would have an impact on every major sheep station in Queensland, including the huge stations owned by Cobb & Co.

The first great Australian workers' strike, the Maritime Strike of 1890, had seen up to 50 000 workers down tools, many for over two months. Initially the strike defended the right of a small union of ships' officers to join the Melbourne Trades Hall, but it turned into a more general defence of wages and conditions, with shearers, coal miners, trolley-cart drivers and thousands of others joining the struggle.

The Maritime Strike was massively defeated, and the victory

encouraged Australian employers to further push their own causes. Pastoralists were one group who realised they needed to unite to protect their interests as employers. They formed a national union, the United Pastoralists' Association (UPA), in effect a mouthpiece for each colony's pastoralist union. At the end of 1890 the group moved quickly to draft a new shearing agreement that detailed the responsibilities of shearer and employer. They weren't going to sit back and be dictated to by their own contractors.

Their 'agreement' stated that employers were to keep shearers fully supplied with sheep to shear, accommodation, cooking and eating utensils, wood and water free of charge. They would supply rations and stores at not more than 10 per cent above cost and cartage. In return, shearers had to agree not to bring liquor onto the station, and to refrain from singing, spitting or using profane language while on the job. The penalties could be dismissal or a fine to the local hospital board (of which their boss was usually chairman).

Shearers were to pay for their own cutters and combs. If a woolshed's shearing machinery was broken, shearers had, if required, to use hand shears. If they cut a sheep badly, shearers were obligated to immediately sew and tar any cut or wound. If they cut the teat of a ewe or the pizzle of a male, they were to pay the cook's rate for the injured sheep. Most importantly, as wool prices were now so low across the country, the employers' agreement attempted to block any rise in shearers' wages by specifying pay of twenty shillings per hundred sheep for wethers, ewes and lambs, forty shillings per hundred for rams.

The shearing rates proposed were close to the average at the time and in the recent past, but the shearers' unions argued that western

Queensland sheep were bigger and tougher to shear, so shearers in that colony should be paid more. The Queensland Shearers' Union (QSU) had been pushing for thirty shillings per hundred. The pastoralists knew they were in for a fight, but they also knew they had the government behind them, so they rolled out their new 'agreement' in Queensland, bypassing any consultation with the shearers' union.

Sure enough, the Queensland shearers refused to sign their new contracts. The station owners responded by standing firm, refusing to employ them. The government rallied its police force and helped station owners ship hundreds of unemployed men from Victoria and New South Wales to take on the work. It was a risky move, for the shearers now had not just a policy to attack, but also their physical replacements. The furious shearers branded the imported workers 'blacklegs' for working on the pastoralists' terms and not being union members.

The Queensland colonial government's action turned a strike into an insurgency. It was at first centred around Barcaldine in central Queensland, but the camps of striking shearers spread quickly until there were dozens throughout western Queensland. Some camps lasted a matter of weeks; others dug in for months. The bigger camps were home to up to a thousand shearers and supporters at a time.

The men were idle, bored and frustrated, and funds were running low. By mid-February 1891 the QSU decided to use force to stop the blacklegs from working. Bent on destruction, they used the easiest tool available to them – fire. They brazenly torched structures and equipment, calculated to anger the landowners – goods sheds, outstations, wool stores, harnesses and wagons loaded high with wool. On at least six occasions they successfully burned acres of valuable grasslands. If they were not going to have their demands met, then they were sure as hell going to make the landowners suffer.

Between early March and mid-April 1891, four Queensland woolsheds were burned down, often with the season's clip inside. A mob of forty men wearing masks raided the enormous Milo woolshed, forcing out two guards before setting the place ablaze, together with close to a hundred bales of wool. Around £4000 damage was recorded – the shed was only insured for half that. In May, attempts were made to burn two more woolsheds.

Bullocks were shot, horses' throats were cut, and cattle and sheep killed. Strikers cut fences, broke gates and threw themselves against blacklegs' huts until they crashed to the ground. They verbally abused and spat at the blacklegs. By March some of the city shearers were being physically attacked. There were reports of some non-union shearers being chased off properties by strikers, and made to walk up to a hundred miles to the railway.

The authorities were vigilant, investigating every crime and arresting suspects. The strikers tried to wreck trains carrying troops and non-union shearers by placing crowbars or huge logs across the tracks, and they destroyed a railway bridge. On at least two occasions, police resorted to loading rifles or fixing bayonets to dissuade a crowd of angry strikers from attacking free labourers. Unable to get at the blacklegs, some strikers focused their hatred on Chinese market gardeners, attacking them or their property in country towns. Dozens of strikers were tried and convicted, and their sentences were harsh.

Our English coach traveller, Constance Ellis, had been living in western Queensland two years. Now married, and living the life of an itinerant worker, she was based at Cobb & Co's Claverton station during the 1891 shearers' strike. She had a poor opinion of the shearers' cause:

> *When I had left home two years before, all my sympathies had been with the poor down-trodden working man. What I saw during this strike cured me completely of that delusion.*

By April the unrest had reached Cobb & Co's territory at Cunnamulla. On 10 April, 250 protesters marched in defiance of the government's support of the blacklegs. Two days later, Cunnamulla's strike camp had swelled to 450 insurgents.

James Rutherford's role in Cobb & Co did not involve overseeing shearers or shearing. This was Arthur Leeds' domain. Leeds must have been concerned when, in mid-May, unionists shifted their focus to the Claverton district, demanding that his station hands and rabbiters strike in support. At the beginning of May, two thousand shearers had marched in protest up at Charleville. On 24 May at Thurulgoonia station, just south of Claverton, strikers set fire to valuable haystacks. Less than three weeks later, a boundary rider's hut and fencing were torched on the same station.

Faced with continuing trouble, police teams were sent from Brisbane and thousands of 'special constables' were sworn in wherever they could be found to suppress the strikers. City teenagers volunteered as soldiers, were given horses and ordered to ride hundreds of miles to trouble spots – sometimes over 60 kilometres a day. Most were not used to the saddle and were so stiff and sore they could hardly dismount at the end of a day's riding.

One large posse of volunteer city soldiers camped a night at Cobb

& Co's Claverton station en route to protect the blacklegs. Arthur Leeds provided new mounts to give their exhausted horses a spell, but Claverton's station hands laughed at the young city recruits. Many were hazy as to the correct side to mount a horse. The young visitors set sentries to guard their camp at night, but the sentries were so exhausted they fell asleep, their guns lying out for anyone to use against them.

In the main Barcaldine camp, rations had run out and infectious diseases and malnutrition were weakening the rebels. The motivation to go on was flagging. By early June, some unionists returned to work rather than face further hunger and sickness. Three days later, strike camps all over the colony admitted their funds were exhausted. They advised their members to go back to work. The pastoralists and huge property owners like Cobb & Co had won.

The significance of these strikes was not only their extraordinary size – virtually the whole labour movement was involved – but the generalised confrontation between the classes involved. Employers had consciously organised to collectively confront the unions and beat them at their own game. So heavy-handed was the government that not only were the strike ringleaders gaoled, they were incarcerated on an island off the Queensland coast.

For the pastoralists it was to become an empty victory, as in just a few years far more powerful natural forces would devastate not only the sheep business but the whole industry, bringing once-wealthy property owners to their knees.

CHAPTER FIFTEEN

FINANCIAL COLLAPSE

It will come as a shock to the public to learn that the directors of the
Commercial Bank have determined to suspend payment . . .
– Sydney Morning Herald, *April 1893*

If an audit of Cobb & Co's New South Wales assets had been carried out in the early 1890s, it's unlikely the firm would have been found to be solvent. Their diversification into railways construction and mining ventures had been disastrous; there was a collapsed wool market and ongoing drought; their properties were worth a fraction of the funds the firm had paid for them; and their share of New South Wales' mail contracts had fallen off sharply after 1885, coinciding with Rutherford's 1886 collapse. In expanding into a monster, Cobb & Co had lost its focus and was haemorrhaging money, having amassed high levels of debts to countless creditors.

This was not a good time to be in financial straits. Thousands of Australians had lost their life savings in the 1890 real-estate crash, and jittery overseas investors had continued to pull their funds from Australian banks. By 1892 everyone was nervous, panicked by the ongoing drought and banks with too many unpaid loans. A once comfortable society had lost confidence in its financial institutions.

In the country's three major cities, Melbourne, Sydney and Brisbane, the public were beginning to worry their own banks would fall, taking the common man's hard-earned savings with them. On Wednesday 9 February 1892, a rumour began to circulate that the Savings Bank of New South Wales was going under. That afternoon, panicked customers mobbed the bank's Barrack Street headquarters, at the bottom of Martin Place, demanding their money. Many banks issued their own bank notes at this time, and if you had no confidence that the bank would honour the note it was payable as gold. So tellers handed customers their deposits as bags of gold sovereigns. A continuous stream of gold poured over the bank's counters, and customers walked away clutching a total of £14000 on that first Wednesday.

On the Thursday morning more than forty people were queuing anxiously for the bank to open. When it did so, the crowd pushed its way through the huge doors, again demanding their savings. As the day wore on, the crowd increased and so did the heat. Staff distributed cups of water to customers who'd been queuing for hours in the scorching sun, while other staff staggered through the crowd loaded with fresh bags of sovereigns. Barrack Street was now choked with customers, and police had difficulty controlling the melee. Customers sweated and grizzled as they fought their way through the chaos, clinging to the iron railings of the tellers' cages with one hand, gripping their bankbooks with the other, until they could force their way to the counter.

Many customers were nonplussed by the readiness with which their demands were satisfied, and even more so when at noon the bank put up a sign – not to announce that they were closing, but that they would remain open for several hours after usual closing and pay every demand on the spot in gold. Then another sign went up, calculated to assuage the fears of even their most panicked customers. It promised that all of Sydney's main banks would stand shoulder to shoulder with the Savings Bank of New South Wales and accept the bank's deposit receipts, by the bushel basket if need be, paying them as cash. Customers had only one fear – if they didn't grab their savings, they would be lost. Across the city, weary bank tellers remained at their counters into the night. In total, the Barrack Street branch handed out £50 000 in gold coins on this second day of panic.

It had all been a false alarm, however. That night in parliament the premier confirmed there was 'not the slightest ground for alarm', promising that if it were necessary the government would 'come to the assistance of the bank' to put an end to the absurd scare.

The ongoing economic depression affected not only city dwellers. Unemployed rural workers were also becoming increasingly desperate. Vandalism of property and the poaching of sheep and cattle were becoming common. On Cobb & Co's Carcoar properties not a week would pass without the sound of a gun cracking in the distance among the blue gums and stringy-barks. Armed station hands would gallop out to the bottom of the paddocks with their weapons but the hungry poachers would have already hauled the carcass of a stolen sheep over a horse and made off, leaving the rest of the flock bleating in terror.

In desperation, the government asked for citizens to come forward to be sworn in as Special Constables for the Carcoar district. The local paper asked the large station owners to provide men.

A call has gone out for each of the larger stations to nominate a reliable man to be sworn in as Special Constable. It is hoped the measure will deter further damages in the district. The managers of Errowanbang, Cliefden, Coombing and Waugoola will be asked particularly to contribute.

So determined was the government to restore order that those nominated for such a role could not refuse to take it on.

Eight months after the Sydney panic, in November 1892, the public's fear that their banks were cracking with the drain of overseas funds was inflamed once again. In Melbourne, the chairman of directors and manager of one of the colony's leading banks, the Anglo-Australian, were arrested in their city offices, charged with conspiracy in concurring in the issue of false balance sheets. A Melbourne newspaper marked the arrest as 'the beginning of what justice-loving citizens have been anxiously looking forward to for a long time'.

The scandal caused a sensation in business circles, but it was just the tip of the iceberg. There were rumours that the banks had far exceeded their lending capacity, and the pessimists were warning that bank funds might be frozen if the large English investors continued to pull funds.

Many property owners, including Rutherford's and Whitney's neighbours and friends, were being ruined under the weight of their bank loans. Loans were being written off, and many building societies, land and mortgage companies could not sustain their losses. It was not until April 1893 that the public's fears really came to fruition. One of the nation's largest banks, the Commercial, found it could not afford to keep meeting its customers' demands for money. Forced into a corner, their only choice was to close their doors and reorganise their entire investment operations.

5 April 1893

THE COMMERCIAL BANK

SUSPENSION OF PAYMENT

CONTINUOUS DRAIN OF DEPOSITS

It will come as a shock to the public to learn that the directors of the Commercial Bank have determined to suspend payment. For weeks past a feeling of unrest has existed as to the stability of that institution . . .

. . . It is officially stated that since the commencement of the year the deposits withdrawn total £1 000 000. With such a tremendous strain upon the resources of the bank the suspension of payment eventually became inevitable, especially as there seemed to be no prospect of stemming this withdrawal of confidence.

The Commercial Bank was one of Cobb & Co's key financial institutions. All the Coombing staff and contractors were paid from this account, and now the firm's access to all monies was frozen.

Within six weeks, twelve more banks in Victoria, New South Wales and Queensland had closed their doors to stem the flow of withdrawals. Over £100 million in assets – two-thirds of the country's wealth – was frozen. Thousands of investors queued hopelessly outside barred bank doors, their money inaccessible. It took three months before the government was able to complete some frantic restructuring of the banks to ensure that those with frozen funds were able to open their doors again. Many customers were forced to agree to leave their funds with their bank as fixed-term deposits, not repayable for five to seven years.

Rutherford was up at Buckiinguy when he heard of the Commercial Bank's collapse. He simply shrugged and announced to a friend, 'It will not make any difference to me; I owe them £200 000, but they will carry me on.' Frank Whitney heard nothing directly from Rutherford. He knew it was up to him to beg Walter Hall once again for a small loan to keep Coombing Park going. Spare funds for the new house Frank and Bella had dreamed of building seemed an eternity away.

Walter Hall's huge private wealth was Cobb & Co's only hope. While Hall was no longer a partner in the Cobb & Co business, he retained a hefty financial interest through his loans to his friends, and continued to help out by covering the firm's interest payments. However, he had his own headaches. His own funds were also largely locked up in the banks' freeze of monies, and he desperately needed security on the £30 000 that remained tied up in the firm. He wrote back to Frank.

Potts Point
7 June 1893

My dear Whitney,
With this I send you cheque for one thousand. You put me in a fix as I had to hunt up to get this together, and expect it to be paid back, as I told Rutherford all I could do before September would be to meet the Interest bills which I am providing for. I am not a Bank – as all my cash is locked up in them – they

cannot pay and I shall have to wait years for the principal, shall be lucky to get the Interest. I have cursed the lot.

Like yourself, I cannot understand why Rutherford should take such a long trip at this time. When I got home tonight, Miss Rutherford – Geraldine – was here. She said she heard from her father a few days since, from Cunnamulla, and that he was going to Yowah and from there to Brisbane. If so, he will still be away some time. I want to get information. All I can say is now things are very mixed. You hear of Reconstruction – in all quarters. Why don't you come down and talk matters over with me?

Yours truly,

W. R. Hall

Frank was very lucky to have a friend like Walter to help him out of a tight spot.

Few letters survive from Rutherford during this stressful period. He refused to sell stock in the depressed climate, so he and Frank Whitney had no choice but to mortgage their entire stock of merino sheep on Cunnamulla station – 220 000 of them – to Hall to raise additional funds. In late July they transferred the title of the firm's huge Claverton property to Hall. The only other asset Rutherford was prepared to part with was the famous Cobb & Co cattle brand, and in due course it too was transferred to Hall. Rutherford knew Hall could have no long-term use for it, and when times were better he could buy it back.

At Coombing, it became necessary to turn away itinerant workers without providing the usual food and shelter the station was known for. Station hands would have to be put off; the housekeeper, governess, gardener and grooms would need to go without pay for a time. Coombing was a relative haven compared with how they might have fared elsewhere. At Hereford, Rutherford came up with a list of maintenance work to keep some of his staff busy, as there was little in the way of farm work.

The debts mounting up in the name of Frank Whitney and James Rutherford looked irretrievable. The pressure on them both was immense. All who knew Rutherford well recognised he was not one to listen to advice or outside opinion, for in his mind he was always right. In these economic times, such a trait was dangerous. Despite the financial crisis, in December 1893, Rutherford continued to expand the company's empire. He and Whitney convinced a competitor in the Narrabri–Moree–Walgett district, John Charters, to join forces, signing over horses and coaches rather than cash in exchange for shares in a new partnership.

In May 1894, Rutherford leant on Walter Hall once more for further assistance. Hall well knew there was little chance of Cobb & Co meeting their interest payments on their huge property loans until the depression and wool prices lifted, and this time he refused to help. Once again, he needed Frank to help shore up his position.

Potts Point

18 May 1894

My dear Whitney,

When are you coming to town – I want to see you and talk matters over – Rutherford has been here the last few days, goes home I think tonight. He wants me to do something more for

him which I have refused to do – and I do not think he has gone
away in a very good temper. All will now rest with you.
    Yours truly,
    W. R. Hall

It was a full day's journey each way for Frank to travel to Sydney – two days' absence from Coombing that he could ill afford. The slow steam train from Bathurst to Sydney took all night, and it's unlikely that Frank slept soundly. A pain in his stomach gnawed at him through the night as he worried about what the future held for his large family. Cobb & Co's intricate financial dealings were stacked like a house of cards, and in the current climate everything could be lost.

No details of this Sydney meeting survive, but one thing is clear: ready cash from Hall was no longer available. Over the next few months Frank Whitney desperately chased up his unpaid debts. Frank had always been a generous fellow when friends came to him for a small loan. His office clerk would write out promissory notes with a due date for payment, but Frank's usual attitude was, 'Never mind the promissory note. You can pay it when I ask you for it.' Now that had to change, and Frank went back through even his smallest debts. Whether £10 or £25, either was enough to keep his household running for another month at least.

Pritchard Bassett was the Carcoar-based partner in the legal firm of Lee, Colquhoun & Bassett, and during the 1890s their business was booming. Bassett and his colleagues worked long hours filing bankruptcies and chasing up debts on behalf of cash-strapped clients such as Frank. These debtors were no criminals – most of them had lost their employment or investments during the financial crisis, and had every intention of paying back their debts when they could find work again. One fellow who owed £12 in back rent to Frank's son-in-law assured him the debt would be repaid (and two years later it was), writing to Pritchard Bassett: 'I have nothing to sell, only the few bits of things in the house and they would not bring much I can assure you.'

By late June 1894 Frank Whitney was so desperate for cash he harassed his solicitor to chase up £25 owed him by a Catholic priest named O'Kennedy for a bay horse the fellow had purchased. A month later just £10 had been retrieved. Agitated letters between the two men's solicitors continued, threatening a court order against O'Kennedy. It would be another eighteen months before this tiny debt was finally paid off. Well before then, an unimaginable event was to distract all concerned.

Frank had not been feeling well for several months. By August he could no longer ignore the pain that festered in his abdomen. He'd likely put off seeing the doctor until the pain was well advanced, and then forced himself to visit a surgeon who diagnosed an abscess on the liver. His prognosis cannot have been good. Just days later the surgeon operated on Frank, and he was sent home to Coombing to recover.

By 4 September 1894 Frank was with his Carcoar solicitor, finalising his will. He nominated his wife as his sole executor, but then changed his mind a few hours later and added a codicil naming Arthur Leeds and his son-in-law William Kelty as co-executors. Walter Hall and Pritchard Bassett witnessed Frank's signature on a document that was to cause years of grief for the Whitney family.

Perhaps the operation had been too late, and infection had already spread through his body, for three weeks after the medical procedure Frank was still in a bad way. Most likely the abscess had burst. The Coombing homestead was in a panic and four doctors were in attendance, desperately trying to curb the infection.

The Whitneys' four-poster bed – that much-treasured wedding present – was singularly beautiful with its pressed-metal frame draped with white curtains. Flower motifs made out of pearl shells decorated the iron bedstead. Apart from the fancy iron bed, the furniture in the room was plain, almost drab – a walnut tallboy and dressing table the main pieces. It was in this room that Frank lay waiting for the systemic infection to put him out of his misery.

For thirty-two years Frank Whitney had slaved to build a prosperous future for his wife and family, only to see Rutherford drag the firm into enormous debt. The assets he and Rutherford had nurtured for so long were now in danger of being called in by the banks to cover their debt. Of the property, stock or buildings, not even the plates the Whitneys ate from were in their own name. Everything was company property. It was a cruel twist of timing and fate.

Another month passed and still Frank was bedridden with infection. On 27 October, Rutherford's *National Advocate* paper, perhaps in an attempt to control the negative talk in Bathurst, reported triumphantly that Mr Whitney was so far recovered he had left his room for a few hours: 'His medical attendants have every hope that in a short time Mr Whitney will be about again.'

At worst it was an outright lie, at best overly optimistic, for it was common knowledge that Frank was dying. Rutherford and Whitney had been partners and friends for more than thirty years, but the Rutherfords were too busy to call at Coombing.

28 Oct 1894

My dear Mrs Whitney,

I feel so dreadfully not being able to come and see you – if I had had any servants to depend on, I would have come last week and it is unfortunate the shearing commencing tomorrow preventing Mr Rutherford coming. I do so wish I could send you something, but hope for better times soon. Poor Mr Whitney, give my kindest regards to him and with loving sympathy for your anxious position.

I remain

Yours very sincerely,

Ada Rutherford

P.S. Not having heard lately we hoped no news was good. Geraldine sends back her thanks for music.

It's not known how honest Frank Whitney was when he spoke to his wife during the last days of his life. Did he confess to her the financial mess Cobb & Co was in? Did he admit what confidence he had lost in James Rutherford, that he had made a mistake in staying in the partnership? Given the great pain he was in, it is unlikely, although Arthur Leeds' granddaughter claims that Frank did warn Arthur to be careful in his dealings with Rutherford.

At 7.15 in the evening of the last day of October 1894, Frank Whitney died in the Coombing homestead. He was aged sixty-eight. The *Bathurst Times* had already prepared a glowing eulogy, which was printed the next morning:

The intelligence will cause unfeigned regret among a large circle of friends in the western district, where the family are well known and highly regarded. The deceased gentleman was essentially a self-made man . . . Mr Whitney was of a peculiarly genial disposition, possessing as kind a heart as ever beat within a man's breast. He scarcely knew a day's sickness and when a couple of months since he was stricken down, he felt it very much . . . Poor Frank Whitney! He was a grand fellow, and we, with many others, grieve over the death of a true-hearted friend.

For Bella, with only one child out of seven married, an increasingly deranged son, two children aged under fifteen and the task of extracting her family from the web of Cobb & Co commitments, life had in a way just begun.

CHAPTER SIXTEEN

DESCENT INTO LUNACY

*I give my share in the business carried on by me in partnership with
James Rutherford of Bathurst . . . to my said trustee Isabella Whitney
upon trust to convert the same into money . . .*

Nineteenth-century etiquette prescribed that neither Bella nor the children should leave the house while preparations for Frank's funeral took place. Social mores also dictated that the diminutive Whitney matriarch would spend the next two years wearing nothing but black.

The family had a large plot put aside in the Orange cemetery, where Bella had already buried two of the three sons she had lost. The funeral was held in Orange, and the church was filled with the family's friends and business colleagues, along with many townsfolk. The grandly beautiful town with its parks, fountains, statuesque public buildings and wide tree-lined streets was farewelling a favourite adopted son. The trustees of Carcoar's hospital wrote to Bella commiserating with her for the loss of one of their great fundraisers. Bella received a card from Rutherford promising that a marble monument would be erected; the Cobb & Co staff throughout the colony were each docked £5 wages to pay for it. The monument still stands in Robertson Park, Orange.

No records exist of Bella Whitney's mental state in the dark days after Frank's funeral. Bella was not one to show her emotions in public, not even to the household staff, but less than two months after the funeral she faced another crisis at home. On the Sunday before Christmas, the family's first without Frank, Bella and her four youngest girls found a nasty shock waiting for them when they returned from attending church in Carcoar. The Coombing hay sheds were ablaze, and smoke was billowing across the garden. A man lay on the ground, blood oozing from his chest.

The men on the property spent all afternoon beating down the flames, and they managed to prevent the blaze from spreading to other buildings. Word had already got out that this had been no accident. Fingers were being pointed at discontented shearers, for tensions between pastoralists and shearers had flared once again, this time in New South Wales. Strikes had begun afresh, and anger in the idle and hungry workforce was growing. The shearers' union had again resolved to take no part in shearing unless employers agreed to dispense with non-union labour.

The man lying on the ground bleeding was Jack Pulsford, a brave young station hand who'd been assigned a revolver and Special Constable status by the magistrate just three weeks before to help deter trouble with striking shearers. When Pulsford was interviewed by the police, there was little he could tell them. He'd seen two figures a hundred metres away from the burning hay shed, but he couldn't make out their faces. Next thing he'd heard bullets and felt a wrenching pain in his shoulder. When he fell to the ground the culprits escaped. The alarm was raised by the head stockman, who dragged poor Jack to safety. Further questioning produced nothing of use.

Christmas Day at Coombing Park was sombre, punctuated by a half-hearted attempt to enjoy the roast turkey. On Boxing Day Bella wrote to Rutherford about the arson episode. She had to show Rutherford she could run Coombing as well as any manager. She was of the opinion that the culprits were almost certainly striking shearers in the district, though there was no record of ill will specifically targeted towards Coombing, and she begged permission for the firm to fund a reward for information.

28 Dec 1894

Dear Mrs Whitney,

Your letter to hand about reward, I was waiting until we see what the government does in the matter. Our loss is in hay but the thing the authorities should consider is that a human life was nearly sacrificed to cover up a criminal act and to endeavour to escape from its consequences. If the government offer a reward we must supplement it and that by making it a liberal one. The only hope now is that a good reward and a full pardon offered to the one who did not actually fire the shot may induce the guilty one to split or his crowd may undermine him for fear of consequences. In the latter case there would be an additional chance of running in of 2 or 3 of the rascals.

I think we should offer £50 for such information as will lead to conviction of the perpetrators of the outrage. Willie might advertise in the Carcoar paper two or three times and I will have it inserted here always supposing the authorities do something.

Yours truly,

J. Rutherford

Billy Whitney wrote to Carcoar's senior constable a few days later to inform him that Cobb & Co would offer a £50 reward for information that would 'lead to the conviction of the outrage committed at Coombing Park'.

Everyone in the homestead was on edge. Billy in particular was exasperated with the lack of police progress in the matter. As he and his mother were due in Sydney in a week, most probably to see Walter Hall, he wrote to the inspector in Orange requesting that a police officer be stationed at Coombing in their absence.

Bella placed a notice in the *Carcoar Chronicle*, warning trespassers off Coombing Park:

> *All persons found trespassing either with or without canine pets will be prosecuted. Poison is laid on the Coombing Park run. Trespassers and those who value their dogs should take the manly warning and make themselves scarce in those quarters.*

Since Frank had fallen ill, Bella, with the help of Billy and her brother Arthur, had been managing the firm's properties, unsure of her family's future. With the drama of recent months, she had allowed herself little time to consider the ramifications of her husband's last will and testament. The document contained one crucial clause, a clause that Bella Whitney flatly refused to accept.

> *I give my share in the business carried on by me in part-*

*nership with James Rutherford of Bathurst in the colony
aforesaid, grazier, under the style of firm of 'Cobb & Co' to
my said trustee Isabella Whitney upon trust to convert the
same into money . . .*

The Whitneys' entire assets were tied up in Cobb & Co, a business
that was largely mortgaged to Walter Hall and the banks. There were
no cash reserves available for Frank's family. Frank Whitney's estate
did not even have the £2000 each his will put aside for Arthur Leeds
and for the care of Frank's demented son, Glassford.

It was clear that Rutherford had no access to funds to buy out
Bella Whitney, certainly not at a decent price. There was nothing to
live on and no way of repaying anything without selling up.

However, it was the worst time to consider selling property, as
values were at an all time low. There was no feed for the sheep, no
markets for lambs or wool, labour was a problem and the country was
in the middle of an incapacitating drought. A forced sale would barely
cover the huge debts. Besides, after fourteen years in residence Bella
knew her family belonged at Coombing. She had promised herself
the place would always be a sanctuary for her family. She was adamant she would not sell, regardless of the law. Bella wanted, *needed*
her own dominion.

If Bella Whitney had been asked about Cobb & Co's mail and
coach routes, she would have been hard pressed to answer. However,
she did know about the firm's stock and station holdings. Her brother
Arthur's correspondence over the past few years meant she could list
them precisely. Despite being faced with her late husband's instructions in black and white, Bella insisted she and her fellow executors

continue in partnership with James Rutherford.

The family's lawyers were left to work out how to challenge the terms of Frank's will. In the meantime, an interim agreement was arranged between Rutherford, Hall and Bella, along with her brother Arthur and son-in-law Dr Kelty, stipulating that no property transactions would occur until the mess could be sorted out. Ultimately, Bella had to take on the colony's legal system to challenge her husband's will, leveraging her connections to have a new law passed by parliament. Bella Whitney was not destined to have a comfortable widowhood, for it would take eight years and enormous legal fees before her actions were sanctioned in law under the *Whitney Estate Act.*

Bella had watched while James Rutherford had pushed his boys into strategic professions. They were given little choice. Norman was dispatched to study engineering, Aleck medicine, Laurence accounting and George into law. Only Rutherford's eldest son was allowed to become a grazier. All of his children were high achievers; even his youngest daughter was to become a doctor.

In contrast, most of Bella's daughters had no such brains and she was determined that they should marry medical men. Marriage into such a highly respected profession would not only solidify their social standing, but keep them on an equal footing with the Rutherford clan. Despite the fact that her brother Arthur's sons had grown up on the Claverton station in western Queensland, Bella strongly suggested that his boys be enrolled at a boarding school nearly 900 kilometres south in Orange, so she could better oversee their progress. Even when her nephews had graduated from school, Bella Whitney had plans for their future.

Now that Frank was gone, Rutherford was faced with the task of rearranging staff responsibilities in Bathurst. With the financial burden of Frank's death upon him he was in desperate need of an accountant he could trust. He wrote an urgent letter to his son Laurence, who was still studying accounting in Scotland, demanding that he sail home immediately. Laurence and Billy Whitney were the same age, and had rowed in the same crew at Geelong Grammar.

As Rutherford put his trust in his family, so Bella relied on her son Billy. She'd chosen Billy to manage Coombing until she could give him a property of his own. But James Rutherford was not about to see the flagship station in the Cobb & Co business managed by Bella Whitney or her 22-year-old son, and he said as much in a letter to Bella: 'You ought to pay for putting a man in Mr Whitney's place or I ought to receive the £520 a year which Whitney did.'

Bella was furious. Her son had been managing the property proficiently since Frank had taken ill. Rutherford had perhaps forgotten he had put his eldest boy in charge of the massive Davenport Downs station at exactly the same age.

Rutherford and Bella Whitney had an impossible task on their hands to bring Cobb & Co back from bankruptcy, and the situation was about to worsen. James Rutherford was on the brink of a mental breakdown that would leave Bella and her brother in charge of the enormous business.

The Hereford homestead was in uproar. In the months following his partner's death, Rutherford's mental stability deteriorated and he relapsed into a deep depression, reminiscent of his collapse of nearly a decade earlier.

Rutherford had always had difficulty sleeping, but in the coming weeks he found it impossible to sleep at all. Instead, he paced the length of his bedroom continually, muttering to no-one in particular, 'I am ruined. I have not a shilling left in the world.' He was so distraught, he again declared his intention to end his life.

Desperate, Ada called in forty-year-old Dr Machattie, Bathurst's leading medical man, whose father had been the pioneer town's doctor a generation earlier. Dr Machattie prescribed sedatives at night and tonics through the day to settle his patient.

To add to the crisis, just weeks before, without consulting a soul, Rutherford had committed company funds to purchase a property called Bunnamagoo west of the mountains near Lithgow, with nothing but a promissory note, heedless of the fact that he had agreed with Frank Whitney's executors that there would be no new purchases. Bunnamagoo had recently been overrun by gold prospectors, and in the past two years over £1000 worth of gold had been siphoned from the area.

When Bella heard of this double crisis, she immediately wrote to her son-in-law Dr Kelty, co-executor of Frank's will. The pair quickly agreed that a power of attorney over Rutherford was necessary. Walter Hall was the only person they trusted who had the necessary background in the firm's affairs to hold such a position. Bella wrote to her solicitors to obtain an opinion on how to handle this sensitive issue.

E. Pritchard Bassett responded in support of her proposed plan.

20 June 1895

Dear Madam,

Re Whitney deceased

As I will not have the opportunity of conferring with the executors upon the subject of Mr Rutherford's actions before they come to a decision as to what is to be immediately done, I have thought it better to write you upon the subject.

As a matter of fact I understand that directly Mr Rutherford had matters entirely in his own hands he, unknown to the executors, committed a breach of trust by embarking upon an adventure at Bunnamagoo, which adventure he was perfectly well aware should never have been commenced . . .

Not only as regards the particular breach of trust mentioned, but as regards any others which may exist without your knowledge, in view of the fact that Mr Rutherford's mind appears to be somewhat unhinged, it is necessary to decide what steps are to be taken immediately . . .

I understand that you and Dr Kelty have come to the conclusion that it would be desirable to get Mr Hall if he is willing to take a power of attorney from Mr Rutherford in a lucid interval, to act for a term of six months.

While it was thought advisable that no unnecessary notices should be served upon Mr Rutherford as it was not considered desirable to cause unnecessary friction. I am of opinion that the proper remedy is to institute a suit against Mr Rutherford and to apply to the court to appoint a person to direct the winding up of the affairs of Cobb & Co.

It may be thought that taking such a step would not be treating Mr Rutherford well! . . . Mr Rutherford has not treated the executors well; in addition to which he has when in possession of his full senses, committed an absolute breach of trust and shown that he is unfit to occupy the position of trust imposed upon him – further the Executors must remember that, as Trustees are not supposed to consider Mr Rutherford's feelings.

Yours truly,

E. Pritchard Bassett

Solicitors

Bella knew that her family's future was lost should Rutherford continue to sign company cheques while so disturbed, let alone purchase new properties. She also knew she must move quickly – she would call on the Rutherfords herself.

Married in the same year to partners in the same firm, the two Cobb & Co wives were the opposites of their husbands. Ada was shy and retiring against her husband's bluster, while Bella was forthright and confident in contrast to Frank's quiet modesty. Despite their different personalities, these two women were now bound by a common goal: securing the financial future of Cobb & Co. That future was largely dependent on maintaining the good health of the firm's surviving partner – James Rutherford.

Few details have survived about Bella's meeting with Rutherford. Perhaps she witnessed him become violent, shout obscenities or, worse, dissolve into tears. At any rate, she made a rapid exit.

Ada desperately needed to find a way out of this nightmare, and with things as they were it was no use making excuses. But could

Bella be trusted to keep her counsel on her husband's mental state? Ada could only hope so. It must have been difficult for Ada to fight off a rising sense of panic. She wrote to Bella, pleading with her to keep her husband's mental state to herself.

> *Dear Mrs Whitney,*
>
> *I regret very much you did not stay over Sunday – my husband had a dreadful night. He is anxious to tell you all, it in no way affects the firm I think. I cannot think. How can I communicate with you? I might tell you and see if you can see any way out of it. We cannot. He is nearly crazy. Do burn this. He must not come up alone. I cannot bear him out of my sight. Do not mention his affairs till you hear from me or see him.*
>
> > *Write by return.*
> >
> > *Best love to yourself and the girls – do destroy this.*
> >
> > *Ada Rutherford*
> >
> > *P.S. It may be a phantom of the imagination. I pray it is. Your clear head may see some ray of light.*

Rutherford's 24-year-old son Laurence was now living at home, helping with the firm's finances. With his mother, Laurie shared the burden of monitoring his father. Rutherford's paranoia was worsening. He began refusing all offers of food and hissing to anyone who would listen, 'The police are about to arrest me.'

The youngest Rutherford daughter was boarding at Kambala, a private girls' school in Sydney, but it is likely that three of Ada's other unmarried daughters had returned home from their studies in Scotland by this time. Kate and Geraldine were old enough to understand what was happening to their father. Ada would dearly have wished otherwise.

Three weeks of agony passed. For the family, the stress incurred by maintaining a semblance of normality must have been unbearable. In his current state, the threat of James Rutherford doing himself in was all too real. Dr Machattie was called in to take charge. It was American Independence Day, 4 July 1895.

Dr Machattie's case notes made no mention of Rutherford's history of extreme shifts in mood and behaviour from his early adulthood, so it is unclear just how clear an understanding Machattie had of the man's history. The evidence was inescapable, however. Rutherford's condition was spiralling out of control. He needed much more than just time away from Bathurst. Presumably with Ada's consent, the doctor made the decision to certify his patient as insane. In his notes scheduling Cobb & Co's lead partner to confinement at Sydney's Callan Park Asylum, Machattie noted:

> He frequently mutters to himself and in answer to a question said, 'Oh Doctor you don't know the crimes and misdemeanours I have committed. I and my family are completely done for.' He is dejected and sad and frequently refers to his ruin. I cannot persuade him to take any nourishment and he states that his food is poisoned.

The colony's laws meant that a second doctor was required to examine Rutherford before he could be certified and admitted. Another Bathurst doctor who knew the family well was called to Hereford that same day. His observations were similar:

Having known him for many years, I observed his manner to have become completely altered from being hearty, cheerful, ready to converse. I found him unable to hold any rational conversation, in a state of restlessness and dejection, maintaining almost without interruption a continuous purposeless walk about his room: during such walk he would occasionally groan, muttering that he 'was ruined' that he had 'undone himself and all belonging to him'. To a suggestion that he needed rest and should go away for a change the only answer I could elicit was 'too late, too late'.

It was settled that Rutherford would be transported to Callan Park Asylum in Sydney as soon as possible. Four days later, just before he was due to depart, Dr Machattie returned to Hereford, in case there had been some change that could prevent this calamity. His patient had not improved. No doubt overcome by a mix of relief and despair, Ada handed over a bag of necessities and James Rutherford was transported directly to Sydney.

On the next day, 9 July 1895, Rutherford's solicitor son-in-law, Hugh Peden Steel, met the train from Bathurst and accompanied the great man to Callan Park Asylum.

Part Four

A Battle of Wills: 1895–1929

CHAPTER SEVENTEEN

A PAINFUL DIVISION

Hospitals are in some sort the measure of the civilisation
of a people ...
– *Sir Ranald Martin,* Medical Topography, *1837*

Seated in the closed carriage next to Hugh Peden Steel, his eldest daughter Katie's husband, on the final leg of his long journey from Hereford, Rutherford was likely too morose to notice the imposing sandstone buildings of Callan Park Asylum, high on a hill in what is now the inner-Sydney suburb of Rozelle. Their carriage passed through the main entrance, punctuated by filigreed iron gates and guarded by a stone gate house, and slowed to follow the long drive lined by camphor laurel trees. The drive wound past beautiful grounds with ponds encircled by neat picket fences, luscious fig trees, tall palms and vast lawns. Around another bend there were formal garden beds, and vines and creepers trellised up outbuildings in the romantic style of gardening then favoured.

On a clear day you could see west as far as the Blue Mountains from Callan Park. The asylum's statuesque slate-roofed buildings with shady verandahs were sited on the water, so that violent or troubled patients could be ferried up the harbour from Sydney on a private steam yacht, beyond the gaze of the wider community. Some members of society saw insanity as potentially infectious; to most, it was a blight best not seen. Self-sufficiency meant less contact with external society, and so Callan Park had its own vegetable gardens, orchards, piggery, poultry farm, milking cows and dairy, as well as an extensive library to feed the mind.

It was a huge complex, with parlours, drawing rooms, patient workrooms, padded cells and a Turkish bathhouse, used for hydrotherapy. The patient wards were surprisingly large, each with ten beds. The wards opened onto a pretty airing yard with a pleasing view of bush and water, and verandahs on three sides. The first pavilion was for convalescent and working patients, the second for the violent and the noisy. The pattern was repeated at the other end of the complex for female inmates. Separate cottages, each designed for patients who had been 'in a better position in life', housed just sixteen patients and an attendant. They were priced accordingly.

James Rutherford's admitting doctor noted that the new patient was too restless even to be weighed. His case notes describe Rutherford as dazed and scared. He refused to answer questions, brushing aside his questioner and shuffling to the far corner of the room like a crippled old man. A diagnosis of senile melancholia, with insomnia as a possible cause, was recorded. A modern-day analysis of Rutherford's case history strongly points to a diagnosis of what psychiatrists now call bipolar (manic-depressive) disorder. The illness affects around 1 per cent of the population, but nineteenth-century doctors had no clear concept of the condition.

As James Rutherford was to discover, Callan Park was more like a resort than a hospital. Each ward had a piano, a selection of magazines, newspapers and a library. Two of the better wards had billiard tables and greater privileges such as a later curfew of nine o'clock. There were workshops offering skills in a trade, and some patients were gainfully employed in making boots and clothing. At certain hours of the day inmates were allowed to roam in the large airing courtyards, surrounded by flowers and creepers. Cricket, tennis and bowls were available, as well as dances in winter and concerts in summer to feed the soul. Down on the bay, cut out of the rock, there was a swimming pool for both patients and the public to use.

Ada Rutherford journeyed down to Callan Park to visit her husband shortly after he was admitted. She found him beginning to take food again, conversing with people and taking an interest in his surroundings, but she was concerned that his recovery seemed so slow.

The facility was fuller than it had ever been. Some felt it was the fault of the recent commercial depression and drought. Many of those who had for a long time supported 'defective' relatives found this impossible once they were struggling to put food on their tables. In addition, New South Wales was the only colony without laws forbidding the importation of the insane, South Australia, Victoria and Queensland having adopted policies to try to protect their societies from such contamination. New South Wales, with its legacy of convicts, perhaps saw itself as so far tainted it was not worth making a fuss. Ships' captains were well aware of this, and regularly dumped those passengers and crew 'of weak and unstable intellect' in the colony, knowing they would find their way to an asylum eventually.

Bella Whitney, Arthur Leeds and Walter Hall were now managing Cobb & Co on their own. In the face of the widespread drought, keeping the vast New South Wales and Queensland businesses afloat seemed an impossible task. Hugh Peden Steel was brought in to keep a watchful eye on business interests, while Hall stepped in to oversee the Queensland arm's coaching operations.

Bella Whitney's dealings with James Rutherford were to be in stark contrast with her husband's quiet and agreeable disposition towards the man. She was a woman in a man's world, but unlike Frank she was determined not to let Rutherford take advantage of her family. Moreover, she had the courage to challenge him. Even decades later, one of her station managers would describe Bella Whitney as 'the most outstanding woman he had ever met' with 'a very clever brain'. Her male peers considered her a handsome woman, her head of wavy silver hair her most striking physical feature. Could Bella's determination and nous, combined with Arthur Leeds' long experience managing the firm's stock and pastoral holdings, save Cobb & Co from collapse?

Arthur had been involved in the Cobb & Co business for twenty-five years, and in that time he had successfully steered hundreds of thousands of cattle and sheep through drought and epidemics. His success was in his timing. Arthur knew exactly when to sell or move stock before their value fell; he could tell which markets were fetching the highest prices and he was not afraid to move stock hundreds of miles in order to pick up a good sale. To his advantage, the firm's chain of properties through New South Wales and Queensland were on hand to use as feed and water depots.

Arthur Leeds was the sounding board any property owner would dream of – utterly unbiased, practical and not one to shy from sharing his opinions. His letters to his sister were always candid and true. Reading them, Bella must have felt she was there at his side as he discussed the problems or successes of the huge stations he managed – Burrenbilla, Davenport Downs, Claverton and Buckiinguy. By taking in the details of his letters, Bella had become wise to weather patterns, sheep numbers, station problems and stock prices. Arthur wrote about the huge stock movements he orchestrated every month like a giant board game – a game in which the objective was to move large armies of beasts from one place to another, selecting a route along watercourses that would maximise food intake until the animals' point of sale.

Arthur was devoted to his sister, and no doubt felt he owed her immeasurably for the opportunities Cobb & Co had given him. Now that Frank was gone, an even fiercer loyalty bonded the pair. Increasingly, it was Bella who advised her brother on how things should be run, consulting him as her private lieutenant when there were staff she wanted removed, stock she felt it timely to offload, station improvements to make or correspondence with government authorities to initiate. If not for his wife and children, Bella would have been quite happy to commandeer her brother to work alongside herself at Coombing.

While her son Billy managed Coombing, Bella spent a good two hours each day reading and replying to her dozens of personal and business correspondents. She worked with Walter Hall and Hugh Peden Steel to come up to speed with Cobb & Co's diverse business interests, surrounding herself with a team of expert advisers, such as her solicitor E. Pritchard Bassett, from whom she sought counsel. From her favourite upright chair at the roll-top desk in her office,

Bella could look out across the creek gully to the flat home paddock and up the steep rise of Bald Hill as she mulled over ways to pay back her debts to Walter Hall. By paring down staff levels and sending sheep to the boiling-down works for tallow, she managed to save a little money every month to put towards the huge loan.

Rutherford showed signs of improvement after just a few weeks at Callan Park. However, those who were close to him knew he must take a proper break from the stresses of work if he was to recover fully. Rutherford could never rest while he remained in a work environment. Ada hurriedly made plans for a discreet departure, booking berths on a ship to London to visit their sons Aleck and George, who were still studying in the British capital. Their daughters Linda and Hettie would remain at Hereford under the care of a governess.

Hugh Peden Steel and Arthur Leeds were to be left in charge of overseeing the New South Wales and Queensland businesses, particularly the signing of company cheques. Ever fastidious, Steel insisted on receiving an estimate for Hereford's running costs before the Rutherfords left Australia. With her husband still in Callan Park, Ada turned to Bella Whitney for assistance.

22 July 1895

My dear Mrs Whitney,

I have to send a statement to Mr Steel of our probable expenditure, what it will cost to keep up Hereford if we go away outside limit. At the present rate of wages I am paying

Cook & laundress £12
Housemaid   £10
Man   £15
and keep of   £6 – without probable visitors.

Do you think £5 a week enough? You said if you could help us you would, so as you have had more experience than I have in this line, I thought before committing myself I would ask your advice. I thought of giving Hettie and Linda an allowance. I have been carefully adding up items and do not think they could dress on less than £25 a year – they want £30 – What do you think? This is to come out of the £5 a week. Perhaps I had better say £25 now, as if I go away I hope to be able to bring them something back.

Mr Rutherford seems to get on very slowly . . . he reads the papers, and seems to understand them, eats and sleeps naturally, but I thought when once he commenced to improve he would do so rapidly.

With best love to you all from your sincere friend,
Ada Rutherford
Please answer by return.

After four weeks at Callan Park, Rutherford was discharged, his physician declaring his recovery complete. A note in his file stated that he was to embark on a trip to Europe in a few days hence.

Just five months after leaving for Europe, James and Ada suddenly appeared back in Bathurst in mid-January 1896. The Rutherfords must have spent little time on solid ground. Bathurst was taken by surprise but the town's Royal Hotel quickly staged an elaborate welcome-home. Rutherford's own newssheet, the *National Advocate*, reported his return from a trip through Europe and America in a piece that waxed lyrical about the town's warm reception.

While the family's inner circle seemed to have successfully concealed the Callan Park internment, it was common knowledge in Bathurst that Rutherford had been in poor health. The town's civic leaders were so delighted to hear Rutherford state he was now 'in first-class health' that the speeches of gratitude and thanks at the Royal Hotel kept coming. The mayor insisted on speaking, as did Dr Machattie, the president of the Progress Association and a colleague from the hospital board. The Chamber of Manufacturers sent a letter to the Bathurst papers to congratulate him on

> *his return, in full health and strength from Europe together with the expression of the hope that he may long be spared and live to see the final success of the cause of native industries . . .*

Good health was hard to maintain for many of Rutherford's contemporaries. Six months on, wealthy Alex Robertson, Rutherford's good friend and old Cobb & Co partner, passed away in Melbourne.

With Rutherford back in Bathurst, Bella was concerned that she and her family would be exposed to further financial risks if he was to resume direction of the company. For the family to survive, she had to disentangle herself from the Cobb & Co web as soon as possible.

Bella well knew that Rutherford commanded enormous influence, and could do great damage if he so desired. However, she had built up a dossier of evidence that convinced her that some of Rutherford's business dealings had done her family out of money. She wrote to E. Pritchard Bassett for advice.

A keenly conservative, urbane man, who was ever eager to keep everybody happy, Pritchard Bassett would have been well aware of Rutherford's aggressive reputation in the court system. His reply was therefore cautious.

> *Lee, Colquhoun and Bassett Solicitors*
> *6 February 1896*
>
> *Dear Mrs Whitney,*
> *. . . Mr Rutherford has committed improper acts and this is sufficient reason, if necessary, to threaten to remove the direction of affairs completely from Mr Rutherford's hands. In addition to this, the executors are in a position to insist upon the whole of the affairs being wound up without delay.*
>
> *Therefore their position in communicating with Mr Rutherford is stronger than it would have been if it were necessary to rely entirely upon the terms of the Deed of Partnership.*
>
> *However, under all the circumstances of the case, we are of opinion that it would be desirable, so far as can properly be done, not unnecessarily to quarrel with Mr Rutherford, but to meet his views so far as they are reasonable . . .*

A compromise was reached, in which the parties agreed that Rutherford would remain in charge of the firm's coaching and property operations but must consult with Bella and Arthur before making any business decisions. Any cheques to be paid from the firm's main

New South Wales bank – the Australian Joint Stock Bank – had to be countersigned by Bella or Arthur. The result was a headache, with all three parties fielding dozens of letters each week regarding the firm's myriad business interests. Bella found herself travelling back and forth incessantly between Bathurst, Coombing and Sydney for meetings related to the business.

By necessity, Bella was developing a close working relationship with Rutherford, though it was not a relationship based on trust. The pair traded letters every week – if not every day – regarding business decisions. Soon each began querying the other on the whereabouts of certain monies.

Petty's Hotel
August 1896

Dear Mr Rutherford,

In reply to your letter I willingly give the asked for information re cottage in Orange and the one I am building in Wellington tho for many reasons would have preferred to let it rest . . . Years ago when Cobb and Co first became Cobb and Co my husband lent Mr A. W. Robertson the money that helped to pay his share . . . He did pay back that money with which the cottage was bought . . . So never in any way did this money come from the firm. Now I do not refer to 21 years ago re America but much more recently. Of course you are incensed at me . . . I have no wish to irritate but you must in some measure receive some of the unpleasantness you gave so readily. The later part of your letter I pass over with more pity than anger that you could have written it.

I. W.

Arthur too began to quarrel with the man. He was past showing Rutherford the respect he once did. In an ongoing and bitter battle between the three, Bella and Arthur began accusing Rutherford of treachery and selfishness. Arthur complained about being short-changed on sheep transactions, and it is clear from his letters that he saw Rutherford as a conniving swindler.

Bella had gone through all the possibilities. She would ask for their share of the firm's properties to be divided as soon as practicable, and Arthur and she could manage on their own. She would finally have the authority over Coombing she craved, her son Billy having already shifted to a manager's house some miles away.

Arthur supported Bella's plan, keen to protect his sister's interests. Besides, Rutherford's interference was continually undermining his own grazing plans. Rutherford would move his sheep onto paddocks Leeds managed for Cobb & Co, without Arthur's knowledge, then move them on when the paddock was eaten down. Rutherford had a number of his own properties outside the partnership – including Miranda Downs in Queensland and Murrumbidgerie in New South Wales – but in Arthur's mind the man was a haphazard grazier at best.

It was September 1896 and just a week before Coombing Park had been blanketed in the heaviest fall of snow Bella Whitney had ever experienced. It lay a foot thick, transforming the landscape to a fresh bright canvas, obscuring every imperfection. But it could not hide her eldest son.

Bella had probably known little of the colony's mental asylums before Rutherford was interred in Callan Park. Such a solution might be suitable for Glassford. She was caught up managing the Cobb & Co business with Rutherford, and simply had no time to care for her incapacitated adult son. With his removal, her daughters would no longer feel anxious about entertaining at Coombing Park – worrying about when their brother would appear and how he would behave.

When a buggy carried Glassford down Coombing's long drive for the last time, rather than weeping it's more likely his four younger sisters breathed a collective sigh of relief for the removal of an embarrassing blemish on their social stature. At twenty-nine years of age, Glassford made the overnight journey by train from Carcoar to Sydney, the same trip he used to make to boarding school. He was examined by two specialists in the city, who both agreed on his insanity, and next day he was admitted to Callan Park with a diagnosis of imbecility.

Glassford Whitney was never again mentioned at Coombing Park. Bella never wrote to her son and seldom visited him herself. Instead, she wrote short notes to the ward manager, asking him to pass on fruit, clothes and the occasional gift. His mother wanted nothing to do with his treatment. Perhaps she found his condition or her loss too upsetting. In close to forty years of correspondence with the hospital, Bella Whitney made a point of never using her son's Christian name. 'Mr Whitney', 'this patient' and, on a good day, 'my son' kept the tragedy at a safe distance.

✼

Burrenbilla

5 Nov 1896

My dear Bella,

We had one day's shearing Tuesday. We make a start again tomorrow. The rain delayed us yesterday and today. We start again in the morning and hope to finish in ten days. Have 40 shearers on for about 30 000 sheep. The rain was not light and did no good. I will start down as soon after shearing as possible. I am certain to be with you long before the end of the month . . . I can talk everything over and arrange what is best to be done. It will never do to let Mr R to do as he likes. I am disgusted with him and the sooner we fix a decision the better. Best love to my boys and all at Coombing.

Your affectionate Brother,

A. Leeds

The decision Arthur was speaking of was when and how to carve up the stations, stock, machinery and thousands of sundry items between the Whitneys and the Rutherfords. Discussions were not progressing well. Rutherford had had enough of Arthur Leeds – a mere company employee, if truth be told – telling him where he could and could not run his own stock. Losing his patience, he wrote to Arthur, ordering him to shift his family from the Burrenbilla homestead to Bathurst. Arthur ignored the request, but sent the letter on to his sister. It was bound to fuel the fire of resentment that was building.

Bella squabbled with Rutherford over who should be appointed general manager of the firm's pastoral business, threatening that she would take steps to ensure that she or Arthur countersigned all cheques for the Queensland business if her brother was not appointed.

The executors decline to leave the management of any station in the hands of so incompetent a man as Mr Tolmer or the inexperience of Mr Austin. We wish Mr Leeds or someone equally competent to be appointed there as General Manager pending winding up of the firm's assets, as otherwise we must take the same steps with the Queensland National Bank that we have been compelled to do with the AJS Bank NSW.

Tired of the arguments, Bella wrote to Rutherford suggesting that they 'sell' the various parts of Cobb & Co either to each other or on the open market. Most of Cobb & Co's New South Wales transport lines had ceased operation by this stage, and as the Whitneys had never invested in the Queensland coaching business their equity lay trapped predominantly in pastoral stations. Rutherford refused, arguing that such a move would be madness in the current climate. He wrote: 'I propose that you keep your share in the firm until such time as the economy improves to make it a more attractive sale'.

As a compromise, Rutherford was pressured into valuing and dividing the most important properties so each side could manage their portion. Once officially valued and the Whitney share separated, steady management would ensure a living for Bella and her family. The decision went against the terms of Frank's will but Bella was determined to hold on.

Dear Mr Rutherford,

You will most likely think we are rather hard in the matter, but you must also remember you said a great deal to me of your actions which makes us most cautious. We are not in any way

trying to shirk the responsibilities of Cobb & Co and most cer-
tainly we intend to do nothing rashly . . .

By April 1897 the valuations of the main properties and Lithgow
Eskbank ironworks were complete. Seven major stations across New
South Wales and south-west Queensland were estimated at a collec-
tive value of over £262 000 ($29.5 million at current rates of inflation).
The sum included the value of some 328 229 sheep, 5364 cattle and
648 horses.

There followed months of arguing over which family would take
possession of which properties. The Whitneys, being restricted to a one-
third share, were in a less powerful bargaining position but they argued
hard to keep Coombing Park and neighbouring Waugoola, valued at
close to £60 000. By April 1897 they had reached some kind of compromise. Rutherford forced Bella to choose between Coombing and
Buckiinguy (by far the most valuable in monetary terms). There was
no competition. They lost Buckiinguy and received Claverton instead.
Arthur was instructed to relocate his family there from Burrenbilla.

Rutherford was to receive Hereford, Burrenbilla, Wyagdon and
Buckiinguy, as well as taking on the assets and considerable debts of
the Eskbank ironworks business. Most of the stud sheep and cattle
were at Burrenbilla, and it was agreed that many of the animals would
be shifted to the Whitney property in order to equalise their share of
the stock.

Two more large Queensland stations, Davenport Downs and
Yowah, as well as the many smaller parcels of Cobb & Co land (bought
mainly for stables, feed storage or mineral prospecting) were set aside
to be sold when the market improved and the monies split propor-

tionately. In regard to these, the legal agreement the pair had drawn up had a safety valve stating that 'in the event of either party declining to authorise sale, the other could sell without the consent and notwithstanding the dissent of the other, after six months' notice'.

Despite this painstaking division, and however much they had fought, the lives of James Rutherford, Arthur Leeds and Bella Whitney had become so entangled that in practice it was impossible to hold to strict divisions. A Queensland Supreme Court case seven years later suggests that Arthur Leeds continued to run stock on Rutherford's Miranda Downs, Davenport Downs and Yowah stations, although it is unclear whether he was ever given authority to do so.

In fighting for management of a third of the firm's holdings, Bella Whitney was taking on huge liabilities brought on by continuing drought and a stock and wool market that had remained flat. Bella had retained some of her own family's land near Montefiores, and she forced herself to sell it, together with the stock it carried, in order to pay the interest on her bank loans.

There remained costs to reduce at Coombing. Putting off fence repairers for the next few years could save hundreds of pounds; Bella was loath to put fellows out of a job, but there was little choice. Then there were the house accounts – large entertainments at Coombing were out of the question.

Sorting out whose stock was whose would continue for at least a year, and Bella and Arthur had agreed they would watch Rutherford like a hawk. Arthur was as bold as his sister in challenging the man. On 4 September 1897, Rutherford wrote back from Burrenbilla, warning Leeds

The sheep you claim, does astonish me somewhat . . . I can only say that a parallel case would be that I demand the sheep which went from here only a short time before and are, I believe, now in Playboy paddock. No such conversation ever took place . . . if it had, it would have been in the agreement. It may be there. If so, it is wrong and my memory of what took place is at fault

It would be as well if you moderated your bluff and bounce. They butter no parsnips and [are] useless except you might like to show someone how you talk to me.

On the same day Arthur wrote to his sister complaining about Rutherford's meanness.

Your letter came safely to hand last mail. Rutherford leaves 'so Austin says' on Monday. He is without doubt the meanest old witch I ever came across, a liar and a rogue – 8,000 of his sheep left yesterday for his son's selections and the balance leave on Tuesday.

Two weeks later Arthur wrote again to his sister, clearly fed up with Rutherford's hard-nosed negotiating.

I have the greatest contempt for Rutherford, and would not trust him in the smallest transaction. You need not be afraid of his threat of any sheep dying on Claverton for some considerable time.

I note what he says in his letter that he feels if 'the business could have been carried on two or three years more, it would

probably have ended better for both of us, but as you seemed
determined, I submit'. I like what he says very much. The
sooner we are rid of him the better. I would not work for him if
he offered me £10 000 a year again.

   I will not at any time buy, sell or lend to Mr Rutherford . . .

The eight years until 1903 marked the worst drought the country
had seen. Centred on Queensland, where the vast majority of Cobb
& Co's property still lay, the drought continued to place enormous
strain on Arthur, Bella and Rutherford. Herds of kangaroos overran
their stations in their thousands, fighting the remaining stock for the
last trickle of water in the cracked landscape.

   Each party was desperate to salvage whatever it could from the
soured partnership. For Arthur, the last straw in the bitter division
came when Rutherford gave instructions for 20 000 Whitney sheep to
be mustered onto his land, claiming the stock were his. The situation
was impossible. Sheep were money – money the Whitneys could ill
afford to give up, as there was a continued risk of bankruptcy.

   Since his return from America in January 1896, Rutherford had
hated having to consult with Bella and her brother before making the
smallest business decision. He complained that quick decisions could
make a huge difference in business, and was irritated further when
Bella began to say no to every one of his suggestions. Her suspicions
regarding doubtful past transactions increased, and she accused
Rutherford of spiriting away funds to family members in America, a
claim he vehemently denied.

   They had exchanged so many letters in the three years since

Frank's death that Bella could likely tell what frame of mind Ruther-ford was in merely by looking at the angle he scrawled her name on the envelope.

> *Cobb & Co*
> *Coach Proprietors*
> *Bathurst*
>
> *Mrs Whitney,*
> *Your darling friend Arthur has taken £400. This man, but for you, would have discharged or sold out long since and at last after leading us along every year for some time, has walked off with £400 . . . but poor Whitney was so wrapped up in him that he would do nothing. If I discharge him, I would have done it to spite you. A part of the money he took has gone to pay for the monument, so that so far, I have paid for it.*

Bella's spine must have tingled. The words he wrote made no sense – and how dare he cry poor over funding the marble monu-ment to Frank in Orange, particularly as he had docked Cobb & Co's employees £5 apiece to pay for it. Bella forced herself to read on.

> *Now you know I pointed all this out to you but your determination not to trust me or adopt any advice I gave re cattle were sacrificed. I wanted to sell or give away Bourke shop but could not move without what amounted to a charge of trying to take advantage of you. Is it any wonder that one becomes disgusted with such disastrous tactics? If you had produced a scintilla of evidence that I had wronged or had attempted to wrong you, the matter*

would have been different. Bourke has lost more than £2,000 the last year and if you had not stood in the way, most of it might have been saved.

Finally, to show you that I do believe, with the greatest satisfaction, that you mean to act in a reasonable manner from this forward, I have tried all I could to conciliate and am in no way to blame for any unpleasantness. I sat silent under the stigma until silence could no longer be evidence and suffered all the vituperative language you were capable of using vs our Bank manager and the charges of stealing money and sending it to America.

Those were stories you told and should have been as well proven in fact at least before being circulated. The American charge is too contemptible – as you must know that there is not a scintilla of evidence to sustain so bold a charge.

To help to ease your mind I may say that I will behest myself in the strongest manner you can devise to give £50 for each pound you can prove that I have wrongfully sent or sent at all from here to America for the last 10 years previous to your husband's death or since, except in a few little instances to keep Norman at school – all of which were properly charged to me. When you refer to it, I cannot but think that after all, you think it worthwhile to badger me as much as you can conveniently. I hope however no more unpleasantness will arise.

The Rutherford–Whitney feud continued, and Bella became suspicious of any irregularity. It was suggested that there were anomalies in the Lithgow ironworks monies due to Cobb & Co – an asset she had at least unofficially offloaded to Rutherford. Bella Whitney had potentially been short-changed thousands of pounds. She wrote to her solicitors demanding that, in view of Rutherford's mental condition, decisions about winding up their problematic Lithgow colliery investments be frozen. Although she knew it meant months of work ahead, Bella located an independent auditor.

When he found out about Bella's intentions, Rutherford was cautious. A week before Christmas 1897 he wrote to Bella

> . . . we do not want auditors dancing up and down. All I want is a fair statement . . . I will agree to any capable and disinterested party.
>
> . . . I cannot consent to this and I will not be a party to pay my share in any way. They may be very good men in their way but I desire to have the accounts audited by someone who will work for both parties not one only. I wish you to inform those gentlemen that their services will not be accepted by me.

Another auditor was eventually engaged, though it would be another year before the results were released.

By now, Rutherford was desperate for cash to keep his many properties afloat in the face of the ongoing drought. Four days after the Christmas of 1897 he mortgaged everything he could to obtain a huge capital injection of £126 000 from the pastoral mortgage company Dalgetys. In return, his lenders held a mortgage over his Murrumbidgerie and Wyagdon properties, as well as close to 178 000 of his sheep, 1000 cattle and 320 horses.

Despite his stubbornness, in his letters, if not face-to-face,

Rutherford was beginning to treat Bella Whitney as an equal. In addition, Bella's mood must occasionally have been heartened by letters of encouragement from Walter Hall, who assured her the economy was slowly recovering. There was also a wave of support gathering for giving women a say in electing each colony's leaders.

Even more significantly, as Bella Whitney and James Rutherford struggled to unravel the entangled Cobb & Co empire, the six British colonies seemed finally to be serious about coming together as a nation.

CHAPTER EIGHTEEN

LEGAL CHALLENGES

*. . . a good deal of litigation . . . might have been obviated by
the exercise of some common sense*
– H. Peden Steel, 1900

Rutherford escaped to San Francisco in mid-March 1898, presumably for some respite from the pressure of his debts and the constant dealings with Bella Whitney and Arthur Leeds. In typical fashion it was another quick visit, and just three months later he was writing to Bella from Bathurst.

As soon as Rutherford returned there were the usual headaches. Three firms of solicitors were involved in sorting out the specifics of winding up Cobb & Co's New South Wales business. Rutherford found it extremely difficult to adjust to the new 'yours and mine' situation, and he continued to interfere in Bella Whitney's share of the divided properties. As relations deteriorated further, heated letters would be traded with Bella one day, and Arthur Leeds the next.

Cobb & Co's as yet undivided Yowah station was in dire straits, turned to dust by the relentless drought. Desperate to keep his stock alive, it was now James Rutherford who was ready to cut off his own arm to be rid of the quarrelling. On 26 July 1898 he wrote to Bella:

While I was at Cunnamulla I went to Yowah and there found a terrible state of things. Kangaroos have completely over-run the place – 7,000 of the beasts have been shot from Feb up to June 1ˢᵗ but that is nothing. Shooters will only shoot large ones that have valuable skins. There is not a vestige of feed and the cattle are in a deplorable condition.

Under these circumstances I wrote to Leeds asking him if he would divide the cattle that I proposed to muster. I stated that if he would and take his we could sweep off many young ones which will die where they are if rain does not come. I thought if we took off all the three year olds which are estimated @ 600 with a lot of old cows and some two year olds we could have relieved the run of probably 1,500 which might save them, and their removal might save the balance.

I can not suggest nor do anything except it is disparaged out and my reasonable reports treated unreasonably. Under the circumstances can you wonder that I am obliged to give you notice that according to the terms of our agreement it cannot go on further than I can prevent. I have always and am now trying to do the best I can to improve our position.

In the same mail there was a similar note, also from Rutherford:

Without prejudice
I am in receipt of yours re removal of sheep from Claverton Park . . . Mr Steel on advice from Claverton gave me authority to remove the 3,000 sheep which I did to save their lives and may hope by that to save the lives of the balance.

*I should get my share of the £1,200 about which Arthur
Leeds kept back from us. I want my proportions say £800 and
until I get that I should think you would have been silent. When
that is adjusted then you may speak with some right and will be
heard in a proper spirit.*

*This is only one of several miserable subterfuges to do me
out of money justly mine – which I hope you do not in any way
countenance.*

Bella Whitney and James Rutherford had become a pair of Siamese
twins joined together for too long, their relationship soured from
knowing too much about the other's faults. The bitter accusations
continued. When Bella was reticent to put Yowah and the huge Davenport Downs on the market, Rutherford insisted. Finally, he was
forced to take advantage of the clause in their private agreement,
allowing sale after six months.

*I hereby notify you that in the event of your declining within
the said period to authorise such sale I shall proceed to sell such
property by public auction without your consent and notwithstanding your dissent.*

In 1899, Yowah and Davenport Downs were put up for auction; Both
parties knew the buyer would be getting a bargain. Sure enough, the
properties were sold for just £14 000 and £5600 respectively, including their starving stock – to James Rutherford. Twenty years before,
Yowah had been worth nearly four times this amount. The cunning
man had done a juggling act with his assets, convincing Dalgetys to

lend him another £35 000 by putting up as security 110 000 sheep, 400 horses and 750 cattle. Rutherford now had control of every Queensland property except Claverton. Bella must have felt short-changed by his sleight of hand.

Two years later, after seven years of drought, only a fifth of Rutherford's 110 000 Queensland sheep remained alive. The workforce of hundreds he had employed to manage his stock and vast lands had shrunk to twenty. His remaining men were sent out to scavenge the wool from the thousands of decaying sheep carcasses. So putrid was the stench as the dead wool was scoured and washed that Cunnamulla's town dwellers 10 kilometres away protested.

A newly opened letter from Mr Bassett lay on the desk in front of Bella: the audit she had demanded months and months ago was finally complete. Rather than old Pritchard Bassett, it was his son who had supervised the work and written the appraisal.

The letter's content was alarming, confirming Bella's fears. In particular, Bassett had calculated a discrepancy of £20 000 owing to the Whitney executors from the Eskbank ironworks. Rutherford disputed the figure outright, but in Bella Whitney's eyes Rutherford's casual attitude to book-keeping had cheated her family of monies that were rightfully theirs. If there was any hope of claiming the missing money a legal case on Bella's part would be required.

Legal disputes are heard in equity courts, without a jury, when the accuser aims to win an injunction directing someone to do something, rather than simply desiring monetary compensation. A person whose neighbour will not return his only breeding bull that happened to wander onto the neighbour's land, for example, may want that particular bull back rather than being compensated for its monetary value.

In practical terms, an equity suit would be more valuable to Bella Whitney. Secure in the belief that her share of the Cobb & Co fortune would one day make her a rich woman, she had the confidence to spend large amounts of money on further legal fees.

Hugh Peden Steel must have grimaced when he heard Bella's new demands against his father-in-law. Perhaps the lawyer thought back to his wedding day in 1890, when Bella had walked up the aisle behind the bridal group, arm in arm with one of the Rutherford boys. She had later been seated at the wedding table. What a sad turnaround.

Peden Steel knew that keeping such a case quiet was important if Rutherford's and Cobb & Co's reputations were to remain untarnished. His father-in-law and Frank Whitney had seemingly been the best of friends; now, his partner's widow was going against him, hard as nails in a barrel. There was a mountain of preparation to be done and the lawyer had no idea when James Rutherford would be back from the bush.

Meanwhile, Bella's solicitors, Lee, Colquhoun and Bassett, had failed in their application to challenge the terms of Frank's will. Without resolution on the clause stipulating the conversion of Frank's share in the business into cash, Bella and Rutherford's painstaking division of the ailing company's assets could be made null and void in the courts. Assuring the Whitney family's future at Coombing Park would require nothing less than a change in the law. The machinations of federating the six colonies into a commonwealth were keeping politicians fully occupied, so such an attempt would take years, but to Bella there was no choice but to fight on. She instructed her solicitor to push her husband's will to the full court, counting on her powerful friend Walter Hall to help. Hall mixed professionally and socially with New South Wales' leading businessmen and powerbrokers, so Bella suggested she might come down to Sydney to 'speak with people'.

Hall's reply was prompt but fairly blunt. He had just returned from the Cunnamulla district, presumably to see for himself how the ongoing drought was affecting the Queensland coaching business, in which he was a major partner.

> *10 Dec 1898*
> *Union Club*
> *Sydney*
>
> *Dear Mrs Whitney,*
>
> *I cannot see that you can do any good coming down. They I know have sent the appeal to the Minister, Mr Reid – although that is the correct thing to do, I am afraid it will not do much good. He is almost sure to stick to what his officers say – especially as it affects the essence of this property law.*
>
> *It's no use me seeing him as although we used to be friends, we are not now. I see him every day – we had a row and are not on speaking terms now.*
>
> *There is no doubt it will have to go to the full court – but there is lots of time as it cannot sit until about March – and you must wait for the Minister's answer.*
>
> *Hoping all the family are well.*
>
> *Yours truly,*
>
> *W. R. Hall*

Months passed while the Whitney family waited. Bella watched her sheep continue to starve, her lambs die and her flocks sold at a loss. Itinerant men came begging for work, but she could give them nothing more than a night's food and shelter before they trudged on.

Months turned to a year, in which Bella lobbied hard. She had a particularly persuasive streak, and the knack of putting powerful men at ease. It was perhaps Walter Hall or her solicitor Pritchard Bassett who had introduced Bella to a bright barrister and member of the New South Wales parliament by the name of Edmund Barton. Bassett had petitioned dozens of prominent landholders, including Frank Whitney, to support Barton's nomination for the Federal Convention a few years earlier.

Following the death of Henry Parkes in 1896, Edmund Barton had become the leading champion for the cause of federation, and he was playing a key role in pushing through a constitution for the new nation. Nicknamed Toby Tosspot by the press, thanks to his fondness for long boozy lunches, Barton was an affable but serious fellow with spectacles that framed a round face and a boyish tousle of curly hair.

Despite Hall's discouraging letter, Bella had likely called on Mr Barton during her spring visit to Sydney and invited him to journey out to Coombing Park to see her home for himself. Perhaps it was Barton who suggested that Bella should lobby for a Special Members Bill to change the law regarding her husband's will. To do so, she would need to rally a sitting member of the colonial parliament to raise such a bill on her behalf, and she thought of Thomas Waddell, her local member for Cowra. Waddell had a passion for cattle and horse breeding, and she and Frank had come to know him well during the 1870s when he had owned the Fort Bourke run north-west of their Buckiinguy land. He remained a close family friend. At last there seemed to be a way forward.

Now that the valuation of properties and stock had been finalised and at least unofficially divided, and the disastrous Eskbank ironworks passed over to Rutherford, Bella Whitney was finally in a strong financial position for the future. Her confidence in securing Coombing Park had strengthened, and by 1899 it was time to build the new homestead she and Frank had so often discussed. The new house needed to make a statement, exuding the confidence of the new century on the horizon. Her chosen architect, George Allan Mansfield, had designed not only Sydney's Hotel Australia and Prince Alfred Hospital, but also Carcoar's CBC Bank and Abercrombie House in her own district.

George Mansfield was a charming man and Bella was soon coming up with excuses to write to him or to visit in person on her trips to Sydney. Mansfield translated her words and diagrams into concepts of beauty and symmetry, her vision made clearer by the common reference points to his earlier work.

The final design of the new Coombing Park included an elegant drawing room for the ladies, a billiards room for the men and, like Rutherford's Hereford and Hall's Wildfell mansions, a grand dining room in which to house the English oak furniture and crystal that had come with the Icely estate. The wide verandahs were to be of marble and every room was to have an outlook.

The old homestead was torn down and foundations were laid afresh. Bella engaged the finest tradesmen she could locate, accepting several of George Mansfield's recommendations but sourcing many others herself. Bella had already sent one of her daughters by steamer to Asia, armed with a generous budget – her task to source decorative arts for the new house and garden. She wanted pieces that could be admired, which would distinguish her family as worldly, as progressive.

Bella Whitney could see a prosperous future. It was time the Whitney family stood apart from Cobb & Co to make its own distinctive mark on pastoral Australia.

The last summer of the nineteenth century was nearly over before the Whitney vs. Rutherford trial began. It was 27 February 1900 when Bella and her brother prepared to take on one of the continent's most powerful businessmen, a strange turn of events when the two families were in other ways so close. In just four weeks, Rutherford's son Laurence was to be best man at Billy Whitney's wedding. The legal stoush was embarrassing for all concerned.

The case was to come before the Chief Judge in Equity, Englishman Archie Simpson of Sydney's Supreme Court, who was just four years senior to Bella. Somehow, former Cobb & Co accounting staff had been persuaded to testify, giving evidence on the first day. Arthur Leeds then took the stand, unused to wearing a suit and the formality of court rooms.

Mr Gordon, the barrister instructed by Bella's own solicitor, began his examination, intent on showing that Arthur Leeds' hands were clean of any meddling in company accounts.

'I think you are a relation of Mrs Whitney's?'

'Yes, a brother.'

'And you are one of the executors under Mr Whitney's will?'

'Yes.'

'On one occasion I believe Mr Rutherford was out of the colony and you and Mr Steel and Mr Rutherford's son acted under the power of attorney?'

'Yes.'

'Did you do anything with regard to Cobb & Co's business in Bathurst?'

'Yes, Mr Brooks was in doubt about how to charge the £520 a year . . .'

This was a response Mr Gordon had clearly not expected. He needed to clarify. 'You gave some directions to Mr Brooks with regard to a particular item of £520?'

'Yes.'

'Well, with the exception of that, did you give any orders to Mr Brooks?'

'No, I do not think so. I may have told him to send me a list of the cheques he had drawn.'

Arthur must suddenly have remembered there was a script to follow. 'Oh no, I did not give him any directions at all.'

'Except with regard to the £520?'

'That is all.'

Not until the fourth day was Rutherford examined. It soon became clear that James Rutherford had no idea about Cobb & Co's financial situation from one year to the next. His thick eyebrows lay low over sunken dark eyes, and his seventy-three years showed.

Bella's legal team began to tear open Rutherford's mental state.

At one stage he reminisced: 'I may say that although there is a good deal of friction now, yet in Mr Whitney's lifetime we were like two brothers.' Some questions Rutherford did not seem to hear; to others he gave cryptic, confused answers. He repeatedly contradicted himself, forgetting what he had said only minutes before; at other times, he quite lucidly claimed that he had tried to minimise Cobb & Co's interest repayments.

'I put the money – all the money I received, all my private money – for the purposes of stopping interest. Because Cobb & Co were so largely in debt that I thought every pound I could put in to stop interest would be an advantage.'

Had Bella wrongly judged the man?

However, Rutherford's responses became increasingly unfathomable, and on day five, worn down by the barrage of queries about his lack of knowledge of the firm's accounts, he lost patience.

'I completely broke down in 1875 and was ordered away. My medical adviser *prohibited* me from going into the accounts . . . I was not able to pay attention to the books.'

This is perhaps the first and only time Rutherford was to publicly admit of his illness. Arthur and Bella may well have cast their minds back to that first long escape Rutherford had taken to America. It had been the catalyst for Arthur's removal to Buckiinguy and the Whitneys to Orange. Had it really been a breakdown at this time that had triggered Rutherford's infamous donkey-purchasing trip to America, or had he simply confused his dates?

By the sixth day it had become clear that the legal proceedings were falling apart. Evidence was being introduced by Rutherford that conflicted with his sworn statements and his recollections kept changing. Bella must have tired of listening to the drone of legal minutiae being swatted back and forth as each legal team bickered over seemingly inconsequential points. Perhaps she was relieved when the judge announced, 'Mr Rutherford's memory is so defective that it might affect the view I take of his evidence.' On 8 March 1900, after just six days in session, the case was adjourned.

More than five years had passed since Frank Whitney's death. Since then, Bella's aim had been to maximise the value of every one of her husband's hard-won assets. But at what cost? Perhaps she had been too unforgiving in bringing Rutherford so low. She had banished her idiot son; now it seemed the same fate could face Cobb & Co's iconic driving force.

Rather than prolonging the pain, both parties agreed to settle the Eskbank issue out of court. Bella Whitney agreed to drop the claim to recover the book-keeping discrepancy of £20 000, along with all other claims against Rutherford, who in return agreed to pay the executors just £2500 in compensation.

Five months later, Bella's solicitor received a letter from Peden Steel:

> It appears to me that since your clients have given up their claim to have the £20,000 odd declared a partnership asset that there are only some minor items between them which might easily be settled amicably without any more expense in legal proceedings . . . It seems to me and has seemed so that a good deal of litigation in this matter might have been obviated by the exercise of some common sense. You might let me know your views on this.

No letters between Ada Rutherford and Bella Whitney have survived from this point on, although it is quite possible each destroyed the other's correspondence. The two families continued to have dealings with each other, and neither could afford continued bitterness when dozens of Cobb & Co assets were still to be sold, the proceeds of which would need to be divided.

The final brick of Bella's new Coombing Park homestead was laid on 1 August 1900. The builders arranged a celebration – the finest new house in the district deserved something special. The house was decorated with flags and bunting, and a plank gangway erected from the ground to the roof turrets allowed the more athletic guests to clamber up and admire the chimneys' latticed detail, set against the view of rolling hills and creek flats.

The builders presented Bella with an engraved silver trowel to mark the occasion, and the local newspaper sent a reporter to cover the event. His article observed that Mrs Whitney placed the last brick in position in a 'most workmanlike manner', wetting the mortar with champagne and declaring 'this brick is well and truly laid', as if it were a nest egg, which of course it was.

The finished house was certainly exquisite, incorporating the choicest features of Mansfield's earlier work: stained glass in the front door and a marble-floored entrance hall that was perfectly aligned with the new driveway gates at the end of the circular drive. The bedroom wing boasted twelve rooms: a private bedroom suite, three ladies' bedrooms and, down another corridor, three gentlemen's bedrooms. Elegant ironwork fittings piped acetylene gas to every room, providing a soft glowing light when lit. The servants now had their own separate wing, complete with a shared sitting room adjacent to an enormous, well-aired kitchen.

Bella had achieved Coombing Park's reconstruction through sheer determination. Soon she would have the house stuffed with fine cedar furniture, exquisite Oriental arts, imported English oak heirlooms. This was to be a place of refuge – a world of its own.

Keeping a homestead the size of Coombing Park running smoothly required significant capital and staff. Bella Whitney's large household staff included gardeners, a book-keeper, a cook and a kitchen maid, a part-time laundrywoman, a house maid and a parlour maid who took charge of the dining-room settings and the preparation of morning and afternoon teas. The house maid had the busiest day of any female staff member. She had to wake the family in the morning, bring hot tea to each bedroom, help set up breakfast, make all the beds and clean the bedrooms, assist the parlour maid in serving dinner, wash up, turn down the beds and ensure there was hot water for washing in each bedroom at night. The yard boy had the toughest job among the men, especially in winter when there was the wood to chop and cart indoors to the eleven fireplaces, the staff dining room, laundry and huge kitchen stove. He also had to clean the boots and shoes, separate the milk, feed the fowls and pigs, and sweep the verandah and yard.

Successful Australian pastoral families spent huge amounts of money to ensure their homesteads were elegant and sophisticated. The running costs, including groceries, repairs, cleaning and entertaining, were sizable. In 1903, for example, Bella spent close to £2000 (the equivalent today of over $216 000) on household expenses and wages in her new home. With all the relatives home for Christmas, December was always a particularly expensive month. Sometimes the December bills surpassed £590, more than six years' salary for the average parlour maid.

Bella's four youngest daughters still lived at Coombing, and she now insisted that evening dress be worn at night. After dinner, both gentlemen and ladies retired to the billiards room, where coffee and a fruit supper were served.

While Bella ran the household, and made the major decisions about Cobb & Co assets, Billy, in name at least, looked after Coombing Park's stock. Bella declined to have herself recorded as Coombing Park's owner. Until she had proved her worth as a breeder of stock, it was better to list her son in the directory of station owners. There were plenty of cattle buyers who would not take a woman seriously.

Bella's most lasting close personal relationship was with her brother, who remained more loyal to Bella than to his own family. Arthur was her regular correspondent, and he regularly made the two- to three-day journey by buggy to visit her from Queensland. There was an understanding that he come alone, leaving his wife, two adult sons and daughter at Claverton.

In mid-September 1900, thousands of miles distant, the elderly Queen Victoria issued a proclamation from Balmoral Castle, declaring that New South Wales, Victoria, Queensland, Tasmania, South Australia and Western Australia would be united in a Federal Commonwealth of Australia to take effect on 1 January 1901. It was to be one of the Queen's last acts as sovereign.

The site of a national capital had been hotly contested by Sydney and Melbourne. In the end, a compromise meant Melbourne would be the capital until a new capital city could be built from scratch in a specially created zone (the Australian Capital Territory) within New South Wales, a project that would take twenty-five years.

Official celebrations were coordinated by committee upon sub-committee. In Sydney, the harbour was the focal point during the first week of January, with fireworks (quaintly referred to as 'illuminations'), a 'monster swimming carnival' at Cockatoo Island and steamer excursions. Military processions stretched around the city, Indian cavalry regiments marching behind English artillery troops, Highland light infantry, and Welsh and Scots fusiliers. A cycling and athletics carnival was held at the Sydney Cricket Ground, along with a public schools display of maypole dancing, musical drills and flag marching. There were luncheons and state banquets at the town hall, and in every major centre around the nation. Five-course French menus were in fashion for formal banquets, so *poisson* followed *potage*, succeeded by *entrées, relevés* and a selection of sweet *entremets*. Up to six toasts were made at each banquet – even the press of the new Commonwealth were celebrated.

Just three weeks into January 1901, still hung-over from their celebrating, the new nation wept as their first prime minister, Edmund Barton, announced that their beloved Queen Victoria was dead.

In late March, Bella Whitney and her unmarried daughters received an invitation to the opening of the new nation's first parliament, no doubt through their friendship with the Bartons. The invitation was enormous and arrived in a specially designed envelope with cardboard supports to prevent it being crushed. When opened, the enclosed card was the size of a huge menu at an elegant city restaurant. Colourful knights in armour and patrician women in long Grecian gowns leapt and danced around the scrolled script on the embossed card.

Opening Parliament of the Commonwealth . . .
His majesty's Ministers of State for Australia have the honour
to invite Mrs, Miss and Miss L. K. Whitney
To an evening reception at the Exhibition Building Melbourne
on 9 May at eight o'clock
to witness the opening of the Commonwealth.

It was a proud moment for Bella Whitney. She and her two most eligible daughters, Thirza and Katie, were on the guest list of the nation's most powerful politician. Katie was a personal friend of the Bartons, and Mrs Barton had even asked the Whitneys to stay at the Grand Hotel with them in Melbourne. The next day's mail brought an invitation to the mayor's concert at the Sydney Town Hall later in the same month. For the rest of the week it would have been impossible to get a word in as Bella's girls chattered incessantly about dresses and plans.

The year 1902 was bittersweet for the Whitneys. The *Whitney Estate Act* finally passed through parliament, now that the federation process was complete, securing the family's right to retain rather than sell Coombing Park, Claverton and Waugoola. But the gain was overshadowed by loss: Bella's most beautiful daughter, Thirza, was dying.

Hydatids is a parasitic disease affecting the liver and sometimes

the brain, and is carried by farm dogs and livestock that have con-
sumed the offal of slaughtered pigs, cattle or sheep – a common
occurrence on country stations. Back in 1894 the *Bathurst Post* had
noted an alarming increase in the disease: too many rural citizens
were contracting the parasite through drinking water already con-
taminated by infected dogs and livestock. By the late 1890s some
doctors felt the disease was at epidemic proportions in New South
Wales. In 1900, as Sydney sweltered in its early-January lethargy, the
Sydney Morning Herald had run a story on the common hazards of
country life – they included hydatids, lead poisoning, consumption,
drowning, snakebite and sunstroke. It would be twenty years before
New South Wales published a Health Act forbidding dogs to be let
loose in abattoirs and forbidding farmers from feeding 'any swine
upon . . . any offal unless such offal has been first thoroughly cleansed
and boiled for at least an hour'.

It was too late for the beautiful Thirza Whitney. She may have
been infected years earlier, for the parasitic cysts grew slowly. The
family would have been oblivious for years until, just as Bella Whitney's triumph in challenging her husband's will was made into law, her
daughter deteriorated. At thirty-one years of age, Thirza, near death,
wrote her own will on 30 December 1902, leaving her share of her
father's estate to her mother. Nine days into 1903, Thirza passed away.
With Glassford banished, Bella had now lost five of her ten children.

CHAPTER NINETEEN

THE DEATH OF COACHING

Having made up his mind on a question of business or
a financial proposition, nothing could cause
James Rutherford to look back . . .

As six colonies became six states and a nation, Cobb & Co's story, in one state at least, was far from over. The delivery of mails was now a Commonwealth responsibility, and Cobb & Co's key customer for its Queensland mail contracts, tendered every two years or so, became the new federal government in faraway Melbourne.

The firm was running coaches over more than 7000 kilometres of Queensland's outback by 1900, and with the drought causing hundreds of men to travel looking for work, their vehicles were full. By 1902 Queensland still supported forty-one mail, passenger and goods services (twenty-nine coach routes and twelve men on horseback). Horse-drawn coaches were to remain a vital service in Queensland's outback for some twenty years.

Somewhat surprisingly, Arthur Leeds now owned a substantial share of the Queensland Cobb & Co business, with James Rutherford's share now just a third of the operation. The reasons for Leeds' turnaround are not clear. Perhaps he trusted Rutherford's management when it came to coaching, rather than properties, or perhaps the level-headed Walter Hall's investment in the Queensland firm gave Leeds confidence. Leeds had been an employee of Rutherford and the Whitneys for most of his life, and there was little Rutherford could do to prevent him from buying up shares in Cobb & Co. Buying into the Queensland coaching business would have put Leeds on an equal footing with the man at last.

George Storey, the firm's general manager in Queensland, was worried. Their Charleville factory had burnt down in October 1897, and while it had been quickly rebuilt so that coach sales were not adversely affected, the fire and reconstruction cost the business over £10 000. After so many years of drought, horse feed was now available only at massive prices, imported from interstate. It was a familiar situation. Back in the late 1880s there had been a similar drought and feed costs had skyrocketed to nearly £28 000 compared to just £11 000 a year earlier.

The firm had an overdraft to the Queensland National Bank of £18 000, not to mention other creditors, and Arthur Leeds and James Rutherford were now the two guarantors to Cobb & Co's massive debt. Their government mail contracts were paying £20 000 a year, but in the past year their feed bill had been around £30 000 and their wage bill £20 000, plus the cost of repairs to coaches and harness. In the six months to June 1901, they reported net losses of over £15 000.

The crunch came early in 1902 when their bank suddenly refused to honour any more Cobb & Co cheques. Overnight, the coaching business had no way of paying its hundreds of staff and contractors; meanwhile, its dozens of government mail contracts still had about twenty months to run. Storey went to the Queensland National, begging the bank to extend the company's overdraft. The bank could see that Cobb & Co was in a worsening spiral of debt, and Storey's request was refused. Only if the Federal Postal Department agreed to increase its contract payments would the bank reconsider.

In April 1902, Storey formally requested an additional subsidy of £150 each month from the government to keep the mail services running. Storey quickly realised his request was not going to be nearly enough and he revised it, proposing a maximum of £1500 in government support per month, up to £18 000 annually.

When interviewed by the press, Storey lied, blustering that the firm's contracts had been entered into under normal conditions. With the great drought now in its eighth year, the lie was obvious.

Cobb & Co's request was sent to the new prime minister, Edmund Barton, in Melbourne, and George Storey was quickly summoned in early May. The new federal cabinet was only a year old and no doubt keen to flex its muscle. In Melbourne, Storey was met with the news that the cabinet had considered and rejected the firm's request. The contracts had been issued with guarantors, Rutherford and Leeds, and it was Cobb & Co's responsibility to call on their assistance, not on that of the government.

Brisbane's Postmaster General well knew that neither Rutherford nor Leeds could afford to bail the coaching business out of its trouble. Storey played hardball, announcing that as of four days hence, on Saturday, 10 May 1902, Cobb & Co would freeze every service in Queensland. The issue escalated to one of national importance, the main players in a panic. The next morning, the Queensland National Bank telegraphed the government to say they were taking possession of Cobb & Co's plant, and asking if the government would pay for wages and the feeding of horses after 10 May. The government in turn telegraphed James Rutherford and Arthur Leeds to warn them that if the Commonwealth was forced to carry the mails, the pair of them would be billed for the huge costs involved.

The firm was flooded with telegrams from commercial travellers stranded in far-off towns, and there was concern that many towns would be cut off from their usual food deliveries. In a nation that depended on its rural sector for wool exports, everybody was talking about the disastrous implications.

The Postmaster General directed his Queensland deputy to take immediate action to continue services by putting on special coaches. Competitor firms agreed to fill the gaps on critical routes, but in some areas Cobb & Co's monopoly was such that they owned all the horses. When Storey received a polite telegram from one competitor asking to borrow a few horses so they could run a one-off service, Storey refused outright.

Thwarted, the government turned to the Queensland National Bank, insisting that they should run the services. The bank refused, pointing out that managing scores of coaching routes was outside its area of expertise. George Storey was by now threatening to disband the entire Cobb & Co operation.

Rather than agreeing to provide Cobb & Co with £18 000 a year in extra payments, the government called for new tenders for all forty-one Queensland coach services. Within days, while they stood fast, Cobb & Co lost three of its most lucrative services to competitors.

Rutherford – now an old man of seventy-five and no longer active in the day-to-day business – realised that the transport empire he had built was on the verge of annihilation. He was adamant he would find a way of raising money to refinance the firm so its coaches could return to work. By Thursday, 15 May, Rutherford was in Brisbane reviving his old magic of conjuring capital out of thin air. Typically, he had just ploughed all the spare funds raised from the much-protracted sale of the blighted Lithgow ironworks into a new property in southern Queensland. He already owed Dalgetys more than £150 000 but, as usual, Rutherford found a way out. His new property came unstocked but the fine print of the Dalgetys mortgage stated that they would advance money to stock new country or restock where losses were due to drought. His solution was to sell sheep from another of his stations to himself, thereby tricking Dalgetys into paying for them.

The swindle meant that by Friday, 16 May, the firm was able to pacify their bankers and telegraph the Postmaster General to announce that they were ready to recommence mail deliveries on all their old routes the very next day.

The debacle made Rutherford realise that, once again, he had not been paying enough attention to the financial aspects of the coaching business. The only way forward was to put the firm into liquidation and reform it as a more structured company. In late November 1902, Rutherford took up just under half the new shares and Arthur Leeds took up over a quarter; Walter Hall continued to hold some shares, though far fewer than his earlier commitment. Rutherford was elected governing director, with Leeds, Ludwig Uhl and Tom Gallagher as directors. To reduce overheads, many employees were dismissed and paid-up capital was reduced. Shareholder value was slashed, but there was no alternative.

Cobb & Co's horse-drawn coaches were soon to be faced with a completely new competitor: motor transport, with lorries carrying goods and cars ferrying passengers. In 1900 the Melburnian inventor Herbert Thomson had driven his steam car from Bathurst to Melbourne, the first interstate road trip by automobile in Australia. Seven three-wheeled De Dion-Boutons had arrived in the country in 1899. The availability of these imported cars coincided with the end of seven years of economic depression – the worst Australia had known since settlement. So quickly did the motor car invade the public consciousness that in March 1903 a group of enthusiasts formed the first motoring club, the Royal Automobile Club of Australia, based in Sydney.

Now an old man, Rutherford was reticent to invest in these new vehicles. Motor mechanics were rare in the outback in the early 1900s; horses were more reliable in the vast interior, and farriers and blacksmiths were plentiful. Not until June 1911 did he, Leeds and the other directors approve the purchase of Cobb & Co's first motor cars, but James Rutherford was never to see the vehicles in action. The firm went on to trial lorries, but these did not appear on the Queensland routes until 1914.

Over the next decade, despite a persistent cough and his advanced age, Rutherford continued to travel thousands of miles in his sulky, supervising the mustering and droving of cattle. The man's joy now lay in the vast plains of his Diamantina River stations – Davenport Downs and Connemarra – in his beloved Channel Country of southwest Queensland.

Rutherford's one concession to age was allowing his son Aleck to accompany him to Davenport Downs for the mustering. Like Bella

Whitney, Rutherford had little interest in having his sons work beside him, interfering in his projects. He had lost none of his stubbornness. Despite his failing eyesight, he insisted on driving his two-wheeler buggy across outback Queensland. Often he would find it impossible to make out the faint markings of a country track, but he refused to admit there were times he became quite lost.

In September 1911, James Rutherford was at Davenport Downs, nearly 500 kilometres west of Longreach, camped out with his swag, salted beef and his son Aleck. Even at the age of eighty-four, he had no taste for the comforts to which his great wealth gave him access, but his health was deteriorating. Rutherford caught cold in the chill spring air, and in concession to a worsening cough he allowed himself to travel home from northern Queensland by steamer rather than overland. On the steamer, halfway from Townsville to Brisbane, Rutherford's condition worsened and he was forced to disembark with his son at Mackay. Four days later, on 13 September 1911, James Rutherford died of pneumonia. He was 2000 kilometres from home, though some might have argued that this remarkable man never had a fixed address.

Bathurst came out in force for Rutherford's funeral. Every person who owned or could beg, borrow or steal a coach, buggy or hansom cab for the funeral had obviously done so. After the short service in All Saints Cathedral, the funeral procession stretched half a mile down the main street en route to the cemetery.

At the open Rutherford vault in the Bathurst cemetery stood two ancient fellows with silvery white hair, doubled over with age. As the grains of dirt fell silently upon the coffin lid, both men surreptitiously drew out a handkerchief and cried like babies for their old boss and for their past. John Barry and Jacob Russert were the only two drivers present that day who had witnessed Cobb & Co's triumphant entry into Bathurst fifty years earlier.

In its report on James Rutherford's passing, the *Bathurst Times* waxed lyrical:

> *As a businessman he had the heart of a lion, and the pluck of a regiment of the bravest soldiers. Having made up his mind on a question of business or a financial proposition, nothing could cause James Rutherford to look back . . . His enterprise, his grit and determination, and his wonderful power of reaching his goal can only be described as his American people would describe them as – colossal.*

Full of energy to the end, James Rutherford had died on the job. He had made a huge impact on those who knew him. At least three men, including his son-in-law Hugh Peden Steel, wrote poems to mark his passing. For Bella Whitney, time and a better acceptance of human weakness had tempered years of distrust into compassion.

The Cobb & Co story was all but over, for the heart of the company cooled with Rutherford's death. Long-serving Tom Gallagher, the company's inspector, had held the day-to-day running of routes and the Charleville coach factory together for decades. He resigned six months later over a dispute with the new directors regarding payment of the firm's Charleville factory staff.

James Rutherford might have felt quietly satisfied had he lived to see the new motor cars struggle with the conditions on outback Queensland roads. Roads were still poor, old coach drivers were antagonistic to the new motor coaches and there remained few skilled mechanics to service the vehicles when they broke down. By 1917 the firm was using Cadillacs and a few Hupmobiles on relatively short outback runs, but there were always a few horses in reserve. In fact, the Queensland Post Office insisted the firm keep horses handy on motor routes, in case of breakdown, right up until 1923.

Company directors Arthur Leeds and Ludwig Uhl were not interested in expanding the possibilities of motor transport – motor cars could not be serviced by Uhl's saddle-making business. Their major motivation for replacing coaches was to save money on the expense of horse feed, the bugbear that had crippled the firm so often in its history. For some time, customers were offered the choice, on several routes, of a coach or the pricier motorised alternative.

In 1917 Cobb & Co's financial position was grim once again. Three years of drought and continued reliance on horses had led to losses of £16000. The spread of railways up to Normanton on the Gulf of Carpentaria and to Cairns on the far north coast, along with the uptake of the motor car, made the firm's main assets redundant. Thousands of horses, sets of harness and dozens of coaches were slowly sold off, and old coaches were left to rot in paddocks.

The end of World War I was a major catalyst for Cobb & Co's eventual collapse. The war had seen accelerated improvements to motor vehicles, and they were now far more reliable and economical than ten years earlier. The roads were still poor but postwar vehicles had high ground clearance, large wheels, long-stroke motors and low-gear transmissions, allowing them to handle even the worst

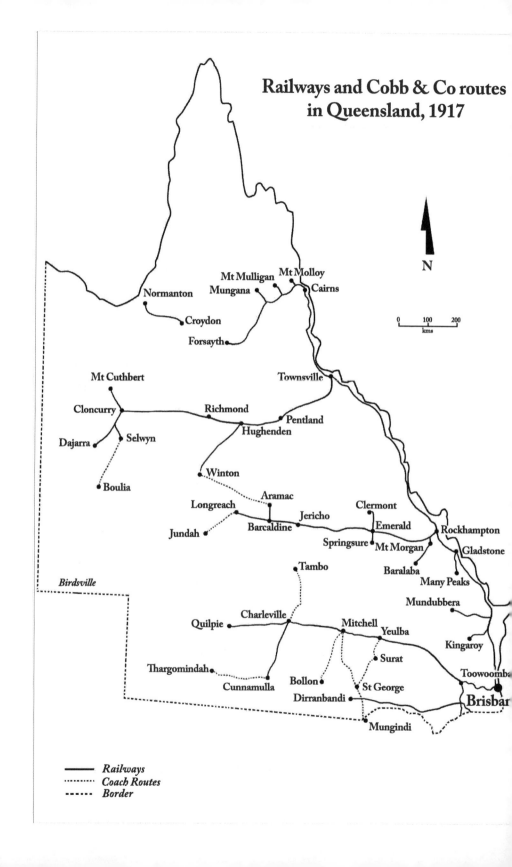

Railways and Cobb & Co routes in Queensland, 1917

N

0   100   200
        kms

Normanton

Mt Mulligan   Mt Molloy
Mungana   Cairns

Croydon

Forsayth

Mt Cuthbert   Townsville

Cloncurry   Richmond   Pentland
Hughenden

Dajarra   Selwyn

Boulia

Winton

Aramac   Clermont

Longreach   Jericho   Emerald
Barcaldine   Springsure   Rockhampton
Jundah   Mt Morgan
Gladstone

Baralaba

Birdsville   Many Peaks

Tambo   Mundubbera

Quilpie   Charleville   Mitchell
Yeulba   Kingaroy

Surat

Thargomindah   Toowoomba
Cunnamulla   Bollon   St George

Dirranbandi   Brisbane

Mungindi

——— Railways
.... Coach Routes
- - - - - Border

bush tracks. Fuel was less of an issue now that oil companies were setting up depots in the outback, and vehicles could be maintained by the hundreds of returned soldiers who had been trained in operating motor cars while serving overseas. The government needed to find jobs for its returned diggers, so they ceased giving major mail contracts to Cobb & Co, instead steering dozens of opportunities to returned soldiers. One fellow with a single truck had lower overheads than a large company and could now operate a mail and passenger service that had once needed a coach and driver, four or five grooms and fifty horses.

Cobb & Co's Charleville coach factory closed in 1920. It had once been the centre of the firm's operations, but they had now lost every mail contract that fanned out from Charleville to cheaper single operators. In 1921 the firm won just three mail contracts across the whole state. Two years later Cobb & Co was still running coaches from places like Yeulba to Surat. A story is told that in late 1924, on the last occasion the firm carried passengers – by motor vehicle – there was heavy rain and the vehicle bogged. The old horse coach had to be recommissioned for the final run.

But it was not only returned servicemen, motor transport and the railways that forced Cobb & Co off the road. Just 300 kilometres west of Cobb & Co's last route, a revolutionary new transport company was challenging the status quo. The Queensland and Northern Territory Aerial Services, eventually to become Australia's national airline Qantas, began to carry both mail and passengers from Cobb & Co's one-time base, Charleville, to Longreach and Cloncurry. Change was in the air.

Horses continued to be used to haul hansom cabs about

Australia's cities until the early 1930s, but the era of horse-powered passenger transport was over. In the event, it was the motor vehicle rather than the railways that replaced the last outback coaches. The firm's effort to move into motor transport had been half-hearted at best, and the business lacked a leader with the energy and drive of James Rutherford to guide such enormous change.

The company had dabbled in the business of storekeeping since the 1890s. It now took over a handful of general stores in country towns to give its dozens of unemployed old drivers something to do. Often these old teamsters did not adapt well to life behind a counter, as a bush jingle of the day suggests:

> *And now we find old Bill behind*
> *The counter, half unsexed;*
> *He's selling hose and women's clo's,*
> *He murmurs 'And what next?'*
>
> *Yes! Driver Bill, whose fame is still*
> *Renowned from Bourke to Hay*
> *Now humbly stands and smooths his hands,*
> *'Yes, madam, step this way.'*

By the middle of 1929, the five country stores were failing and the Queensland directors wrote to shareholders:

> *The directors have come to the conclusion that owing to the risk sometimes incurred in the running of country stores due to drought, credit, bad debts and the occasional difficulty of secur-*

ing capable and trustworthy branch managers, all in addition to heavy taxation and oppressive award rates, it would be advisable to further reduce the stores in operation with the ultimate idea of winding the company up and returning the capital to the shareholders.

On 16 June 1929, Cobb & Co went into voluntary liquidation for the last time. Gordon Studdert, Cobb & Co's general manager since 1921, bought the Cobb & Co store at Surat, along with the region's mail run and the company name. Twenty years later, Studdert sued W. R. F. Bolton when he took the Cobb & Co name for his modern trucking business centred in Toowoomba. They settled out of court and joined forces to form a new Cobb & Co – but that's another story.

Decades before, Henry Lawson had immortalised the coaching giant in a number of his poems, particularly 'The Lights of Cobb & Co'. The firm was the first great home-grown service provider Australia had known, and its legacy continues to burn strong in the Australian psyche. Born out of the country's gold rushes, the Cobb & Co name has come to represent the pioneering spirit, a willingness to battle against the odds, to reliably connect far-flung communities in a vast, unforgiving land.

Cobb & Co's main players all combined qualities required by today's most successful corporate executive teams: James Rutherford's stamina and energy; Walter Hall's financial skills; Bella Whitney's sharp mind; and Frank Whitney's unerring loyalty.

Since Cobb & Co's demise, a commemorative stamp has been issued, re-enactments of great outback coach journeys have taken place and a tacky Hollywood-produced television series based on the legend has been made. However, the only lasting signposts of the once vast business empire are the Cobb & Co museum in Toowoomba, the few restored coaches and buggies in towns around the nation, and the occasional coaching inn scattered along a forgotten back road.

EPILOGUE

Back in 1907, Billy Whitney had tired of being his mother's lackey. It had been his hard work, along with his uncle Arthur's efforts, that had reduced the debt to Walter Hall in less than nine years. But what thanks did he get? He wanted out of the family business.

Billy was also tired of being ordered around by his brother-in-law Dr Kelty, one of the executors of Frank's will. Plus, his best friend Laurence Rutherford had just died – out of the blue – from some rare disease they called pernicious anaemia. Life was too short and unpredictable to let people walk all over you. It was time to force his mother's hand, to force her to pay off all of Walter Hall's loan so Billy could have his name on a piece of his own land. He would no longer live caught up in his stubborn mother's complex web of mortgages and obligations.

Billy submitted a letter of demand for his interest in the Whitney inheritance, together with his resignation as manager. He'd already written to his eldest sister to warn her of what he was about to do:

I am very sorry to have to take this step as it perhaps means making a breach which should never have been. I am aware I could have avoided it if I was agreeable to do what I know is bad business and this I declined to do.

One hundred years on, exactly what 'bad business' Billy was referring to is not clear. It is likely he was referring to the kinds of clashes that countless generations of pastoral families have experienced. He successfully obtained the family's Waugoola station for himself and his young family, but it meant a parting of ways for Billy and his mother. Coombing Park and the Cobb & Co inheritance were now completely in the hands of Bella Whitney and her four daughters.

Over the years, Bella Whitney built a formidable reputation as a survivor. In 1910 she formed a shorthorn stud at Coombing and became a renowned breeder of top-rate cattle. The lady enjoyed close friendships with governors, wealthy stock breeders and ambassadors, and often hosted visiting dignitaries. A Coombing soiree or wedding reception for a Whitney grandson or granddaughter featured in the social pages of the Sydney papers at least once a year.

Unlike James Rutherford, Bella was keen to embrace the motor car. Dr Machattie had been the first person in the Bathurst district to invest in the new horseless carriage, having owned a motor car since 1904. In 1910 Bella paid £800 for an Austin – more than $81 000 in today's terms. Like many ladies of her day, Bella never learned to drive. Instead, she employed a chauffeur who not only drove and maintained the car, but dutifully recorded the details of every journey. Few private citizens had a motor vehicle and the excitement of this novel means of travel was so great that the family thought of any excuse they could to journey in it. Bella would take her daughter Katie to Sydney in the new car, then spend a week or two motoring around the town. The Austin was employed for shopping trips to Blayney,

Bathurst and Orange, to inspect the family's mining operations or to visit neighbours on the next property. In her first year of ownership, Bella's chauffeur carefully logged over 3700 miles of travel (almost 6000 kilometres), more than six times the distance from Sydney to Melbourne.

The 1910 New South Wales motorists' manual established elementary rules for drivers. Speed limits of 15 miles (24 kilometres) per hour were set on the open road, 6 miles an hour when crossing intersections and 4 miles an hour when turning corners in a city. In this age before headlights, night driving was forbidden unless the vehicle carried gas lamps at the front and back. Before the invention of indicator lights, drivers were required to make a clear hand signal out the window to indicate that they were making a turn.

A few years later Bella upgraded to a six-cylinder 40–50 horsepower 1909 Rolls-Royce, costing more than £2000. She was one of the first people in New South Wales to purchase this luxurious import. The huge car had one of the biggest engines on the market, and could seat up to seven passengers comfortably. It had a retractable canopy to shelter passengers from the elements and was nearly 5 metres in length.

Bella Whitney had been quicker than the nation's greatest transport firm to invest in motor transport.

Walter Hall proved Rutherford wrong and outlived him, though not by much. Exactly a month after Rutherford's death in 1911, Hall passed away quite suddenly at his harbourside Sydney mansion, aged eighty years. His wife's family orchestrated his burial hundreds of miles south in their own city of Melbourne. Never one to court publicity, Walter had been a generous though anonymous philanthropist in recent years. To the end, he could be found at the Randwick racecourse during the season. Eliza Hall, left with a magnificent fortune and no heirs, made a gift of a million pounds to her country (equivalent to $100 million today). In 1912 the Walter and Eliza Hall Trust was formed, devoted 'to the relief of poverty, advancing education and Anglican religion as well as for the general benefit of the community'.

The bequest was the largest of its kind ever made by a woman in the British empire. Travelling and research fellowships and scholarships were founded at the universities of Sydney, Melbourne and Brisbane, while the Walter and Eliza Hall Institute of Medical Research at the Royal Melbourne Hospital continues to conduct leading medical research to this day.

The couple's exquisite Wildfell mansion at the tip of Potts Point was knocked down to make way for a block of units in 1958. Even the wreckers pulling down the property were overawed by the fine workmanship of each room they reduced to rubble.

After her husband's passing, Ada Rutherford moved out of Hereford into a smaller though rather elegant townhouse in Bathurst. Of her ten sons and daughters, only her eldest son, James junior, had settled in the Bathurst district. Her other offspring were dispersed throughout Australia and overseas. Ada lived alone, surrounded by James' personal papers and her favourite pieces from Hereford, spending her time studying her husband's letters and crafting the extraordinary story of his life. She refused to let even her children see her work until it was completed. In 1916, when it was close to completion, Ada's research and all her husband's private letters were destroyed in a mysterious fire that engulfed the rear section of her home. Was it an accident, or was someone trying to protect a reputation? The cause was never identified by Bathurst police. An important record of the Cobb & Co story was lost to history.

Ada Rutherford died in 1920. Bella Whitney had promised her she would never speak of James Rutherford's illness to another soul. However, rather than destroy the letters as Ada had requested over two decades earlier, Bella locked them away.

In March 1935, Arthur Leeds died at Coombing Park with his beloved older sister Bella by his side. He was eighty-eight years of age. His younger wife, Margaret, estranged from her husband, was thousands of miles away on a cruise to North America with her granddaughter.

Bella was heartbroken. To assuage the grief and emptiness that threatened to overwhelm her, she insisted that her brother's body not be sent home to his Claverton family in Queensland. He would be interred as close to Bella as possible – in the Church of England cemetery at Carcoar, looking over her beloved property. By having Arthur's grave close at hand, she could keep him alive – in her mind, at least.

For the first time, ninety-year-old Bella Whitney found herself unable to concentrate on company business. Distracted by grief she fell ill, and her accountants, stock agents and buyers had to deal solely with her nephew, Arthur Leeds junior, who was now running the Whitney pastoral business, having taken the place of Bella's estranged son Billy.

Bella had always dealt far more comfortably with men rather than women and her remaining confidant after Arthur's death was her mild-mannered chauffeur, Ferson. She would spend long afternoons being driven around the district in her Silver Ghost Rolls-Royce, insisting that the car be taken cross-country to inspect some beast or other in a distant paddock.

Ferson would whinge about the vehicle's suspension being ruined, but to no avail. The poor chauffeur often found himself on his back under the chassis, wrestling with the spare tyre and cursing the rocks on the rutted tracks for wrecking his day. He was sure his elderly mistress looked forward to a puncture. It was the way she sat there so content in the front passenger seat, her black parasol angled against the heat in summer or shielding her from the bitter winds in winter, while he jacked up the car. Ferson would look up and catch Bella Whitney gazing out at the cattle or timing the movement of clouds across the sky. She had such a glint in her eye, she seemed to be counting the beasts or perhaps estimating their collective age.

In August 1941, as a second world war raged in distant Europe, Bella Whitney died in her sleep. The grand lady's death at ninety-six was not unexpected, though her mind had stayed sharp until the very end. Gran Whitney, as she had been known to her large family for decades now, was buried in the family vault in Orange, next to Frank, though she would perhaps have preferred the Carcoar cemetery next to her brother Arthur, looking over her Coombing landscape. The female side of the family had the strength and longevity: by the time of her passing, Bella Whitney had buried all five of her sons and her three sons-in-law but just one of her five daughters.

The Coombing homestead and many of its convict-built structures – shearing sheds, stables and cottages – are now listed by the National Trust of Australia. It is the only Cobb & Co property still owned by direct descendants of the firm's partners. In recent years, Bella's great-grandson has spent many thousands of dollars on restoring the turn-of-the-century homestead, and has brought the long-neglected, cobwebbed rooms alive once again. Much of the telemovie of Bryce Courtenay's *Jessica*, a fictionalised nineteenth-century story, was filmed at Coombing Park in 2003.

Nothing seems to have shifted since Bella Whitney's death. Hanging beside portraits of English kings and queens, Bella and Frank stare down at their descendants from the dark, creaking hallways. Bella's bone-handled hairbrush and mirror lie on a dressing table beside her wrought-iron four-poster bed – the same bed the couple received as a wedding present back in 1863. Her Maltese lace wedding dress lies packed away amid thousands of family heirlooms, but one can almost smell the scent of her perfume. In the grand dining room, with its oak, marble and cedar, Bella peers at the camera from the snow-covered garden of a nineteenth-century Coombing. Though almost seventy years have passed since she lived here, Bella Whitney's spirit still defines Coombing Park.

SELECT BIBLIOGRAPHY

COBB & CO AND COACHING HISTORY

Aspinall, Clare, *Three Years in Melbourne*, L. Booth, London, 1862.

Austin, K. A., *The Lights of Cobb & Co: The story of the frontier coaches 1854–1924*, Rigby Limited, Adelaide, 1967.

de St Hilare Simmonds, D., *Cobb & Co Heritage Trail: Bathurst to Bourke*, Lynx Printing, Mudgee, 1999.

Durack, Mary, *Sons in the Saddle*, Constable, London, 1983.

Lee, R., 'By Track and Road: Animal Power and Australian Transport 1788–1920', *Linking a Nation: Australia's Transport & Communications 1788–1970*, Commonwealth of Australia, www.ahc.gov.au/publications/national-stories/transport, 2003.

Oakes, A., 'An American-Australian James Rutherford', *Daily Telegraph*, 29 November 1924.

O'Carroll, J. J., 'When Cobb & Co Came to Cunnamulla, Lower Warrego Pioneers', *Queensland Country Life*, 17 September 1953.

Rutherford, Joan, *Cobb & Co*, Central Commercial Printers, Bathurst, 1971.

Tranter, Deborah, *Cobb & Co: Coaching in Queensland*, Queensland Museum, Brisbane, 1990.

Trollope, Anthony, *Australia and New Zealand*, Chapman and Hall, London, 1873.

White, Charles, *Short-Lived Bushrangers*, NSW Bookstall Co., Sydney, 1900.

AUSTRALIAN EMIGRATION AND GOLD RUSHES

Aitchison, R., *Thanks to the Yanks: The Americans and Australia*, Sun Books, Melbourne, 1972.

Kelly, W., *Life in Victoria, or, Victoria in 1853 and Victoria in 1858*, Chapman and Hall, London, 1860.

Melvin, J. W., *The Emigrants Guide to the Colonies*, Simpkin Marshall & Co, London, 1850.

Potts, E. D., & A., *Young America and Australian Gold: Americans and the Gold Rush of the 1850s*, University of Queensland Press, Brisbane, 1974.

Serle, Geoffrey, *The Golden Age: A History of the Colony of Victoria 1851–1861*, Melbourne University Press, Melbourne, 1977.

Smyth, R. B., *The Prospector's Handbook: A Catalogue of Useful Minerals which may be Sought for and Found in Victoria*, F. F. Baillère, Melbourne, 1863.

NINETEENTH-CENTURY AUSTRALIA

Blainey, Geoffrey, *A Shorter History of Australia*, Random House Australia, Sydney, 1997.

Blainey, Geoffrey, *Black Kettle and Full Moon: Daily Life in a Vanished Australia*, Penguin, Melbourne, 2003.

Capel, Hugh, *Where the Dead Men Lie: The Story of Barcroft Boake, Bush Poet of the Monaro*, Ginninderra Press, Canberra, 2002.

Clark, C. M. H., *A History of Australia*, vol. V, *The People Make Laws 1888–1915*, Melbourne University Press, Melbourne, 1981.

Clune, Frank, *Wild Colonial Boys*, Angus & Robertson, Sydney, 1982.

Crotty, Martin, *Making the Australian Male: Middle Class Masculinity 1870–1920*, Melbourne University Press, Melbourne, 2001.

Ferguson, Charles, 'Eyewitness Report from a Californian Ranger', *History of the Australian Goldfields: By Those Who Were There*, ed. Nancy Keesing, Angus & Robertson, Sydney, 1987.

Furphy, Joseph, *Such is Life: Being Certain Extracts from the Diary of Tom Collins*, Bulletin Newspaper Co., Sydney, 1903.

Hughes, W. M., *Crusts and Crusades*, Angus & Robertson, Sydney, 1947.

Hunter, Marcella, *Australia Post, Delivering More than Ever*, Focus, Sydney, 2000.

Kingston, B., *The Oxford History of Australia*, vol. 3, *1860–1900 Glad, Confident Morning*, Oxford University Press, Melbourne, 1988.

Ruhen, Carl, *Pub Splendid: The Australia Hotel 1891–1971*, John Burrell/Murray Child & Company, Sydney, 1995.

Svensen, Stuart, *The Shearers' War: The Story of the 1891 Shearers' Strike*, University of Queensland Press, Brisbane, 1989.

Taylor, Peter, *Station Life in Australia: Pioneers and Pastoralists*, Allen & Unwin, Sydney, 1988.

United Pastoralists Association of Queensland, *The Great Queensland Strike of 1891*, Black, Keid & Co, Brisbane, 1891.

Unstead, R. J., & Henderson, W. F., *Transport in Australia*, A & C Black, London, 1970.

Victorian Yearbook, 1893.

Willoughby, H., *Australian Pictures*, The Religious Tract Society, London, 1886.

BIOGRAPHIES

Australian Dictionary of Biography 1850–1890, Melbourne University Press, Melbourne, 1976.

Campbell, Ellen, *An Australian Childhood*, Blackie & Son, London, 1891.

Ellis, Catherine, *I Seek Adventure: An Autobiographical Account of Pioneering Experiences in Outback Queensland from 1889 to 1904*, Alternative Publishing Co-operative, Sydney, 1981.

Jeffery, R., *Pioneers of Australia: A Biographical Review of Australia's Landed Gentry*, Pioneer Publishing Co., Melbourne, 1938.

Rutherford, D. A., *The Life and Times of James Rutherford*, Fast Books, Forster, 1994.

LOCAL HISTORY

Barker, Theo, *A History of Bathurst*, Crawford House Press, Bathurst, 1998.

Faces of Mandurama, National Library of Australia, Canberra, 1997.

Greaves, Bernard (ed.), *The Story of Bathurst*, Angus & Robertson, Sydney, 1961.

McDonald, D. L., *They Came to a Valley: Wellington 1817–1967*, Wellington Commercial Printing, Wellington, 1968.

Porter, Robert, *History of Wellington: A Record of the Growth of the Town and District from the Earliest Days*, W. C. Penfold, Wellington, 1906.

Reynolds, Gary, *The Kings Colonials: The Story of Blayney and District*, G. K. Craig, Orange, 1982.

Schiffman, P., McCowen, F., McCowen, D., & Halliday, K., *Bolivia: A Century and a Half*, National Library of Australia, Canberra, 1988.

ORIGINAL MATERIALS AND MANUSCRIPTS

Boake, Barcroft, Personal letters (unpub.), Bulletin Magazine archives, 1888–1889.

Boake, Barcroft Capel, Personal memoir, www.boake.net, 1896.

Callan Park Hospital, Case papers 14/10006, Admission Papers 3/3340, Medical Case Books 1877–1910 3/4674–7, NSW State Archives, Kingswood.

Lee, Colquhoun & Bassett, Legal papers, Carcoar Office, Mitchell Library, Sydney.

Lowe, G. E., Private letters (unpub.).

Lowe, William, An Account of Coaching Days (unpub.).

Rutherford, David, *Sons and Daughters of James Rutherford* (unpub.), 1995.

Rutherford, George, *History of Cobb & Co*, Mitchell Library, Sydney, 1949.

Rutherford James, *Diary of James Rutherford*, Mitchell Library, Sydney, 1863.

Rutherford, Joan, Personal letters and correspondence, Mitchell Library, Sydney.

Rutherford vs Whitney in Equity, Court transcript 1900, Whitney Pastoral Company Records, Mitchell Library, Sydney.

Whitney family letters, Mitchell Library, Sydney, NSW.

MONOGRAPHS, PAMPHLETS AND MAGAZINE ARTICLES

A brief history of the Rozelle Hospital, 1990.

Fair, R., 'Coaching in Australia', *Queensland Geographical Journal*, May 1953, pp. 47–52.

Fraser, D., *Bridges Down Under: the History of Railway Underbridges in New South Wales*, Australian Railway Historical Society, 1995, pp. 42–43.

Holmes, L., 'Bolivia GNR: A Country Railway Station', *Byways of Steam*, no. 15, May 1999.

Lees, W,. 'Coaching in Australia: The History of Cobb and Co', *Australian Pastoralist*, June 1917–June 1918.

Moore, H. E., *The Australia Hotel*, John Sands, Sydney, 1893.

National Trust of Victoria, Timber Bridges Study, The National Trust, Melbourne, 1997, p. 42.

NSW Department of Main Roads, *Old Coaching Days*, vol. XVII, no. 2, pp. 40–45.

Rules of the Reform Club, Mitchell Library, Sydney, 1884.

'Sydney in September', *Temple Bar*, September 1890, pp. 113–14.

The Official Record of the Sydney International Exhibition 1879, Thomas Richards, Govt Printer, Sydney, 1881.

Trangmar, E. R., *The Saga of Cobb & Co 1852–1924*, Coleraine Historical Society, Coleraine, 1961.

OTHER SOURCES

Ayto, John (ed.), *Brewer's Dictionary of Phrase and Fable*, 17th edn, Weidenfeld and Nicolson, London, 2005.

Cumpston, J. H.L., *Health and Disease in Australia: A History*, AGPS Press, Canberra, 1989.

Manning, Fred Norton, *Report on Lunatic Asylums*, NSW Government Printer, Sydney, 1868.

NSW Police Act, 1855.

The King's School Parramatta Register 1831–1990, The Council of the King's School, Parramatta, 1990.

The Whitney Estate Act, NSW Parliament, 1902.

Tuckey, Bill, *Australians and Their Cars: 100 Years of Motoring*, Focus, Sydney, 2003.

Walsh, K., & Hooton, J., *Australian Autobiographical Narratives: An Annotated Bibliography*, vol. 2, *1850–1900*, National Library of Australia and Australian Scholarly Editions Centre, Australian Defence Force Academy, Canberra, 1998.

NEWSPAPERS

Australian Pastoralists Review
Bathurst Free Press and Mining Journal
Bathurst Post
Bathurst Times
Carcoar Chronicle
Daily Telegraph
Illustrated Sydney News
Mount Alexander Mail
National Advocate
Queensland Country Life
Sydney Mail
Sydney Morning Herald
The Star
The Worker
Town and Country Journal
Wilcannia Times

PHOTOGRAPHIC SOURCES

King P. Whitney and King Family photographs, Mitchell Library, Sydney.

MAP SOURCES

Department of Lands, Pastoral Map of NSW, 1883.
Postmaster General NSW, Postal Services Map, 1852.

ACKNOWLEDGEMENTS

In the years between starting this book and publishing it, there have been many people whose advice, knowledge, expertise or simply patience deserves the fullest thanks. These include Berkeley King, who originally provided the inspiration for the book and gave me unfettered access to the Whitney family history; David Rutherford, for access to his wonderful archive of material; John Whitney and Peter King, as well as the many other descendants who provided family documents, such as Mary Hill, Bernie O'Shannessy, Neil Robertson, Rosalie Counsel, Georgette Schmidt and the research of the late George W. Rutherford and Joan Rutherford.

I would also like to thank the Writers Centre of NSW, whose writers' groups provided invaluable early critique and whose funding provided me with a mentorship to help develop the manuscript. In addition, I thank the manuscripts staff of the Mitchell Library of NSW, along with archivists from the King's School Parramatta, Ascham School for Girls, the Bathurst Historical Society, Jeff Powell of Toowoomba's Cobb & Co Museum, Heather Nicholls of Orange City Council and many others.

The professionals who have guided my development as a writer through this process and who deserve thanks include Patricia Cortese, Janet Austin, Ben Ball, Anne Deveson, Corydon and Brenda Unwin, Clare Forster, Rose Creswell and Lesley McFadzean.

Additional images were provided by Museum Victoria, the National Gallery of Victoria, Queensland Museum, and the state libraries of New South Wales, Victoria and Queensland. Thanks to Darren Keating for his tireless support in preparing the maps, and to Katie Hudson for coaxing me to look at a camera.

I particularly want to thank Philip Copeland, Michael McKelvie, Dominic Thurn, Catherine Shaw, Anthony Blair and all my friends and family for their support, understanding, patience and inspiration throughout the long years of research, writing, re-writing and editing, and during the time spent hunting for an agent and finally a publisher who believed in the story as much as I did.

A NOTE REGARDING CURRENCY CONVERSION

Where pounds sterling have been used to indicate the prices of goods and services (including fares), use the following calculation to convert into today's equivalents: £1 = $113.

INDEX